AF206990

Stefan Stammer

The Horse in Positive Tension

Harnessing Equine Kinetic Energy for Top Performance

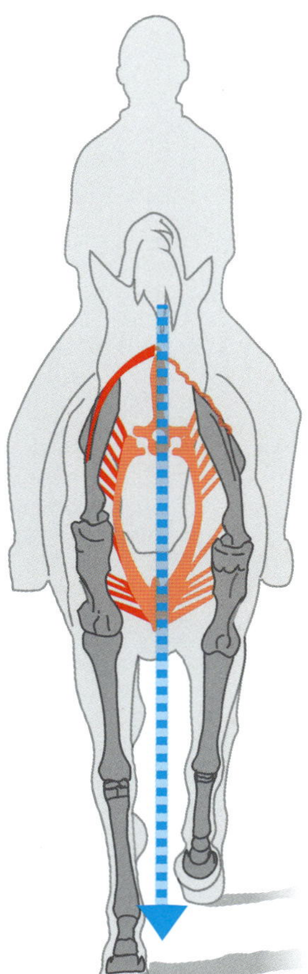

Translated by Lena Rindermann with editorial consultation from Dr. Anastasios Moschos

Trafalgar Square
North Pomfret, Vermont

First published in the United States of America in 2023 by
Trafalgar Square Books, North Pomfret, Vermont

Originally published in German as *Das Pferd in positiver Spannung*.

ISBN: 978-1-64601-129-2
Library of Congress Control Number: 2022951772

Illustrations by Jeanne Kloepfer, Lindenfels (Germany) except: Cornelia Koller, Dierkshausen (Germany): p. 36 and p. 91 bottom: Taken from Basic Training for Riders and Horses–Guidelines for Riding and Driving, Volume 1 [Grundausbildung für Reiter und Pferd - Richtlinienfür Reiten und Fahren, Band 1], FNverlag 2014.

Photographs by Kiki Beelitz, Hanstedt (Germany): pp 118 top, 118 bottom, 120. Katharina Dickel, Vieux-Ferrette (France): pp 115 top, 115 middle, 115 bottom. Tobias Dinslage, Baiersbronn (Germany): pp 134, 140 top left, 140 top right, 140 bottom, 141 top, 141 bottom, 142, 149 bottom, 153. Andrea Ehret, Mannheim (Germany): pp 4 top, 14, 15, 18 top, 24 top left, 62 top. Foto Tammo Ernst, Ganderkesee (Germany): pp 4 bottom, 5, 25 middle, 25 bottom left, 25 bottom right. Werner Ernst, Ganderkesee (Germany): page 110 (2). Bernhard Fauser, Heidelberg (Germany): page 67. Corinne Foxley (USA): 7 top, 9 bottom, 24 top right, 25 top left, 25 top right, 29 top left, 29 top middle, 29 top right, 29 bottom, 32, 37 bottom left, 37 bottom right, 38 top left, 38 top right, 38 bottom right, 39 bottom, 63 top left, 63 top right, 63 bottom left, 63 bottom right, 66 top left, 71 left, 71 right, 78, 79, 88, 89, 98 top left, 98 top right. Kurt Fuchs: page 172 top. Stefanie Fuchs, St. Remy (France): pp 154, 155, 161 top, 161 bottom, 165 bottom, 170, 172 bottom, 173 top left. Hengststation Ludger Beerbaum Stables GmbH, Riesenbeck (Germany): page 111. imago/Pressefoto Baumann: page 7 bottom. imago/SprintPress: page 11. imago/Werek: page 13 left. imago/Colorsport: page 13 middle. imago/Camera 4: page 18 bottom right. imago/Sven Simon Barfuß: page 44 right. imago/Science Photo Library: page 56 bottom. imago/GEPA pictures: page 133 top. imago/Thomas Zimmermann: page 133 bottom. Jessica Kellner, Warendorf (Germany): page 121. D. Matthaes/RJ: page 77. Mary McKenna, Silver Spring, Maryland (USA): pp 136, 137. Ricarda Mertens, Mannheim: pp 112 top, 124, 127 bottom, 131 bottom, 135 left, 135 right. From the private collection of Eckart Meyners, Lüneburg (Germany): page viii. Ralf Michael, Weinheim (Germany): pp 147 top left, 171. From the private collection of the Nepper family: page iii. Felicitas von Neumann-Cosel, First Choice Farm (USA): pp xii, 66 bottom, 74, 123 left, 123 right, 143, 150 top left, 150 top right. Julia Rau, Zornheim (Germany): pp 98 bottom, 122. Beat Sax: pp 112 second from top, 112 bottom left. Werner Scheidegger, Sankt Pelagiberg (Switzerland): pp 147 top right, 147 bottom. Caroline Schunk: page 112 bottom right. From the private collection of the Stammer family, Baiersbronn (Germany): page x. Eveline Stammer, Baiersbronn (Germany): pp 13 right, 24 bottom left, 24 bottom middle, 24 bottom right, 128 left, 128 right. Stefan Stammer, Baiersbronn (Germany): pp 16 top left, 16 top right, 18 bottom left, 66 top right, 83 bottom, 86 top left, 86 top right, 86 bottom left, 86 bottom middle, 86 bottom right, 87 left, 87 middle, 87 right, 97 left, 97 right, 102 left, 102 right, 104 bottom left, 104 bottom middle, 104 bottom right, 105 top left, 105 top middle, 105 top right, 105 bottom left, 105 bottom middle, 105 bottom right, 106 middle left, 106 middle center, 106 middle right, 106 bottom left, 106 bottom middle, 106 bottom right, 125 left, 125 middle, 125 right, 126 left, 126 right, 127 top, 129 left, 129 right, 131 top, 132, 138, 144, 145, 150 bottom left, 165 top left, 165 top right, 166, 168, 169 middle, 169 top, 169 bottom. Cord Wassmann, Badbergen-Langen (Germany): page 119. Aline Wicki, Kerzers (Switzerland): pp 157, 173 top right, 173 bottom. Page 158: image capture edited by Michelle Oeschger, Haltingen (Germany). Page 167: taken from Halla, My Horses, and I [Halla, meine Pferde und ich], page 112, FNverlag 2008 (photographer unknown)

Interior Design: mf-graphics, Marianne Fietzeck, Gütersloh
Cover Design: RM Didier
Translation into English: Lena Rindermann with editorial consultation from
Dr. Anastasios Moschos

Printed in China

10 9 8 7 6 5 4 3 2 1

Dedication

*For H.U. Nepper, because he taught me to question things,
even when they seemed plausible at first sight.*

H.U.Nepper

H.U. Nepper, who passed away too early in 2008, was the most important influence on my professional career. He was my teacher and mentor at the Sports, Gymnastics, and Physiotherapy School in Waldenburg, Germany, and one of the early developers and tutors of medical training therapy in Germany. For him, function and therapy were always directly linked. Once a new "form" of therapy or a new "miracle tool" hit the market, he simply and critically analyzed how useful it really was. Yet, he always remained innovative, never clinging to the past, but actively shaped medical training therapy in Germany. He defined the largest obstacle in shaping this process to be recalling therapeutic reflexes, when questions within a closed system suddenly arose. From his point of view, the solution lay in overcoming exactly these reflexes by objective analysis. Just as in other areas of life, this path has always been arduous and rocky at times, but once one has gone down that way, there is no turning back. From day one, when I told him about my journey into equine physiotherapy, he has given me all the support I could have wished for. Ezra Pound, American poet, wrote: "You catch fire or you don't catch fire." H.U. Nepper lit a fire for my profession in me, and my greatest wish would have been for him to read this book and for this book to make him smile.

Contents

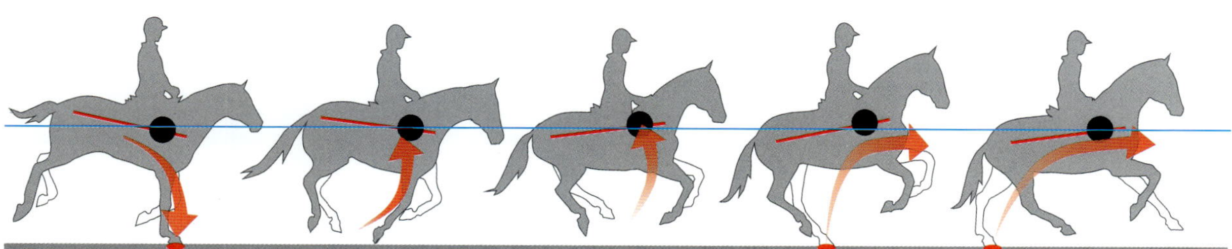

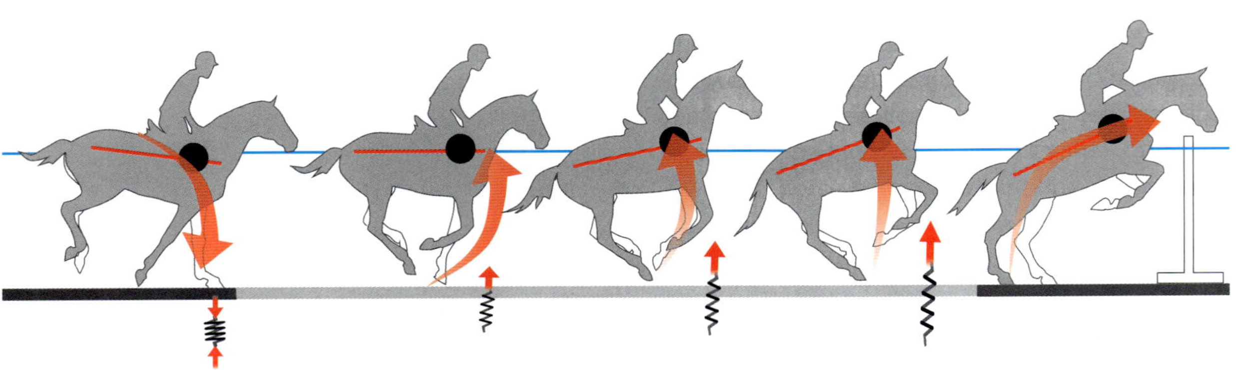

Foreword

One may ask why someone like me, who is not an active trainer in equestrian sports, provided input on this book, as it's about fundamental links within the horse and the effects on the horse's training. Nevertheless, I will attempt to give an assessment of this book from my perspective, a perspective based on the general nature of movement science.

Many equestrian professionals will likely have stumbled over the term "tension," and it is usually connected to something negative. However, this book mainly focuses on "positive tension." With his hind end as his engine, the horse generates kinetic energy, which must flow through the horse's body, "arrive in the horse's mouth," and is to be fine-tuned with the rein aids (modulation), to positively re-affect the hind end. This is "positive tension." This movement flow can be disrupted in several places on its way "through the horse," as the rider often unintentionally interferes with its transmission. That is how the rider creates negative tension, which she does not want.

I use the term "unintentionally" because in riding lessons, certain "looks" for horse and rider are very often sought, which, on a functional level, do not work with the biomechanical system of the horse (or the rider). Chasing such a "look" is unnecessary; once the natural functions within the horse have been stimulated through the correct application of biomechanics, the outer shape of horse (and rider) becomes fluid and smooth, and is in "positive tension."

"Positive tension" means the "rhythmic" stimulation of all neuromuscular functions of the horse in accordance with his system. The term "rhythm," in the context of "positive tension," is understood to refer to the temporal, spatial, and dynamic order of a movement. It is about the rider's overall or partially recurring movements of contraction and relaxation.

Rhythm may further be defined as either "object rhythm" or "subject rhythm." The horse sets an object rhythm for the rider. Due to his features (size, muscles, angles, disposition), he can only move in a given way at a given moment and not (yet) any differently. Initially, the rider has to adapt to this object rhythm to achieve a successful, harmonious interaction of all sections of the horse's system (without tension).

The rider has to share an identical rhythm with the horse from the beginning, in order to be able to (subjectively) influence the horse's rhythm (object rhythm) with her body, and ensure that the horse can always move in "positive tension" according to the classical theory of riding.

The external indicator of an ideal rhythm is the constant, soft, and harmonious flow of movement in all transitions and repetitions.

And this is exactly Stefan Stammer's goal. He wants to clarify what the natural movement of a horse looks like and which references need to be made to riding theory. The knowledge of this theory is by no means questioned but supported and made clear with reference to the horse's biomechanical function. Both trainers and riders will pick up valuable background knowledge concerning the horse's natural development of movement skills, the better to keep him healthy and able to perform throughout his life.

The author does not only apply this knowledge to the horse, but also includes important considerations such as how to achieve functionally correct riding, how this information is a factor in different horse sports, and how it applies in general horsekeeping scenarios, according to horses' natural needs—for example, when they are turned out in the pasture.

As someone who is not a professional horseperson, but a biomechanical scientist, I have gained an in-depth insight into how the horse moves, which I can connect with the movement patterns of the rider. In doing so, harmony between horse and rider can be achieved.

Eckart Meyners

Former Lecturer,
Leuphana University, Lüneburg
and Coauthor of Rider + Horse = 1

Preface

When, five years ago, I decided to write a book about the functional background of my work and classical riding theory, luckily, I was not aware of the true complexity of the journey I was about to embark on. It was always my goal to find a structure that would appeal to both individual riders and professionals alike. In the end, the real obstacles turned out to be images and definitions that had solidified in the heads of this particular audience—images and definitions that did not always correspond to the actual functional circumstances. And even though any individual image or definition was not always inherently wrong, in the aggregate, they sometimes conformed more to the feeling in the saddle rather than the biomechanical and physical facts.

The struggle of reason is to overcome what the mind has fixed in place.
GERMAN PHILOSOPHER G.F.W. HEGEL

There's no mistaking the first time a rider feels the state of her horse's optimal movement—she seems to float together with her horse. Gravity seems to have been suspended, and everything feels light and relaxed. This feeling may lead the rider to believe this state should be equated with relaxation, when the term "suppleness" corresponds solely with the non-existence of negative tension. The athletic basics that are necessary to achieve positive body tension in the horse can only be assessed accurately by those who understand the principles of functional stabilization.

This book intends to establish these basics. I am going to illustrate them by means of an examination of movement patterns in the horse's body.

The writing process for this book expanded its scope from the basic rationale of describing dry biomechanics to the desire to make the fascination of movement tangible. This fascination has been a constant throughout my entire career.

"Those who are in love with practice without knowledge are like the helmsman who gets onboard a ship without rudder or compass, and who can never be certain where he is going."

LEONARDO DA VINCI

This book is also intended to make movement patterns and their foundations, the way they emerge in the horse, visible, and to explain them in a comprehensible manner. Images will form in your mind's eye that will help you better understand the principles of movement at work within your horse's body. You'll begin to see an extended trot or a transition from walk to canter very differently.

There is always an outer view and an inner view. The outer view is the superficial perspective of an onlooker, which can easily be manipulated with a few tricks. The inner view, however, observes and assesses the core of the movement. The inner view should always be that of the athlete herself, the trainer, and of a judge at a competition. When this is the case, the outer view of the movement is simply decorative.

The inner and outer views often differ significantly. The athlete may feel as if an exercise was performed successfully, but the trainer can attest to significant deficits. Or the trainer is satisfied, but the athlete can feel a "wrinkle" in the horse's movement she would like to iron out, in order to feel better about her ride. An audience can be ecstatic about a performance, but the judges may mark it considerably lower than expected.

The alignment between the inner and outer views in equestrian sports is of particular importance due to the "horse factor." And compared to human sports disciplines, it is a lot harder to judge. Laying out the differences and distinctions between the inner and outer views is precisely the task of this book. The inner view of how exactly a horse moves ought to enhance coordination between the participants; this will improve communication for some riders, and for others, it will cultivate an understanding of not only their horses' body movement, but their own.

Having said this, I wish you many moments in "positive tension," and hopefully some new insights for the good of the horse.

Stefan Stammer

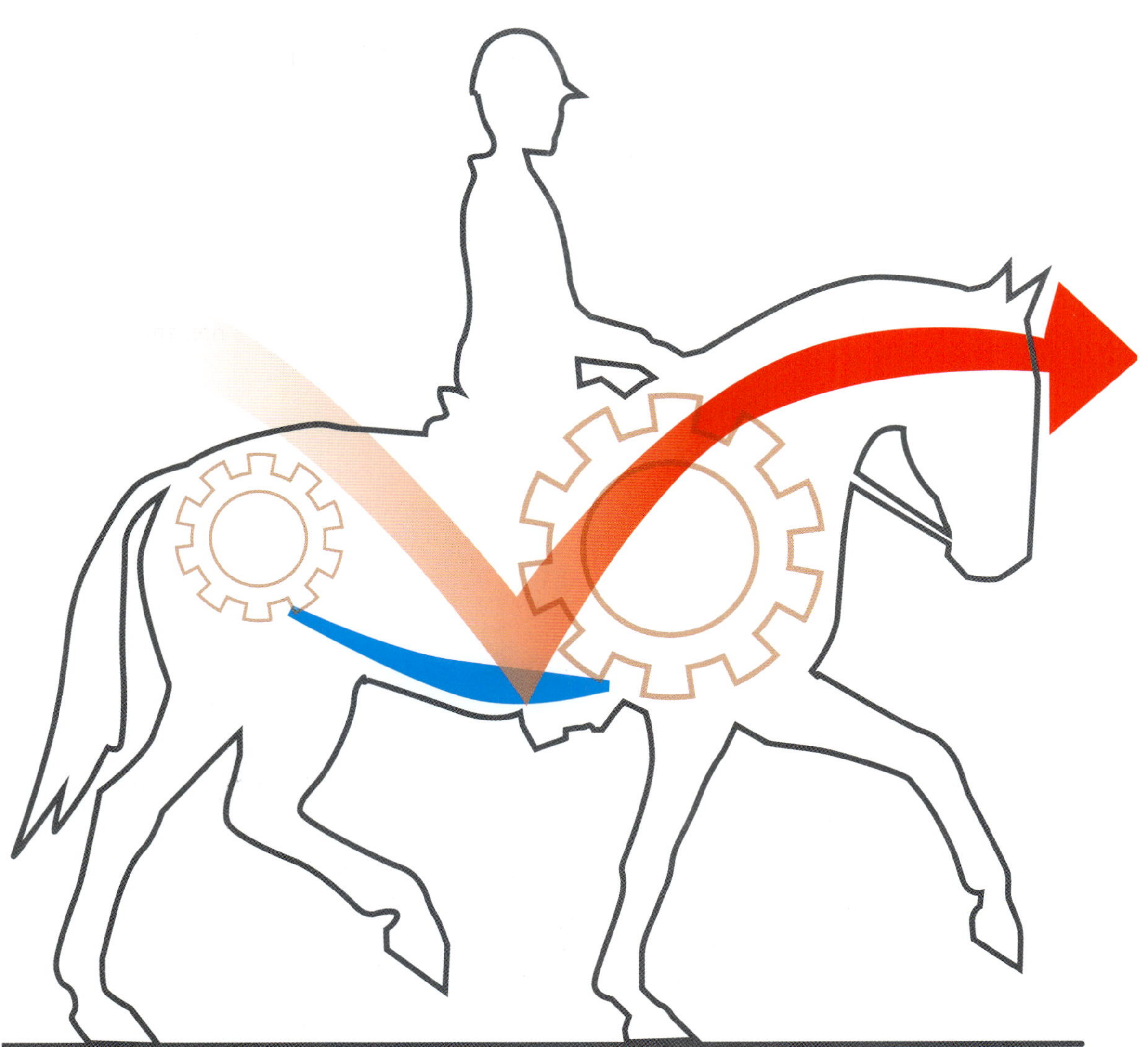

1 Equestrian Sports at a Cross-roads–A Critical Assessment

Leg mover or back mover? Opinions differ on this question.

Developments in Equestrian Sports

The Art of Riding at a Crossroads is the title of a book by Erich Glahn, published in 1956. In this book, he aptly, analytically, and correctly analyzes the rides at the Olympic Games in Stockholm. He did so as a journalist and a great horseman of his time, in the hopes of addressing flawed developments in equestrian sports and illustrating ways to move toward a cleaner and more technically challenging equestrian sport. One of the core statements of the book is as follows: "It is the noblest task of a judge to separate a leg mover from a back mover."

What progress has been made toward realizing Glahn's hopes? If we are honest—not much. The difference between a leg mover and a back mover is just as visible at international championships today as it was 60 years ago. But what has happened in the meantime? In my opinion, something a lot worse: The crossroads of the art of riding has turned into deep rifts within equestrianism. Equestrian sport, which used to involve a broad and versatile training of the horse at all levels, has split more and more into individual styles of riding. Riders now can be categorized into different groups such as *Western riders, recreational riders, classical riders*, or *English riders* early in their careers. In the process, every faction has claimed to be the most horse-appropriate, gentle, and ultimately the best. Just as in other parts of our leisure-oriented society, the troubles of everyday life are often avoided and replaced by worldviews. As a result, the comprehensive schooling of fundamental elements of riding theory such as coordination, strength, and endurance for rider and horse is frequently neglected.

Chronic Overload through Instability

In principle, a young horse should be able to perform a casual, forward flying change in canter during a change of rein. If he does not do so, he is usually lacking in balance and stability. If the rider asks for this change regardless, without creating the necessary foundation—for example, adequate preparation of hind end musculature—the resulting unnatural movements in the horse's hocks can lead to inflammation. Several supplements offered by the feed industry may promise a remedy for these cases, but the underlying causes can only be usefully and effectively reduced through sensible training.

"Gurus" on the Rise

The aforementioned "rifts" within the equestrian world can also be found on a completely different level. Many riders who are riding for fun, relaxation, and recreation have parted with the traditional classical way of training a horse—with unforeseen consequences for the health of their horses. Numerous "gurus" and "horse whisperers" have set out to preach and sell new, holistic, gentle, horse-friendly training methods. All of them have the following in common: They are expensive, they promise quick success, and they develop a system where everyone can become a trainer themselves quickly, should they desire. All are features of a Ponzi scheme, where, in the end, only a few will make money and the rest will inevitably fail.

What Is Training?

The same system can be observed in many so-called "equine therapy" training programs. Here, the rift between reputable therapy and ripoffs is equally deep and wide. The temptation is big, if you believe in the promises of various service providers: An investment of about $7,000 will turn you into a therapist over the course of 15 weekends, no educational background required. Subsequently, it will earn you a monthly revenue of $5,500 to $11,000 for a full-time job. (By comparison, people who decide to become a vet or a physiotherapist, and engage in many years of university and training, must seem rather foolish!)

Knowledge Is Necessary

What can reunite these divergent ideals? I think the answer is information: knowledge of the basic principles of the "genius system" that is the horse. What is it that makes these fascinating creatures so unparalleled? Where does their movement energy come from, and which basic elements of their training allow us to control them?

By the end of this book, the goal is for you to ride better, although you may not do so immediately. First, the aim of this book is to teach you a few new ways to think about the horse's movement. This will automatically lead to practical improvements in daily work with your horse. As long as a rider has the standard mental image of the "bending" of a horse in her head, she will always be tempted to pull on the inside rein–even though she knows this is wrong. But once she grasps the process of the horse's movement on a curved line at a deeper level, her visualization of that movement will change, and it will be much harder for her to make this very common mistake again.

You will recognize that no piece of tack, no matter what it is called, is either good or bad on its own. It can function as an "auxiliary rein," a "disruptive rein," or simply as "force," depending on who uses it and how. You will see the difference between riding a horse, his training, and the correction of incorrect movement patterns, as well as the difference between movement, movement therapy, and rehabilitation. You will realize that the wonderfully simple instructions in many magazines and books cannot be as easily applied as it might seem.

Once you've learned to understand the basic principles of the biomechanics of a horse in movement, most of all, your feeling in the saddle will improve. And that's an important building block for the small and subtle steps of progress, which should accompany a rider for her entire life.

Example: Trot Poles

"To strengthen your horse's back, you should regularly longe over trot poles." This is the kind of thing you'll see in magazines, monthly, repeatedly, almost mantra-like, and copied numerous times. However, this assertion is not always correct. It could just as easily read: "If you want to damage your horse's back as quickly and thoroughly as possible, you should regularly longe over trot poles." Longeing over trot poles does not automatically strengthen a horse's back. Only under certain conditions, individually adapted to your horse, does it have the effect you wish.

All these truths can be summarized in three statements:
- Riding is not easy.
- Training a horse is the highest form of riding.
- Correcting a horse that was not trained correctly is an art.

To really learn riding, you have to do it every day for years, and even decades. Even under ideal conditions, perfection will only be possible for one moment at a time. For those who despair of this situation, I would like to clearly state that imperfection is a normal part of our lives—as is the quest for perfection. Understanding the horse's soul, his body, and his biomechanics will support you on this quest. I would like to expand and deepen this understanding with my book. However, in order to achieve even those brief moments of perfection, simply reading a book might not be enough!

Those who simplify the art of riding just to make it "fun" and accessible to the maximum number of people abuse the creature "horse." The art of riding is meant to be embraced with body, spirit, and soul, and not meant to be simplified.

Equine Studies

Foals have the same baseline speed as adult horses.

At this point in the book, I would like to show the horse in his natural movement patterns that have not yet been altered by training. The fascination the horse holds over humans mainly arises from his untamed energy: the power and dynamics, which humankind can feel directly and utterly–unlike in other animals. The horse becomes part of humans only through training, his energy is transferred directly onto the human body, and he becomes "controllable." The manner of control can be completely different from human to human and often mirrors the "inside" of a rider. Riding makes all facets of human character traits visible–from violent domination to perfect harmony between both individuals.

Example: Foals in the Field
A foal is born–wild on the open steppe. He is licked dry and nudged by his mother. It is essential for his survival to get up on his four feet. The original habitat of horses is the steppe–an open landscape, where a four-legged hunter can appear on the scene and pounce at any moment. Only those ready for flight have a chance. The foal makes several attempts and is up on his legs after a few minutes. As soon as the system of bones, tendons, and joints springs to life and is ready to go, the foal is able to follow the herd at full speed. He has the speed of a grown horse–without training, without grain, without a physical therapist–but with positive tension in every fiber of his body.

A four-year-old horse with impressive movement mechanics, at an auction.

Example: Four-Year-Old Dressage Horse at an Auction
Who wouldn't be fascinated by this picture? Look at this horse, floating across the diagonal in an incredibly expressive trot. Who doesn't want to get on and dream a little about the Olympics? You only have to imagine sitting on this horse, and you are transported there. The horses at the biggest shows shown on TV don't really trot any better. But we can all see how the sales price for certain horses soars to dizzying heights. As many believe, only those who have a horse with fantastic basic gaits can be successful in equestrian sports–and such a horse is expensive.

But why does this animal still need training?

*A three-year-old horse, equipped with sufficient
potential but without any training to date, can, on
occasion, jump 6' (1.80 meters).*

Why train, if a four-year-old already jumps 6' (1.8 meters) and the
highest fences at the international level are only 5'6" (1.7 meters),
according to FEI jumping rules? Jumping high certainly no longer has to be a training goal.

Anything Left?

There is nothing left. What else do we need? These young horses have everything a sport horse will need later. Or are these performances the result of manipulation? If you give credence to various internet forums, top performances
can only be achieved through medication and force. To find a credible answer
and to expose true manipulation, we first and foremost have to learn to understand how the complex movement system of a horse actually functions.

Good or Bad?

Positive examples really do exist, without any questionable or prohibited medication. It's neither good nor bad to test a young, talented horse's performance
ability with fair means. It is an important part of the analysis needed to plan an
individual training program for a horse. The exceptional performances that
do occasionally happen can be ascribed to the individual quality and need for
movement of a "talented" horse. These horses want to show their movement
energy, and they want to please—just as any individual wants to show off her
assets and prove she deserves to be the first choice when it comes to repro-
duction. But this significantly increases the trainer's responsibility, especially
for talented horses. In other words: The *natural movement energy* present in
young horses can be transformed into a *negative,* destructive tension or a *positive*, relieving, and controllable tension, depending on the manner of training.

In the process, classification of the performance ability, motivation, and commitment of a young horse is a first and important step of training, essential in order to understand the individual horse in all his particularities and to optimally further his development.

Even very young horses can quickly lose their movement energy.

Example: Recreational Horse
A six-year-old horse is led into the indoor arena. He stayed with his breeder for his first five years, was outside every day (except in the winter), and was started gently under saddle as a five-year-old. First, four months of groundwork in walk, then another four months of walk and trot on the longe … After, work under saddle was introduced gently and carefully. The horse is well-behaved when hacking and on the ground. "Still a little unbalanced under saddle, but we have time."

Is it enough to simply give a young horse time? What happens if you take away a horse's natural body tension? He is obedient, but loose. The energy he needs to move with impulsion is no longer present.

Training Is Everything—and Without Training, Everything Is Nothing
Whether your focus is dressage, jumping, Western, classical, or trail riding, every horse that is supposed to carry a rider needs training to develop positive body tension. Not for the same duration and intensity and not in the same manner, but every equestrian discipline requires training in the sense of classical riding theory.

And yet any of these horses will be able to perform with incorrect training, or even without any training at all. The jumper jumps, the dressage horse "dances," and the trail horse is a "good boy."

The crossroads appear, depending on the kind of training conducted. Admittedly, the pathologies found in these cases are almost identical. The badly trained trail horse runs the risk of developing the same problems as the badly trained show jumper. Both perform within their means, and both get hurt. The good news is, all horses with professional training will be able to perform for many years without seriously jeopardizing their health, whether over fences of 5' (1.6 meters), in the Grand Prix in dressage, or as a "hobby horse." 17-, 18-, and 19-year-old horses are regularly at the top of the results at the Hamburg Jumping Derby, the most difficult course in the world—an obvious demonstration that intensive athletic activities don't have to cause strain or injury, if a jumping horse is correctly trained.

As it is, this is not a book about classical riding and training—there are many of those nowadays, both good and questionable. But to understand the principles of training according to classical riding theory, it is necessary and useful to discuss the horse's movement system. Only those who understand what they want to develop can meaningfully ask—and answer—the question of how to do it. Our focus shifts to the *systematic analysis of the horse's movement*. This is, honestly, just as difficult as riding in itself, since many different components have to be combined and many misunderstandings have to be ironed out. To be able to plan a horse's training development in detail, it's crucial to dive deeply into the subject matter.

"Supple" Does Not Mean "Light"

We all want to make our horses supple—riders of all kinds of different disciplines have this much in common. And they all experience the same truth over the course of their careers: Riding with *suppleness* is anything but light. But if supple is not light, what does riding theory mean by the terms *suppling, lowering the neck, relaxation, light hands,* and *lightness*? The basic problem is that the definitions and meanings of these terms are often taken out of the context of riding theory, and so they drift through indoor arenas as empty buzzwords.

"Supple" Does Not Mean "Relaxed!"
The meaning of "supple" in equestrian sports has been influenced by its use in other athletic environments. In addition, relaxation is only one part of the movement cycle. A 100-meter sprinter has to stay supple over the last 30 meters of an Olympic final to win. Once this sprinter "clenches up," she loses. But if her body tension is too low, she also loses. She is only truly relaxed 20 minutes later, sitting in a chair with a glass of champagne.

"Supple" does not mean "light."

A soccer player before the decisive penalty shot has to be supple to score safely. If she's relaxed, she'll fail, just as much as she'll fail if she is mentally or physically tense. This is what *inner and outer suppleness* means in equestrian lingo—developing positive body tension and concentration.

Developing this kind of suppleness is not easy, but it's at the core of any good or very good athletic movement. The most important goal of any gymnast, skier, or track-and-field athlete is to embark on their performance in a state of suppleness. Only then can that performance be considered *optimal.*

This brings us back to the deep, wide rift in equestrianism. Today's equestrian magazines and books are very often characterized by the depiction of extremes. If you believe these publications, there are mainly two types of riders.

"Formula 1" Riders

The attitude of these riders is that if suppleness cannot be achieved through lightness, that might mean it's necessary to "take a good grip" now and then. Horses aren't made of glass, after all, and those who expect performance have to occasionally train past the limit—with predictable results.

Chronic overload clinical signs ("symptoms" are what the horse feels and "clinical signs" are what we see, although I'll stick with the term "symptoms" for the most part in this book in reference to both) can be expected from this kind of attitude, an attitude that makes medication to treat the back, hoof joints, and stifle joints an accepted part of a sport horse's health management.

If this is the case, it can then be assumed that the training and showing of a horse in competition is, at least potentially, connected to wear and tear as well as pain. Neither the equestrian world nor the rest of society should accept such an assumption in the long run.

This places the fascinating living being that is the "horse" on the same level as a Formula 1 engine, which can be expected to fail after a certain number of laps. The effort of engineers is only to delay this failure for as long as possible, until the finish line has been crossed.

A lot of effort doesn't automatically equal a good performance.

The Other Side: "Light" Riders

Meanwhile, another group, which we'll call "light" riders, has begun to design their own training philosophies. Particularly relaxed horses that are never ever pushed to or past their limits, and a mindset that everything can be learned easily are what these riders have in common. Their horses live their lives mainly falling from one front leg onto the other, with a low head and a long neck—to the applause of so-called "trainers," whose most important character trait is that they "love" horses. Afterward, these horses are treated to a wellness massage, because they worked so incredibly hard. Completely lacking here is a serious approach to the horse's nature as an animal of movement, full of pride and natural dignity.

It is, of course, by no means a disadvantage if a trainer loves horses. However, her *professional competence* is much more important, including her *regard* for the animal entrusted to her care and her respect for his nature. The outer effortlessness with which a well-ridden horse moves in the end is the result of skillful and experienced training within his first few years of being started. And this is certainly not a "light" task!

You can tell I'm ready to elbow my way into the middle of this! Not so much because I have masochistic tendencies, but because I firmly believe this is the best position for building bridges between the divergent viewpoints in the riding world.

Working only a little doesn't necessarily equal only a little strain.

What Happens in the Middle?

There are still many riders and trainers who do not settle for empty words and quick "wannabe" success. They value their profession and the horses and students entrusted to their care more than themselves, and give it their best every single day. They do not feature monthly in magazines because they have just reinvented equestrianism. They have *equestrian skills, sound knowledge,* and *experience.* That is nothing spectacular, but rather the only option in order to build the movement patterns that horses and riders need to stay healthy long-term and reach their goals, over months and years. Whether this takes place in the competition arena or out on the trails, it is always carried out with joy and respect for the wonderful creature that is the horse.

Suppleness means the development of positive body tension.

Balance, Athleticism, and Suppleness

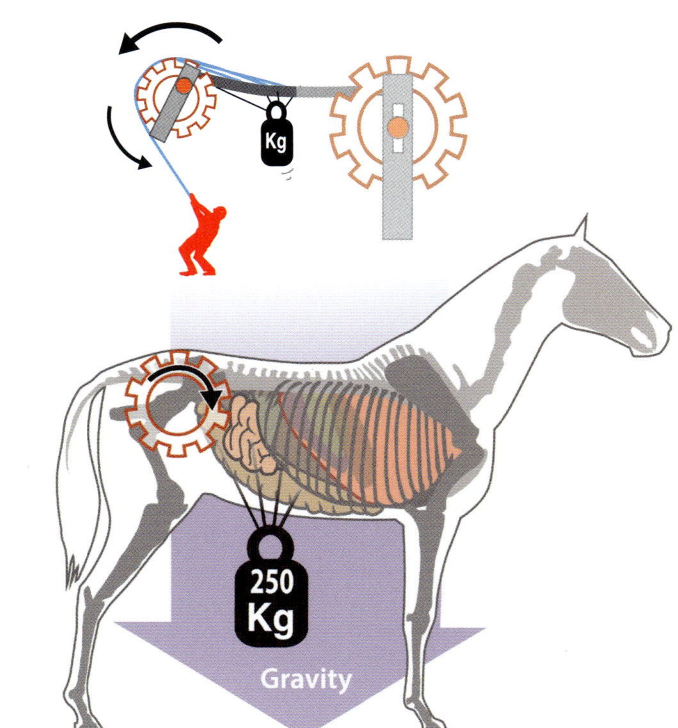

The difference in a static stance for horses and for humans can be found in the ways in which the system must stabilize itself against gravity.

For human beings to stay upright, they *only* have to balance on a vertical axis. However, a horse, as a quadruped, generates power in both the shoulders and pelvic girdle, horizontally; this force can be many times higher than his body weight, due to a leverage effect. If the horse is too weak and *drops* his torso, including his back, instead of energetically going forward, he will become tense. If an overly ambitious rider forces the horse into a position for which he is not prepared, he will also become *tense*. Both *demanding too little* and *demanding too much* thus lead to similar problems and *pathologies* in a horse's movement. The active-dynamic balance as required in riding theory can only be achieved through the development of sufficient athleticism: the foundation for inner and outer suppleness.

Why Biomechanics?

The findings of *biomechanics, functional anatomy,* and *training theory* can help to understand the significant differences between a *correctly* and *incorrectly* trained horse. When visualizing a movement pattern in your mind's eye, pressure lines, leverage ratios, and shock absorption systems become visible. These complex factors have to be clearly described and thought through. In the end, though, your findings can help you determine the best way forward for each individual horse—when he is first started, for his daily training session, when correcting him, or during therapy.

Positive Body Tension as a Primary Objective

One thing may not be neglected under any circumstances: A horse needs *positive tension* to transform his natural *movement process* into one correct for a riding horse. The overall training plan of a horse must never lose sight of this fundamental principle. A generally tense horse will definitely need relaxing exercises and movements for body and mind, first. By contrast, a horse with little basic body tension will need stimuli again and again to build positive body tension and motivation. The *content, supple, and swinging horse that can carry himself well* will, in the end, always be the result of the development of *positive tension*.

Gravity as the Cause of Joy and Sorrow

Observed from a physical standpoint, the reason positive tension is so necessary is gravity. Together with centripetal force (or, subjectively, the sensation of centrifugal force, which is the term I'll use going forward), gravity has an effect on every athlete and every piece of sports equipment. The basis of most athletic movements is overcoming these forces in various elegant variations, or performing despite them—*higher, faster, wider*. Hence, "suppleness" describes the ability to overcome the physical forces involved in an athletic movement. The athlete has to develop athletic skills to reach this goal.

A ski racer going through a turn at 62 miles per hour (100 kilometers per hour) experiences forces three or four times her body weight. She has to brace against these forces with her muscles to be able to endure them. To find the ideal line for the turn at the same time, her muscles also have to be able to perform fine-tuned steering. If her muscles are exerting all possible strength, they start to tense up and the brain goes into "survival mode."

Generally speaking, this automatic process can be summarized as follows: The main cause of cramping during athletic activities is normally an insufficiently trained or overstrained musculature.

Suppleness at maximum strain.

Example: "Lowering the Neck"
Let's tune in to an imaginary riding lesson, where a trainer says, "Now he has finally dropped his neck," because, at that moment, the horse is stretching forward and downward into the hand, and accepting the bit. He is starting to carry himself, and the rider can feel the rein connection become elastic. After having read much on the subject, the rider may now think: "Finally, the horse has relaxed his neck." The logical choice for the rider is to remain passive, to avoid interrupting this relaxation and stretching. The rider sits as still as possible, and holds her breath in awe. She may even visualize the often-portrayed image of the long nuchal ligament lifting the horse's back, in her mind's eye. The moment will last perhaps four to five trot steps before the horse lifts his head again and starts pulling against the rein. Why does this moment come to an end this way?

What is the reason? The answer is: a basic misunderstanding of cause and effect. The rider thinks that a long neck and relaxation are the cause, and the swinging back is the effect. The relaxation of the horse led to the desired result, and the trainer was referring literally to the horse having *dropped his neck*.

This is a classic example of basic misunderstandings in equestrianism, where terms used by professionals have a completely different meaning than their literal interpretation implies. For a horse to raise his back, structures other than the long nuchal ligament have to be activated. A horse that is *truly without any tension* cannot go forward with impulsion. If the rider takes the term "lowering the neck" in the sense of *dropping it* and showing no tension, entirely literally, then the horse will come on the forehand or the rider will have to "carry" his head and neck–which will lead to further (negative) tension.

Back to our imaginary student … Once she has understood that suppleness is the development of positive tension, she will automatically try to *maintain* this body tension. She won't have to wait for her trainer's instruction to continue using a driving aid, which will likely come when it is already too late. She will think and feel in a forward direction, once her mind develops the correct picture of the horse's movement.

Forward Tendency as the Basis of Movement

Anyone who has felt what is meant by the horse "stretching into the hand in a forward and downward direction" on a well-schooled horse will not be easily fooled. The horse does not drop the neck, but elastically swings his entire body with seeming effortlessness in the active muscle chains, against the influence of gravity.

The most important difference that can be felt, compared to incorrect movement patterns, is the continuously engaged, swinging forwardness of the horse. Any disruption of balance (where the horse is either too rushed or too restrained) automatically means a mistake in the complex system of active elasticity. The term "suppleness," in its correct interpretation, describes this perfectly.

"Suppleness" Means "Active Elasticity"

To *carry himself* and work with a *swinging back,* the horse has to elastically absorb his own weight, working against gravity through the lever systems of his limbs and joints, and transform it into new movement energy–and all this has to be navigable for the rider. Therefore, *training* the riding horse means the development of an *active muscular system,* which makes the horse's movement more beautiful and elevated and also relieves strain on tendons and joints. Why this is the case, which exact forces take effect, how classical training guides us through these tasks, and what this *requires of horse and rider* will be explained in the following chapters. *Biomechanics, functional anatomy,* and *sport-scientific research* are important sources of information that will accompany us through this book.

Transformation of the "Human Being System"

The complex system of moving parts that constitutes a human being, as a biped, has to synchronize individual portions of the body with each other vertically. Humans also rely on the development of *positive tension* for optimal functionality in their daily lives, and when doing sports. Examples of different levels of tension in various runners illustrate this concept. Let us compare a more recent top runner, Ethiopian Haile Gebrselassie, to the miracle runner of the 1950s and 1960s, Czech Emil Zátopek. Both were leaders of their sport at the time. The progress that has taken place in running is not only visible with a stopwatch–Gebrselassie ran the marathon distance in about 20 minutes less than Zátopek–but mainly in the change of body tension, from *maximum* to *optimal* body tension. (The amateur runner *without* body tension shows exactly this in recreational sports, where many people participate in "fun runs" without sufficient athletic preparation and accept damages to their joints, tendons, and ligaments, even though their original motivation was to benefit their health).

Different levels of body tension in runners: supple (left), tensed (center), and lacking in body tension (right).

2 Development and Transmission of Power

The functional muscle chains in the horse's legs gather and store movement energy in the supporting leg phase …

Development of Power

In contrast to human beings, the movement patterns of a horse are that of a four-legged prey animal from the steppe. As a quadruped, the horse has been equipped by nature with the ability to elastically engage and flex his haunches. Tendons, muscles, and bones are organized so as to support each other, once they have "sprung open"–think of an umbrella–and are in working mode. They are then actively arched. Complex fascial systems connect the individual structures and permeate them. The haunches function as "catapults": they store the horse's movement energy during the supporting phase of the stride, when the horse sets his foot down, and then convert this energy into forward movement. This enables the horse to always access his maximum performance ability within this catapult

… and then propel the horse forward, through a "catapult" effect.

system. The limits of his performance ability are defined by the elastic force of the tendons and the fascial system inside and outside the muscles.

To understand complex systems, it's best to start thinking in concepts. I would like to introduce a conceptual framework that makes it possible to appropriately record and depict the basic movements of a horse.

The central components of this conceptual framework, which can be applied to any kind of equine movement, are the development and transmission of power.

The Development of Power in Detail

How is the movement energy of the horse actually created? How is it that a foal, barely up on his legs for the first time, is able to canter with the herd at full speed when necessary? As asked previously, what do I have to work on over the next four to five years, if a four-year-old horse can already jump higher than an international course set at the maximum height allowed by the governing body? Can the extended trot of a four-year-old horse, out in the field, be at all improved in preparation for performance in the dressage arena? How is it possible that my backyard horse developed a tendon injury or arthritis in his back or hocks, even though I only rode him on trails, and he was deliberately started late and never exposed to heavy work?

The mighty muscles of hind legs act like "catapults."

A "Catapult" in the Legs

Scientists have been interested in the generation of movement energy in human athletes for decades. In the process, they have used nature as a reference to better understand certain phenomena in humans. What is the ideal ratio of different muscular structures in proportion to each other? Are there other systems that contribute to the development of movement energy? A kangaroo, for example, has approximately the same muscle mass and muscle structure as a red deer, but its development of power when jumping is much higher in relation to its weight.

A kangaroo can jump up to 45 feet (almost 14 meters)! What causes this difference in ability?

To examine the phenomenon of elastic energy originating in the tendons, Finnish sports scientist Paavo Komi conducted special studies in the 1980s.

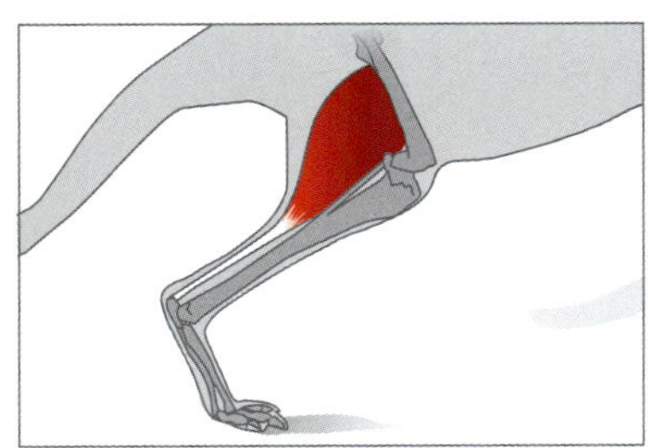
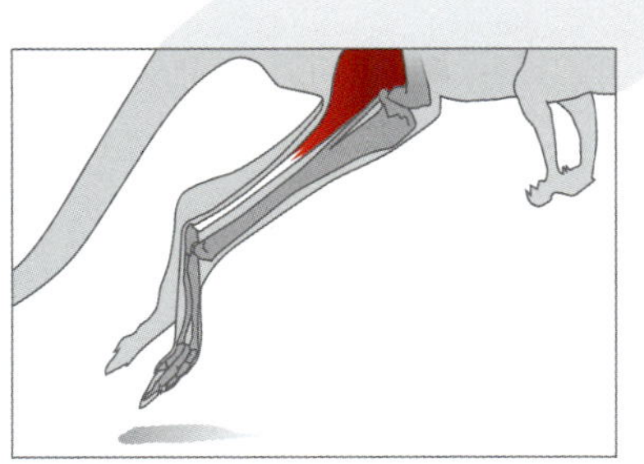

The kangaroo's "catapult" is one of the most effective in the world of mammals.

In the course of his research, surgeons attached measuring strips and fiber optic cables to the Achilles tendons of volunteer student athletes, to collect precise data about their movement patterns. The results were just as revolutionary as they were plausible.

Long elastic structures of tissue store energy during the supporting leg phase through stretching, which is immediately made available to power movement. They function like rubber bands. The quality of the rubber band is genetically determined, and ultimately a decisive criterion for the performance ability of the body. African runners, whose specialty–genetically speaking–is long-distance running, do not have more or longer calf muscles than anyone else. On the contrary, they have significantly longer tendons, and therefore shorter calf muscles, on average, than their competitors. The elastic energy stemming from those long tendons makes them more resistant to fatigue.

The British zoologist Robert McNeill Alexander from the University of Cambridge precisely described these principles in his book *Elastic Mechanisms in Animal Movement* (Cambridge University Press, 1988). Now, it's possible to understand that the horse generates substantial parts of his movement energy from the elastic structures of his tendon and muscle systems. New studies have expanded the possibilities by demonstrating the elasticity of fascial tissue.

The Secret of Fascial Structures

Fascia are tissues that enclose and permeate every muscle fiber, fiber bundle, muscle, and muscle group in the body like a three-dimensional cobweb. They are an important element of effortless energy transmission in the horse, as they connect the individual muscle chains of the legs with the torso, in addition to connecting the different movement centers of the body with each other. New research around this highly elastic and dynamic tissue immensely expands the possibilities for the tendons' "catapult effect." Fascial systems have a significant impact on the transmission of movement energy; additionally, they transfer information and transport oxygen.

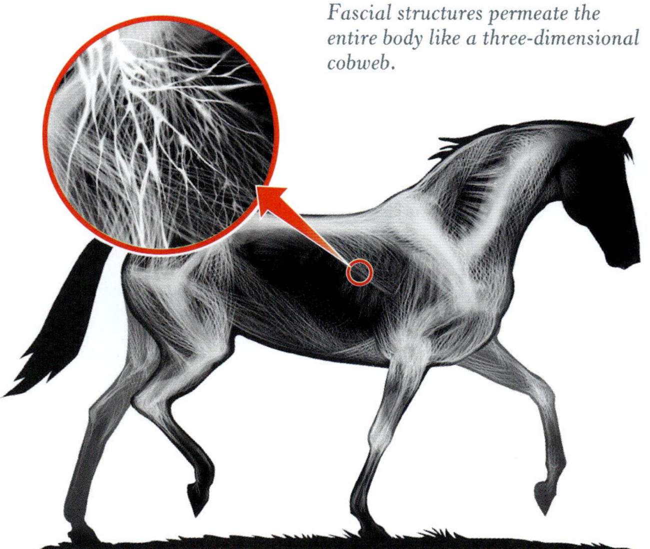

Fascial structures permeate the entire body like a three-dimensional cobweb.

Highly Efficient

The construction of a horse's legs is perfectly adapted to effortless forward movement at higher speed. This *tour de force of nature* guarantees that the natural enemies of all grazing quadrupeds of the steppe do not always emerge

victorious, if it comes down to a chase of life and death—although they undoubtedly reach higher speeds over a shorter time than their prey. The outcome is decided in approximately the first 10 feet (3 meters). If the horse survives those 10 feet, then he is at an advantage, since he needs a lot less energy to maintain his speed than his four-legged pursuer. The "gas tank" of a tiger becomes emptier with every jump forward; it has to decide whether its limited physical resources might better be used to hunt a slower animal. The catapult effect created by the legs of horses, however, is at its most efficient at a fast run and literally catapults their bodies forward, consuming relatively little energy. Therefore, only injured or weak animals that cannot react or tire quickly are in danger, in the wild.

A racehorse remains in his natural movement pattern—flight—and can thus achieve his top speed at two and a half years of age.

The Human System

A human needs about one year of development after birth to take her first steps. Once a human being is upright on two legs, her body has to be continuously stabilized in a vertical position to defy gravity in various situations. Due to the human body's many flexible parts, this coordination is highly demanding. The strength to stabilize the body seems to build up almost playfully, in the early stages of movement development.

Compared to some species, human beings take a long time to achieve this degree of development. An infant can stand upright within about nine months, and

If a child moves actively and playfully, then ideally, her movement and coordination systems are constantly working—and improving.

Olympic and World Champion discus thrower Robert Harting needs constant systematic training to reach his maximum performance ability.

can typically walk around 12 months of age. Approximately two to three years will pass before a child can achieve a true moment of suspension. Before reaching seven years of age, the foundation, at the level of coordination, is laid for all other movement patterns. During this time, regular and sufficiently versatile movement guarantees a body's healthy development. Deficits during this development phase can be difficult to correct later. Once you turn 14 or 15, it's very hard work to run a tenth of a second faster or jump an inch farther.

Humans need good body tension and coordination to maintain their upright position. This should ideally develop within the first seven years of age. Their maximum athletic performance ability can only be reached after the completion of puberty, and is dominated and defined by athletic training.

Performance Can Be Bought ...

Horses, as precocial animals, have structures that equip foals with astonishing movement potential from birth. As a result, the maximum performance ability of a young horse is not determined by the degree of training of his muscles, but by the genetic foundations of his "catapult systems." This includes the elasticity of his tissue, the lengths of his bones, and the angles of his joints.

This means the equation for the young horse is: ideal elasticity plus *ideal lever systems result in maximum performance.* In other words, for horses, maximum performance ability is genetically predetermined and can only partially be influenced by training.

That is why the maximum performance ability of a horse has to be primarily bred or bought—the effect of athletic training is only ever secondary!

... But Training Is a Skill

A fast racehorse is immediately fast, a good jumper can jump very high very quickly, and a dressage horse does or does not have outstanding gaits. Why, then, is years-long training needed at all? The answer is as simple as it is meaningful: *Existing power must be steered in new directions, which are controllable for the rider but protect the horse against chronic overload.* This is the key and a necessity for any athletic training of a riding horse.

Maximum performance cannot be developed. But pre-existing maximum performance can be directed. Thus, the task of training is to control the transmission of power—that is what distinguishes a horse from a riding horse.

Money or Health?

Looking at the horse's movement system helps us understand many scenarios we may have seen or experienced at competitions. A top performance horse can be bought. If I drill him with spurs and sharp bits, I can direct his existing elastic force in prescribed directions or teach him tricks. Unfortunately, even poorly muscled and badly ridden horses can win a competition. The result is short-term success, paid for with money and the horse's welfare at the same time.

If I buy this top performance horse and have him trained well, it will take a lot longer to develop his movement quality. The trainer has to restructure the foundations of movement in a riding horse and actually strengthen and train the muscles needed. This is the only system that will create success in the long run. But it has a high cost of its own, as this kind of training is time-consuming and expensive.

What makes the difference is the sustainability of this second type of training, which enables the horse to perform well for many years. Above all, this system does not waste the horse's health, but rather promotes it.

The question now is: Do you give your money to veterinarians, physical therapists, and horse dealers, or to a respectable trainer? The latter is definitely cheaper. But the real reward is a horse that *loves what he does* and *stays sound* over many years, in body, mind, and spirit. This does not put vets and physical therapists out of work; it simply shifts their focus, for the well-being of the horse.

Summary

The movement energy of a horse originates in long, elastic tissue structures and is immediately fully available upon birth, essentially without any training. The combination of bones, joints, tendons, and muscles works like a "catapult," storing movement energy and transforming it, in a manner similar to a spring, into forward movement. Most importantly of all, the overall system needs tension for the maximum development of performance. The horse's training transforms the negative tension of a tensed back in flight mode into positive, elastic tension. In the process, muscle chains actively carry the horse's front and hind ends, due to the rider's aids. This system differs fundamentally from the movement development of humans, which means what works for human training or therapy does not necessarily work for horses.

The Transmission of Power

What does it mean, from a functional perspective, to say the horse *carries him-self,* or his *back is swinging,* or a *leg mover* has become a *back mover*? Is it enough when he *lengthens the neck,* or is a horse categorically *in front of the leg* when the *hindquarters are engaged*? All these catchphrases are only small parts of the horse's complex system of *active stabilization*. To clarify matters, it is worth pursuing the path of movement energy further.

The Transmission of Power in More Detail

The most important interfaces within this system are those regions where the movement energy from the legs is transferred to the torso. They are called the "front center of power transmission" (FCPT) and "hind center of power development" (HCPD) in this framework.

Structure of the Front and Hind Movement Centers

The neck-chest complex, which connects to both front legs through the shoulder girdle, forms the FCPT.

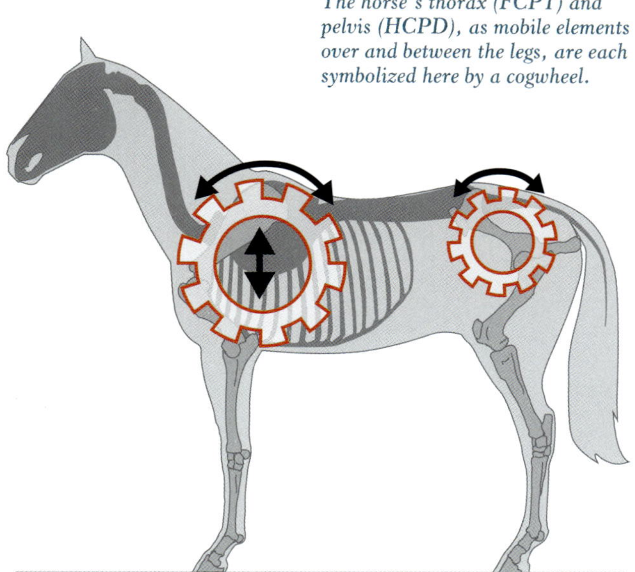

The horse's thorax (FCPT) and pelvis (HCPD), as mobile elements over and between the legs, are each symbolized here by a cogwheel.

The HCPD includes the bony pelvis ring, the lumbar column, the sacrum, and the coccygeal vertebrae. The biggest difference between the HCPD and the FCPT is that the HCPD has a stable joint connection to the legs. While in both cases, this connection is only achieved through tendons and muscles, the hind end has the two large hip joints, which represent a nearly fixed rotational axis. Thus, movement energy from the hindquarters can generate a larger leveraging effect through the hip joints, in a forward movement direction, than movement energy from the forelegs.

Both the FCPT and the HCPD are mobile. Viewed in profile, the FCPT can be raised and lowered, as well as rotated toward the head and the tail. The HCPD can also rotate toward the head and the tail. Depending on how these movement centers are positioned, the direction and manner of power transmission can change.

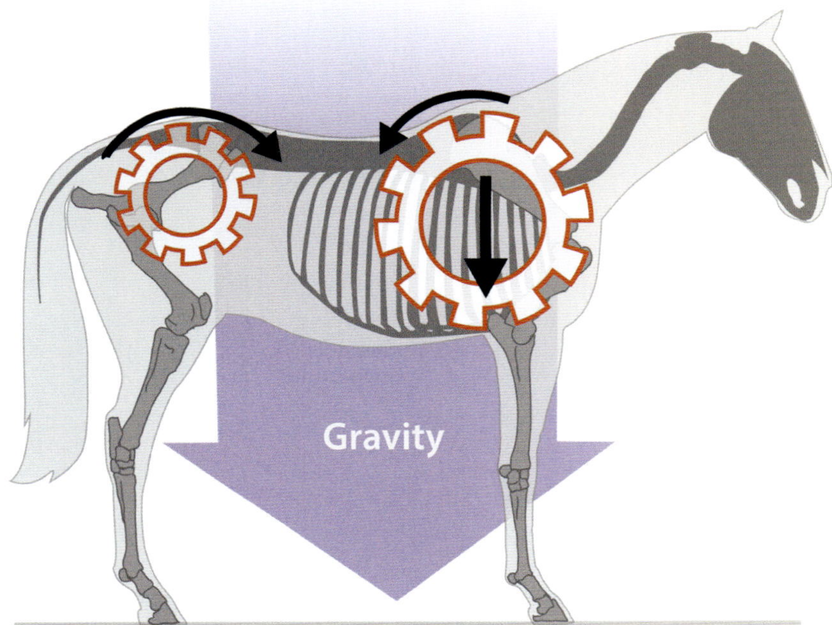

When gravity is exerting a downward force on the horse, these two cogwheels move toward the center of the horse and approach one another.

Horse or Riding Horse?

There is one fundamental difference between an untrained horse and a riding horse. That difference is in *how* stabilization works against gravity. The untrained horse's natural movement pattern is geared solely toward efficiency. Initially, flight is essential for survival. At top speed, a tense back presses the torso downward and exerts force on the tendons and joint systems of the spine. This system is comparatively stable with little effort. All energy reserves can be used for forward movement. The horse's motor skills, geared toward maximum performance during flight, develop to accomplish this.

Once flight mode has ended, any strained structures can recover over several hours or days, grazing at the walk, at maximum relief.

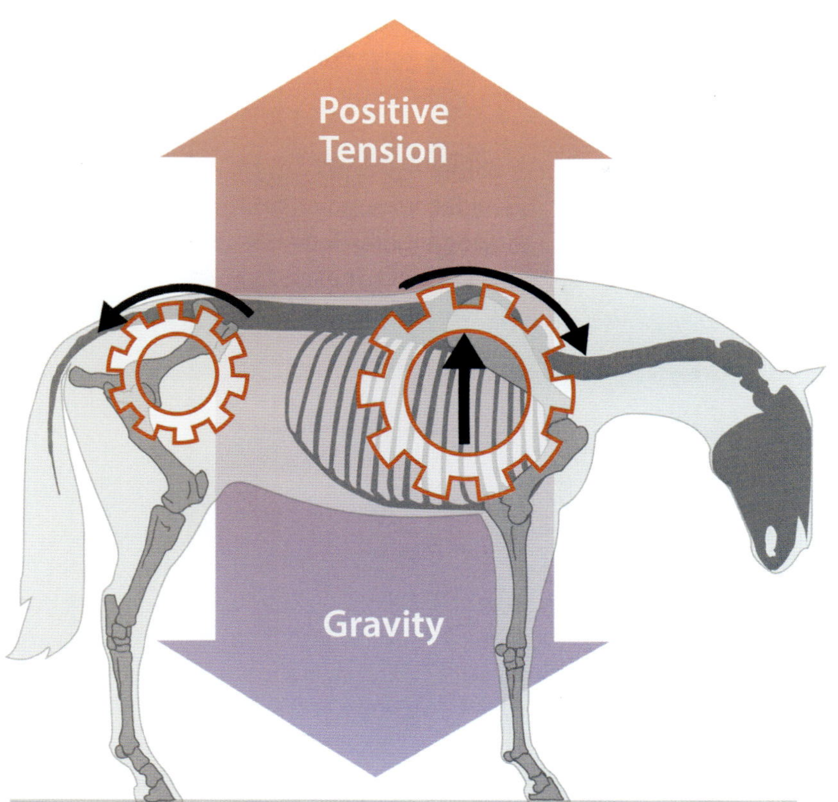

Positive tension works against gravity and opens the horse's topline, reversing the rotation of the cogwheels.

The riding horse, however, is supposed to follow another movement plan. He is expected to carry himself actively, and take direction from the rider's very light aids, on straight and curved lines. This can work successfully, but the manner of power transmission has to change. The horse's torso must be raised upward against gravity and cushioned by his muscle slings in the supporting leg phase. This kind of positive body tension creates an active equalizer for the force of gravity, but one that is still manageable for the rider. The horse feels light and elastic. The lightness felt is ultimately dependent on a functional, athletically organized movement pattern.

The natural movement of the untrained horse and of a riding horse.

The phrase "the horse needs to carry himself" can absolutely be taken literally.

With respect to methodical training, it isn't maximum performance that needs to be developed, but the direction in which this performance is guided. For this, the riding horse particularly needs those muscles that cushion his mass against gravity. This is the proper way to approach training any riding horse, as well as the focus of athletic training.

Riders can only indirectly have an influence on the development of power. Developing control over the transmission of that power is their sole and most important task.

To fully understand this process, we will first analyze the two movement centers independently of each other.

A long way from crawling to walking …

An Interesting Comparison

In terms of the time involved, this process is definitely comparable to the movement development of humans as they work to achieve their erect posture. It takes at least three to four years before horse and human can *actively stabilize themselves against gravity*. For humans, this takes place at the very beginning of movement development from infant to toddler. About four years pass until a child is able to cushion an upright posture against gravity, when walking, with a true moment of suspension. The horse has this ability from the onset, but active, muscular stabilization against gravity is reserved for the training of the riding horse, and also takes approximately four years to develop. For the horse, this movement pattern is the basis for the optimal transmission of power, which is manageable for the rider in any equestrian discipline.

No training is necessary for the development of leg movement—but it's essential for the development of activity in the back.

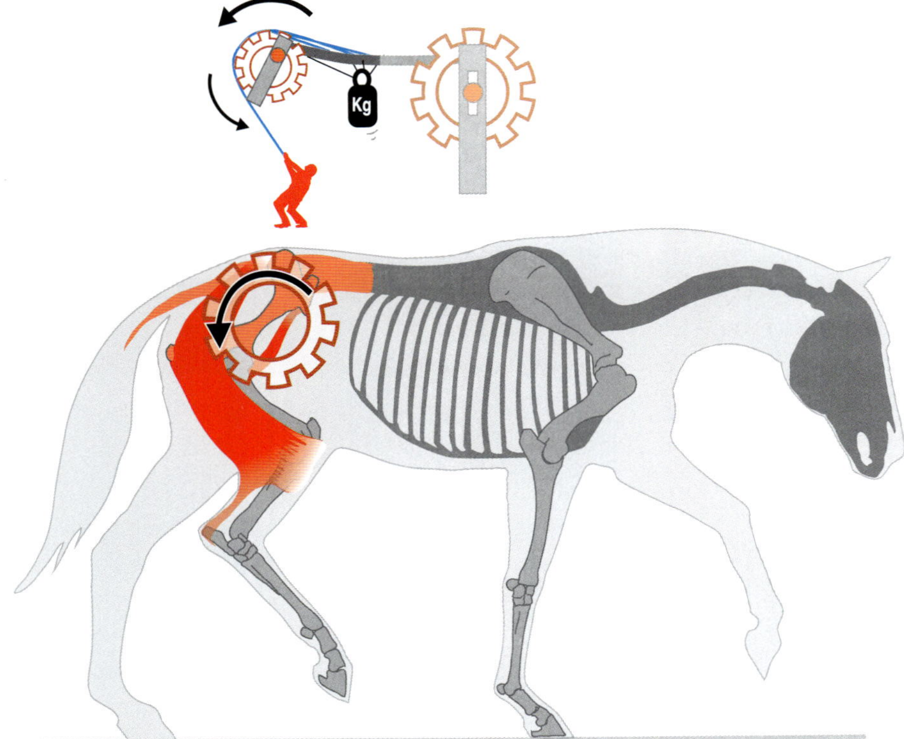

The active rotation of the pelvis in a backward direction organizes the increased absorption of energy and thus the elasticity of the hindquarters.

The Hind Center of Power Development (HCPD)—Carried Actively

If we don't limit ourselves to seeing the legs as part of the horse's hindquarters, but widen our perspective, functionally speaking, to the loin-pelvis region, fascinating mechanisms become apparent.

The change in the position of the HCPD means a rotation of the pelvis toward the tail. Riding theory calls this *stepping under* or *engaging the hind legs*. In well-schooled horses, this position of the pelvis leads to an ideal positioning of the hind legs for the conversion of forward thrust into carrying capacity. Bringing the hip joint closer in the direction of the horse's center of gravity shortens the horse's frame and makes the lever effect of the hind legs more favorable for maximizing carrying capacity. The muscles of the hind legs do not carry more weight, but change the position of the pelvis to raise the basic tension of the HCPD.

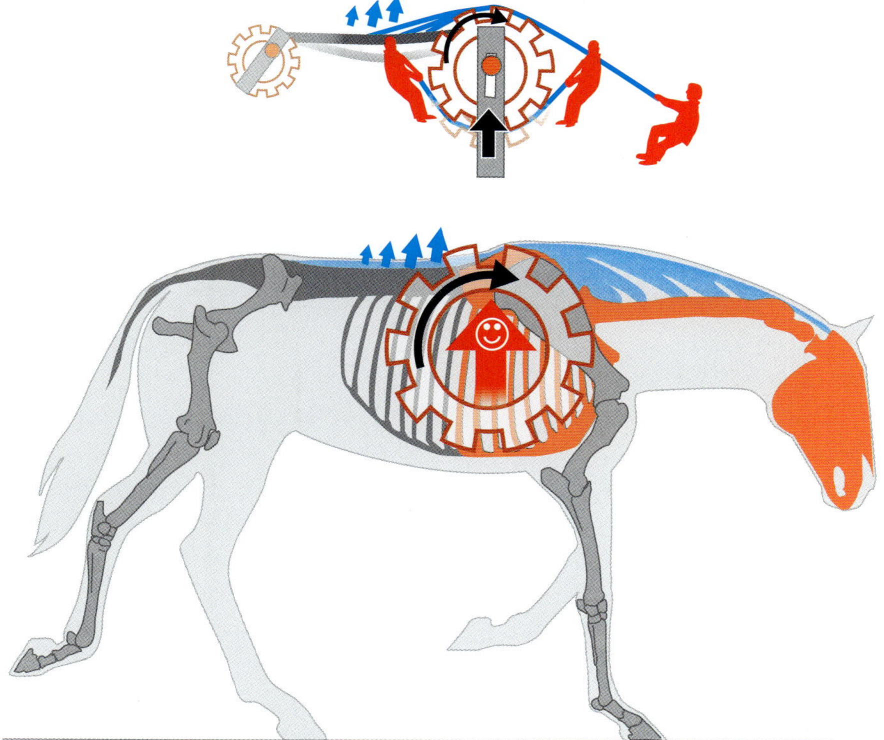

The Front Center of Power Transmission (FCPT)—Carried Actively

This conceptual framework for understanding movement ascribes a much more important role to the horse's forehand than is the case in other common frameworks.

The thorax in trained horses is centrally raised above the shoulder girdle; it is in balance, and its position is controlled by the muscles. This makes it possible for the horse to react to the rider's aids and optimally manage his movement energy for the task at hand. The muscle group of the shoulder girdle is responsible for lifting the thorax.

Only an actively carried ribcage can enable the topline to do its job.

Only by raising the withers, for example, are the topline muscles able to carry the neck in its entire length. Only active musculature can functionally stretch, and thus actively arch passive structures—for example, the long nuchal ligament (again, comparable to opening an umbrella). Depending on the horse's level of training, this position is infinitely flexible, used for everything from a forward and downward movement with impulsion to high-level collection.

Structure and Function of the Front Center of Power Transmission

The horse's "engine" is in the back. In equestrianism, this statement is set in stone. And in general, this is correct, where forward movement is concerned. But the FCPT has, at minimum, an equal share in performance ability, since it is mainly responsible for transferring movement energy from the hind end. That energy can be slowed down, or redirected into forward or cadenced uphill movement.

Balance as a Feat

The horse has to perform with astonishing effort to reach a balance that demands active muscle engagement and hold it for every step. The thorax weighs about 450 pounds (200 kilograms). This weight has to be lifted and balanced.

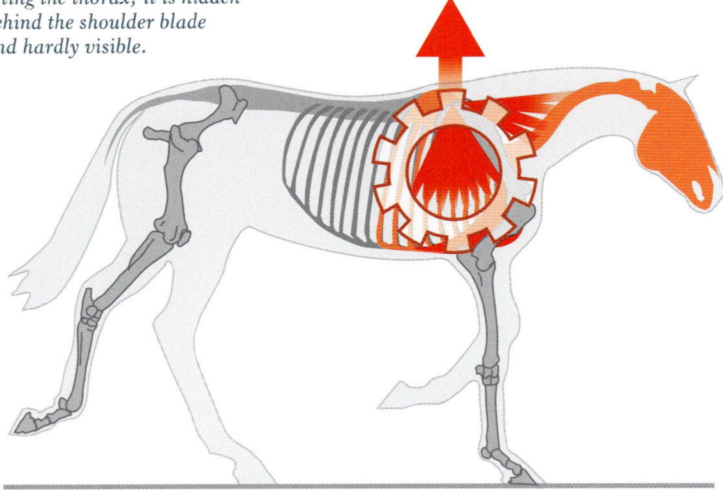

The shoulder girdle, depicted schematically here, is the most important muscle for lifting the thorax; it is hidden behind the shoulder blade and hardly visible.

The development of this new position is no different from riding theory asking *for the horse to carry himself*. Yes, he quite literally carries himself. In this context, the responsibility of the rider's leg also becomes clear. It certainly does more than simply engage the hind legs. Together with the rider's other aids, the legs create the pivotal impulse to lift the thorax between the scapulae, particularly in young horses.

The Neck as a Balancing Pole

It is the responsibility of the upper neck muscles to develop and maintain the horse's balance in every step or stride. The *actively carried neck* functions as a counterweight for the torso weight of the horse and the weight of the rider. The individual balance of the horse, as well as its dynamic adjustment, are criteria for determining the position of the neck. The muscles of the topline are supported in this task by abdominal and thoracic muscles.

Neither "the higher, the better" nor "the longer and lower, the better" applies. Training takes place between these two extreme positions: the constant use of the neck to balance actively.

There are many decisions to be made: a little more or a little less forward, a little more leg or the neck a little deeper, restrain or encourage, support with the hand or not, back on the longe line or trot poles, trail riding or riding in the outside arena, free-jumping or being out in the field …. Any of these decisions can be right or wrong, depending on whether it's helpful for any individual horse in a particular situation to develop an *active balance with muscular engagement* or not.

The neck as a balancing pole and training element for the shoulder girdle.

There is no one correct position for the neck. On the contrary, since the neck has to be actively carried together with the torso, it's imperative to constantly change positions slightly. Fatigue of the active muscle chains can only be avoided by shifting between fascia bundles, engaging new areas and giving previously engaged areas a break. That's all—but "that's all" doesn't mean it's simple.

Active Muscle Chains
- torso support muscles
- topline
- straight abdominal muscles

Signs to Look For
- a beautifully developed topline, tapering evenly from the neck base toward the head
- a well-filled-out area behind the upper part of the scapula
- broad chest with a straight alignment of the legs

The pattern of muscle engagement in an active FCPT.

Structure and Function of the Hind Center of Power Development—Active Structures

Equestrian literature frequently assumes that in the development of collection over the course of a horse's long-term training, *weight is truly shifted from front to back.* New scientific research has shown that this does not describe the actual processes in the horse's body. The distribution of weight between forehand and hindquarters only changes minimally if collection is correctly developed.

Therefore, the phrase *the hind legs taking on and carrying additional weight* actually means an increased storage of movement energy in the muscle slings of the HCPD, when visualized using the cogwheel model. The more the pelvis rotates backward, the more movement energy is absorbed. Due to this change in angle, the oscillating weight of the intestines bounces more vertically, downward and back up at the same time. Forward thrust turns into the carrying capacity of collection. In the end, the highest form of collection, the piaffe, requires a balanced angle change in the positions of the thorax and pelvis. The horse moves elastically on the spot, as if he were on springs, with maximum energy storage in his torso.

In young or untrained horses, it is initially necessary to suspend the negative movement or the lowering of the loins respectively. The horse's intestines alone weigh about 550 pounds (250 kilograms).

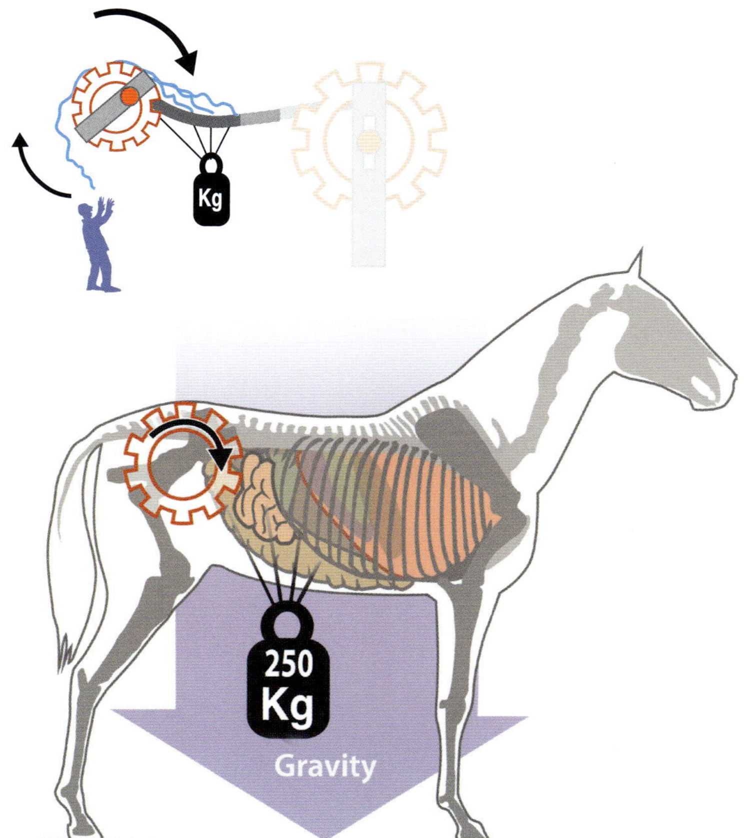

Without active, positive body tension, the horse's spine is subject to massive strain from the weight of the intestines.

Only hind legs that are stepping actively under the horse's body, toward the center of gravity, can achieve stabilization of the pelvis and provide relief for the spine. Over the course of a horse's training, the large muscle chains of the HCPD change the entire balance of the horse, once an increased engagement of the hind legs in the early stages of collection transforms forward thrust into *carrying capacity*. The movement energy stored in these powerful flexed springs increases with every step or stride, and is released into different directions, depending on the type of movement asked of the horse.

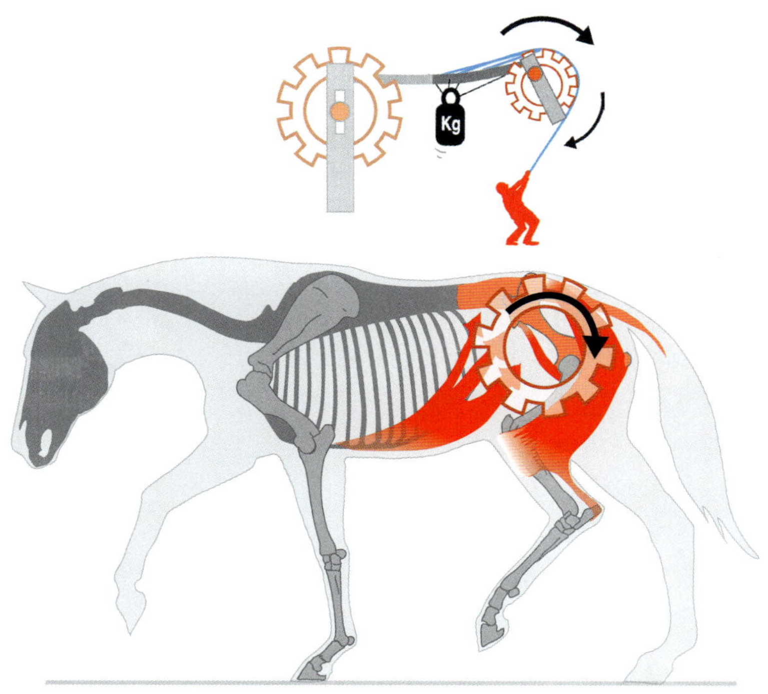

The long muscles of the hindquarters and the abdominal muscles support the rotation of the pelvis backward, as long as the spine can move freely upward.

Therefore, the increased engagement of the hind legs under the horse's body is not controlled by the hind legs themselves, but by changing the position of the pelvis in relation to the spine. In the process, the horse's frame is indeed shortened—not in front, but rather behind the rider!

The hind legs maintain the same overall movement pattern, but shift farther toward the center of gravity through the lowering of the pelvis, and thereby change the direction of movement energy from forward thrust to carrying capacity. An increased angle in the large joint is the result of rotation of the pelvis—and not vice versa. Strengthening the hindquarters isn't just about the hind legs; it also involves the muscle chains of the HCPD and the lumbar column.

The rider can only support the backward rotation of the pelvis and the active engagement of the horse under his center of gravity if she sits "into the movement."

Muscle Chains Involved
- croup muscles (gluteal muscle)
- straight and oblique abdominal muscles
- inner loin muscles

Signs to Look For
- beautifully angled, round croup
- slim, flat flanks
- evenly soft loin section

Carrying of Weight—A Common Misunderstanding

Carrying of weight is often interpreted very differently by different people, and commonly misconstrued. If the horse is supposed to only transfer weight onto his hind legs, this result could be achieved by bringing the horse's head up and back, and putting pressure on the reins. The resulting shift in the horse's mass would lead to increased weight on his hind end. From a functional perspective, however, this does not make sense, and only leads to wear and tear on the hind legs. What is actually meant in discussions of *carrying of weight* is more a matter of *shortening the horse's frame.* Functionally speaking, this takes place through the backward rotation of the pelvis, as described previously (see p. 30). The croup is lowered, and the hip joints are brought closer to the horse's center of gravity.

A low croup is the visible sign of *flexion in the haunches,* and therefore of increased flexion in all major joints of the hindquarters, including the loin-pelvis passage. The lever of the weight placed on the hind end is shortened, and at the same time, muscular elasticity is intensified.

In simple terms: The development of collection, though exhausting to the muscles, will ultimately relieve strain on the joints of the horse. The goal is not to take up and carry more weight, but to alter the effective direction of the existing weight with changes in basic tension.

Summary
*A well-trained riding horse needs to follow a different movement pattern than
an untrained horse in the wild. If he is to trot and canter for long periods of
time, follow fine aids, and perform tight turns, his natural way of going has to
be fundamentally changed to avoid any damage to body or spirit.*

*During the active stabilization of a riding horse, his thorax is lifted between
his shoulder blades and balanced in a forward direction. This movement pattern opens the door for movement energy from the hind end to flow to the
front end, and at the same time, it allows for the control of this movement
energy through the straightening of the pelvis. The horse arches and opens
up his topline.*

*Both the front and hind movement centers of the horse are autonomously
stabilized against the effects of gravity. This is only possible through the effort
of active muscle engagement, not just through the use of passive structures
such as the long nuchal ligament. From a functional perspective, a trainer
develops two gigantic muscular springs, one in the horse's shoulders and one
in the pelvic girdle. These muscular springs have two significant effects on the
horse's movement pattern. For one thing, they develop what the rider calls
"cadence": They slow down the movement while extending range of motion.
Secondly, they function as a shock absorber and relieve strain on passive
structures like tendons and joints.*

*Therefore, equestrian sport training, correctly executed, always promotes the horse's
health and welfare up to the highest level. It is never damaging.*

A "trampoline effect" develops between the two movement centers, in addition
to the spring-like properties of the FCPT and HCPD. The next section explores
the mechanics of actively stabilized oscillating mass and will show how this works
in more detail.

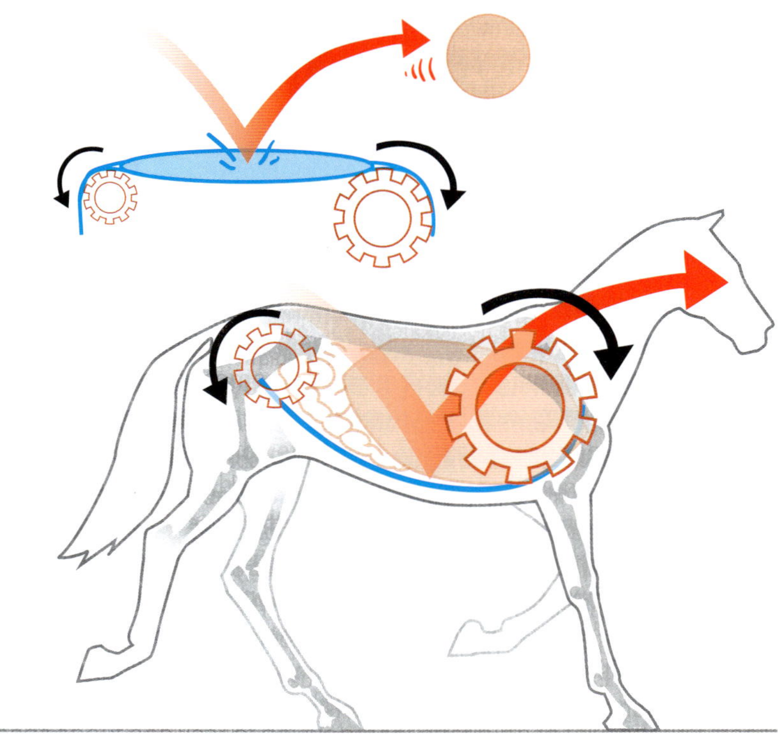

Interaction Between the Two Movement Centers

The "Trampoline" Inside the Horse
The ultimate logic of classical riding theory derives from the functional interaction of both the front and hind movement centers.

The movement centers can only work interdependently during movement. Once the thorax and pelvis are optimally positioned, both are elastically held in position by actively organized muscle chains. If the torso mass swings into this elastic system, it is ejected—it bounces back out, you might say—with little loss of energy. This is what happens if a horse is *correctly on the aids* and *carries himself*. He builds up *inner positive tension,* or—to stick with the metaphor—he unfolds a "trampoline" in his body, which turns movement into a "game with his own body." In addition, another "catapult system" is created in the horse's torso, which is responsible for the development of cadence during movement.

The rider's first major task is to facilitate this unfolding of the "trampoline"—to actively *support* it and to *synchronize* it. Over the course of the horse's long-term training, this mechanism is developed further to maximize cadence, collection, and forward movement.

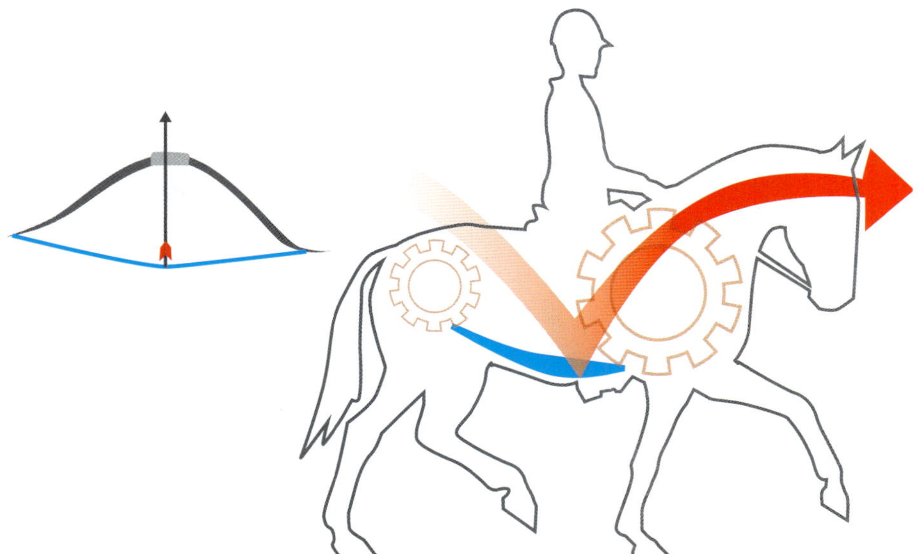

From a biomechanical perspective, only the effective direction of the horse's mass is changed through the positioning of the pelvis and the thorax. This is true for the entire movement range, from extended trot to piaffe—from being catapulted forward to standing almost vertically upright.

The FCPT as a center of power transmission has an increased forward and upward effect, and, for the most part, it controls the development of cadence. The HCPD, as the center for power development, also changes the effective direction of its power: from a relatively flat pelvis position for the extended trot to a steeper position to develop collection.

Yet all this only works the way it should if the trot remains perfectly synchronized—within the diagonal pair of legs as well as across the movement sequences of the two diagonals. This explains pictures where the horse momentarily shows a one-legged support phase in extended trot: there is a lack of synchronization of the movement centers. Very often, this issue can then only be compensated for by exaggerated overriding, seen in riders who are leaning far back and literally thrusting the horse forward.

The "Trampoline Effect" in Trot

The "trampoline effect" performs two important functions in the movement of a trained horse. Firstly, it functions as a *shock absorber,* and secondly, in a manner similar to the spring-like elasticity of the legs, it transforms the horse's movement energy into *forward movement.*

In trot, gravitational force has a profound effect on the horse's center of gravity. The diagonal support phase means that both movement centers have to become active at the same time. Each movement center is responsible for its own elasticity. Ideally, the active springs of the front and hind movement centers combine to become one large "trampoline."

The "Trampoline Effect" in Canter

The effect of gravitational force is dictated by the sequence of footfalls. Only one front leg is affected in the fifth phase in canter, and only one hind leg is affected in the first phase. The "trampoline effect" is significantly stronger due to the line of action of the front leg's power and is mainly responsible for developing "uphill movement" in canter.

In this context, you'll often hear the following: "The horse has to sit on his haunches," or "The horse has to take up more weight to lighten the forehand." Every rider wants to feel uphill movement.

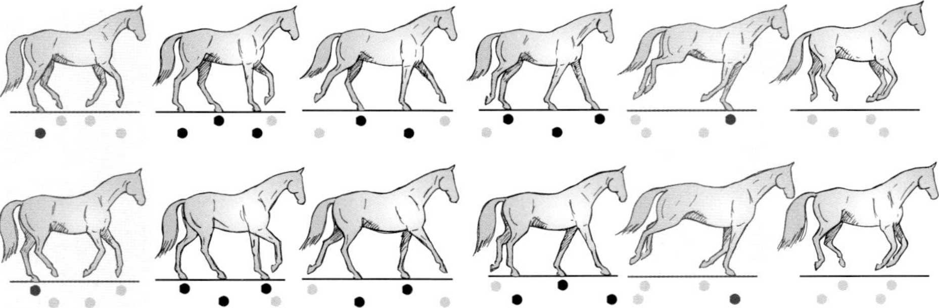

The six phases of canter in the horse's natural movement.

But the mental images that are created in the rider certainly call for further discussion. The emphasis on hind-end activity in canter leads to the idea that the hind legs, pushing powerfully off the ground, sort of propel the horse's body upward.

If we take a closer look at the causes of and reasons for uphill movement, we have to ask ourselves which muscle groups actually do lead to lift along the

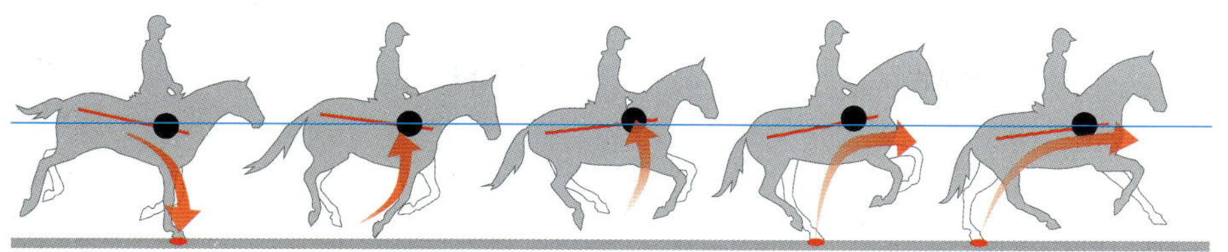

longitudinal axis of the horse's body. A look at the entire movement sequence in canter shows what is actually happening.

The horse supports himself with the forehand on his last contact with the ground before the moment of suspension. This impulse is what lifts the forehand during the moment of suspension. The hindquarters cannot support this movement process, as they are in the air for the entire time that the longitudinal axis is lifted. The hind leg only touches the ground at the end of the moment of suspension—the moment where the downhill movement begins. The hind leg develops forward movement and has to lower the forehand in a controlled manner at the same time. However, the hind end is not responsible for the development of uphill movement during this movement pattern. It can only control the lowering of the forehand and powerfully push the horse's body forward at the angle created by the forehand.

Ultimately, you have to differentiate between a transition to canter and cantering. This is why Colonel Waldemar Seunig strongly emphasized the sequence of legs in transitions between gaits in his classic work *Horsemanship* (Trafalgar Square Books, 2003). For example, to start the canter from walk, a gait without impulsion, the horse has to actively arch his body in a way that is a lot more strenuous for the muscles. The same applies to all downward transitions, where the movement energy of the diagonal support phase (third phase) has to be absorbed

The rider's seat has to be effective in the supporting phase of the inside front leg, to allow room for the uphill movement in the very next moment by "sitting into the movement."

by the body and cannot be transferred into forward movement. That's why the quality of transitions is so crucial and so demanding for the horse's muscles.

The Ensemble Interacting—Active Structures
The muscle slings of the movement centers, described earlier, now have to work together in a *synchronized* manner. This creates an overall picture that will convey a sense of effortlessness to rider and spectator alike, and give the horse his noble and powerful appearance.

A trained horse changes from "untrained horse" mode to "riding horse" mode within very few steps.

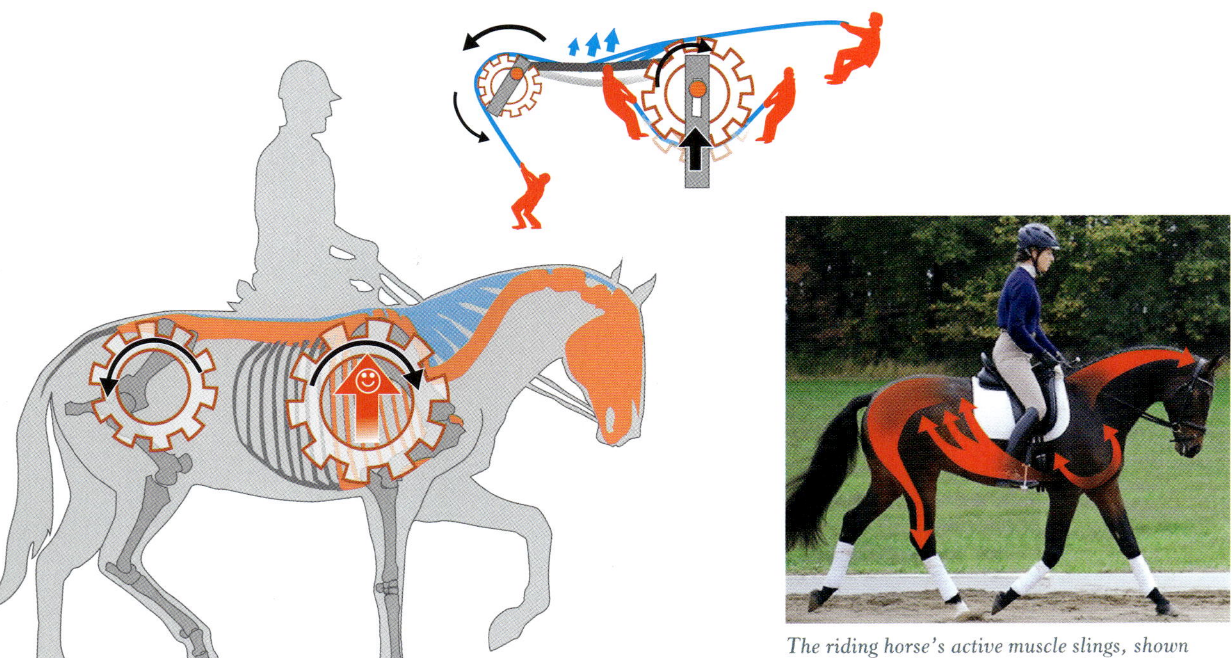

The riding horse's active muscle slings, shown in a diagram illustrating the cogwheel model and as an overlay on a photo depicting the pattern of muscle engagement.

Breathing as a Center of Movement

There is a muscular structure I would like to particularly emphasize in discussing the interplay between the movement centers: the *diaphragm*.

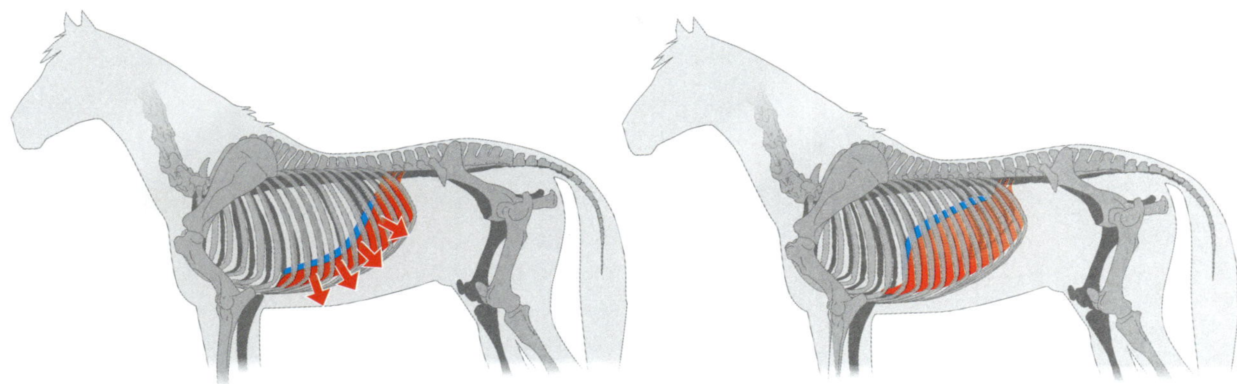

The diaphragm when breathing in and breathing out.

Only the previously described interplay between FCPT and HCPD allows for a riding horse's relaxed breathing. This quickly becomes clear once we look at the diaphragm's anatomy. It's strung up between the rear part of the sternum and the lumbar spine. If the horse rotates his pelvis backward when engaging the hindquarters under his body, the lumbar spine automatically lifts up. The sternum has to follow this movement if tension between the two movement centers is to be maintained.

Inside the working "trampoline effect": the effective direction of power can be guided through the use of very refined aids.

In my opinion, the diaphragm, as a central muscle, plays a significant part in the interplay between the two movement centers. It represents the connection between forehand and hindquarters in the correct movement pattern of a riding horse, to an even greater degree than the abdominal muscles. It has to carry out its task as a respiratory muscle between the two actively arched movement centers. In addition, it is involved in the development of positive tension between the movement centers.

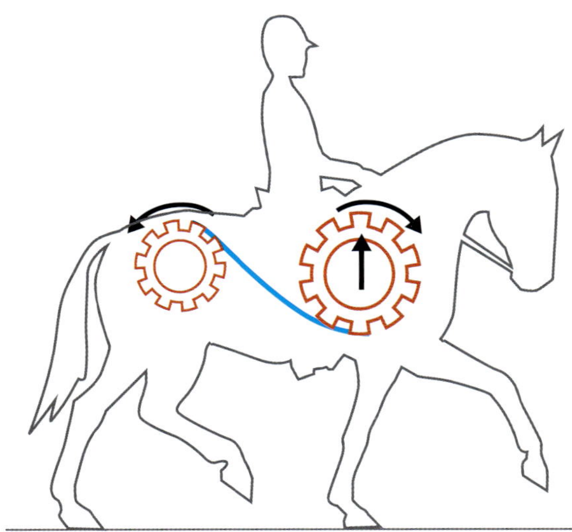

The diaphragm connects the two movement centers.

This alone is reason enough to never train so much that the horse is performing past the point where suppleness, and subsequently the correct breathing rhythm, are lost. A tense diaphragm is strong enough to pull the lumbar spine down and completely obstruct the movement of a swinging back.

Summary

The laws of physics also apply to equine movement. Energy never vanishes; you can either guide it in different directions or transform it. If you drive your car toward a wall, you can transform movement energy into friction and heat by braking, or you can use the same energy to deform the vehicle's body by crashing. Nowadays, electric cars can also use the energy of braking to recharge their batteries. The diversion of a horse's movement energy works very similarly when it actively stabilizes in his muscle chains—only it does so more directly. Every time the horse supports himself, coming out of the moment of suspension, movement energy is stored in the muscle slings of the movement centers and is converted into either forward thrust or carrying capacity, depending on the position of the thorax and pelvis.

The Scale of Training, the guiding principle of classical riding theory, describes exactly this approach to developing additional muscle elasticity in the horse.

One factor makes all the difference—namely, how the two movement centers of the horse are adjusted and synchronized.

- The horse is only in front of the rider's leg if the FCPT is adjusted upward.
- The horse can be forward-oriented at all times only if he is in front of the rider's leg.
- The horse can maintain his willingness to stretch only if he is in front of the rider's leg.

There is no way to directly, correctly engage the hindquarters farther under the center of gravity, if the FCPT has not made room to do so.

Incorrect Movement Concepts and Their Consequences

A conclusion can be drawn from what I have described so far. There are three basic states of tension in a horse: *positive tension, negative tension,* and *"negative relaxation"* (muscular exhaustion). The latter two are equally damaging for the horse. Health problems are bound to occur if these two states are included in a horse's training paradigm.

During flight.

Passive Elasticity—Tensed

The stability of the points of intersection is the sole criterion for the transmission of power. In a horse's natural movement pattern, this stability is achieved through *maximum downward tension* of both movement centers. This means that when the horse sets his foot down in the sequence of his gait, the thorax is pressed backward and downward into strong tendon structures, the back muscles pull the pelvis forward, and maximum tension is created between the back muscles and the bones of the spine. The energy from the legs is converted to *maximum forward movement,* with very little loss.

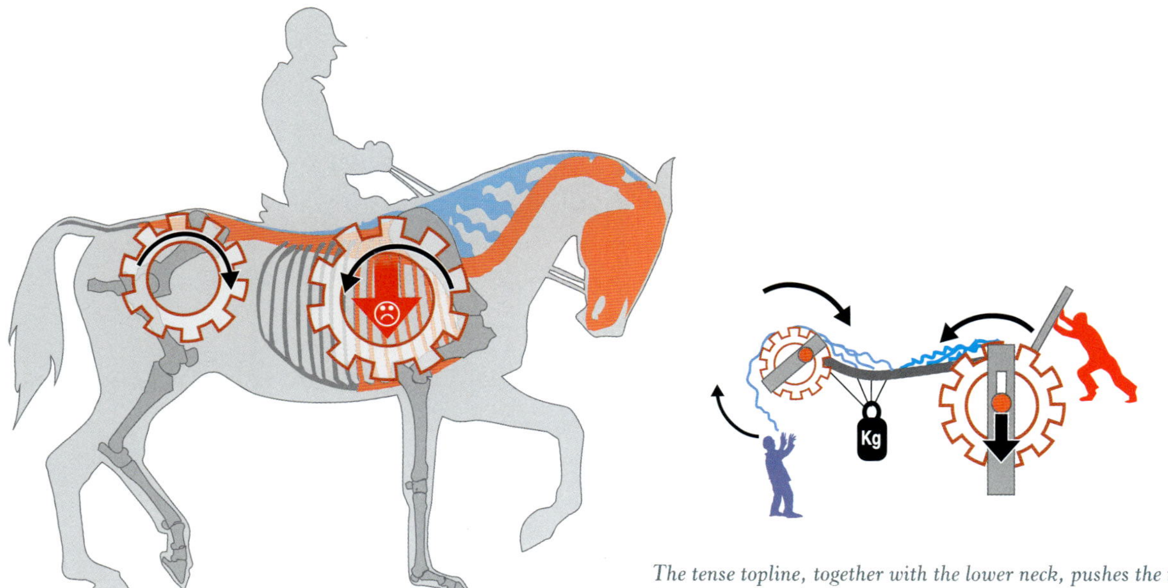

The tense topline, together with the lower neck, pushes the thorax into the passive structures of the FCPT.

This is more or less equivalent to the horse's natural flight mode. The back is *extremely taut* and the forward-oriented transmission of power works like a catapult. The horse's movement energy is maximally utilized, but the strain on the passive system is also at a maximum. In dressage, these mechanisms correspond to those of a "leg mover."

FCPT–Passively Stabilized–Tensed

The horse lifts his head and neck, and presses his thorax backward and downward. His natural movement pattern during flight is mimicked and controlled with minimal effort. The horse loses his natural willingness to go forward due to the position of the FCPT and has to create increasing amounts of thrust to continue going forward. The rider typically steps on the brakes (hard hands, strong bit) and the gas pedal (sharp spurs, heavy use of the whip) at the same time. Within this movement pattern, the additional strain caused by the raising of the forehand is directed in a straight line into the joint structures of the spine as well as the tendons and joints of the front legs, without any buffer.

The positioning of the FCPT can be useful in nature during a short-term flight response, and without a rider's influence. However, it is an extreme strain for a riding horse in the long run, as the backward and downward position of the thorax also diverts movement energy directly into the tendons and joints of the front legs, as well as the bones of the spine.

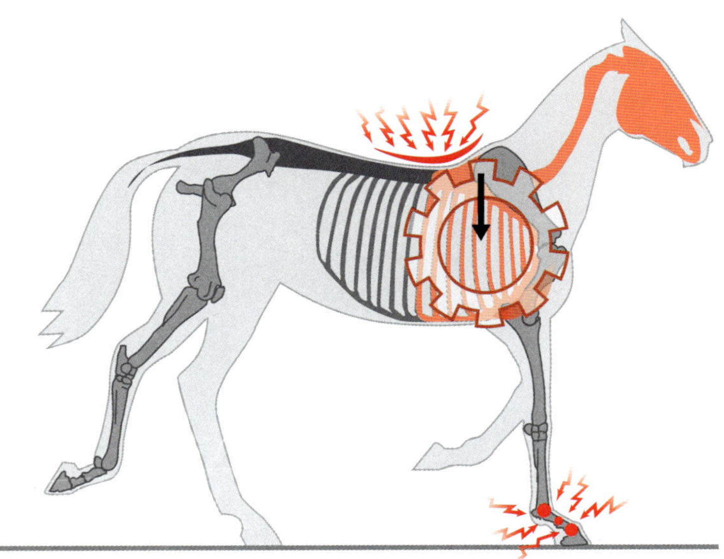

The FCPT, in the passively stabilized and tensed state: head high, back hollow.

Signs to Look For

- distinctly pronounced and tensed lower neck muscles
- insufficiently developed neck muscles
- apparent muscle atrophy behind the shoulder blades
- false bend
- stiff poll area

Symptoms in Motion

- a saddle that continuously slides forward and has to be secured in place with a foregirth, a tighter gullet plate, or any kind of padding
- lack of willingness to stretch
- tensed back
- breaking the parallel alignment between the humerus and the rear cannon bone
- general "leg mover"
- jumping without using his back or landing hard, where the horse needs several strides before he is back on the aids

HCPD—Passively Stabilized— Tensed ("Stiff Loins")

The "leg mover" locks the passage between loins and pelvis securely in place. This presses the spine downward and the pelvis forward at the same time, and places maximum strain on the structures of the lumbar spine, as well as the area between loins and pelvis. An additional rotational movement of the pelvis to the left or right occurs at the end of the movement, which has a detrimental effect on the sacroiliac joint.

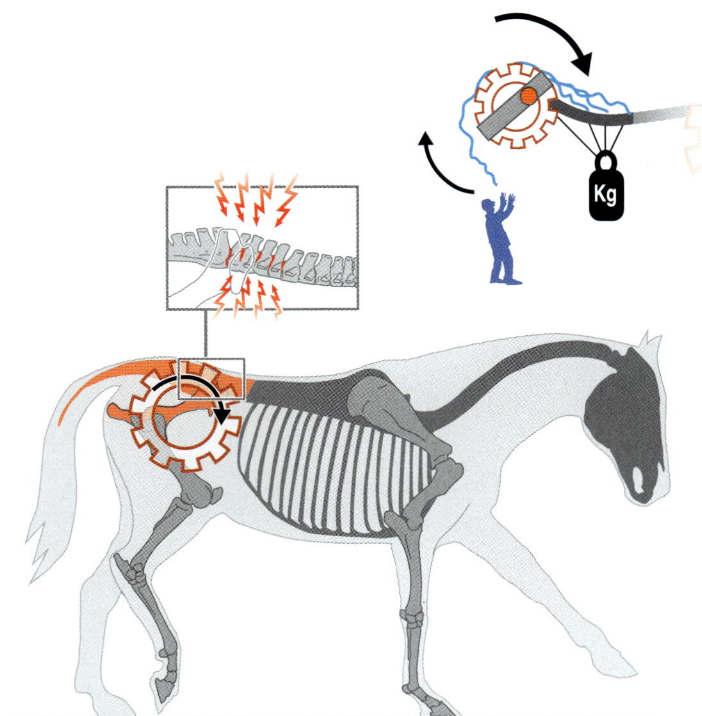

Without shock absorbers, all the movement energy of misconceived collection directly affects the rear parts of the spine and pelvis.

A rider shifting her center of gravity *back,* either due to misconceptions about forward-driving weight aids, an incorrect center of gravity of the saddle, or simply insufficient control of her balance, triggers exactly this reflex in a horse. The horse will remain stuck in flight mode, and only has two options to avoid going faster and faster: Either he tenses backward and upward in the neck, or he enters into a dependency with the rider where he continuously requires an extreme amount of rein aids. The latter usually looks more like water skiing than riding.

Leaning far back and literally thrusting the horse forward may be an elegant position for water skiing ....

Signs to Look For
- muscle bulges along the lumbar spine
- a straight croup with a tensed tail that is carried high
- pseudo "grass belly"
- fat deposits in the loins

Symptoms in Motion
- horse travels out with the hind legs (instead of engaging them under his body)
- shortened, pace-like walk
- tense loins
- high neck position, stiff lower neck
- horse travels wide behind in walk and trot
- horse tends to canter in a four-beat

Passive Elasticity–Sagging Down

If the thorax is "falling through," the topline muscles close to the thorax are not engaged, due to a lack of basic positive tension. The neck cannot perform its role as a balancing pole.

The horse may be relaxed but he does not develop a new dynamic way of going that is stabilized by his muscles. The FCPT does rotate forward, but slides back down between the shoulder blades, making active elasticity impossible. The HCPD rotates forward and is also pulled down by the intestines.

This negative movement pattern can mostly be found among the horses of recreational riders. Many riders in this group have turned their backs on the classical method of equestrian training and toward alternative training systems, due to negative experiences with the former. If, in these cases—with only the best intentions in mind, but based on an incorrect understanding of biomechanical processes—the literal relaxation of the horse becomes the only goal, this again causes strain inside the horse. The back will start to swing, but it will also "fall downward" into the passive structures of the bones of the spine during movement. This uncontrolled *passive "falling through"* causes rotational and shear movement within the spine and the leg axis, which are undoubtedly damaging.

Without positive body tension, the horse just falls from one leg onto the other.

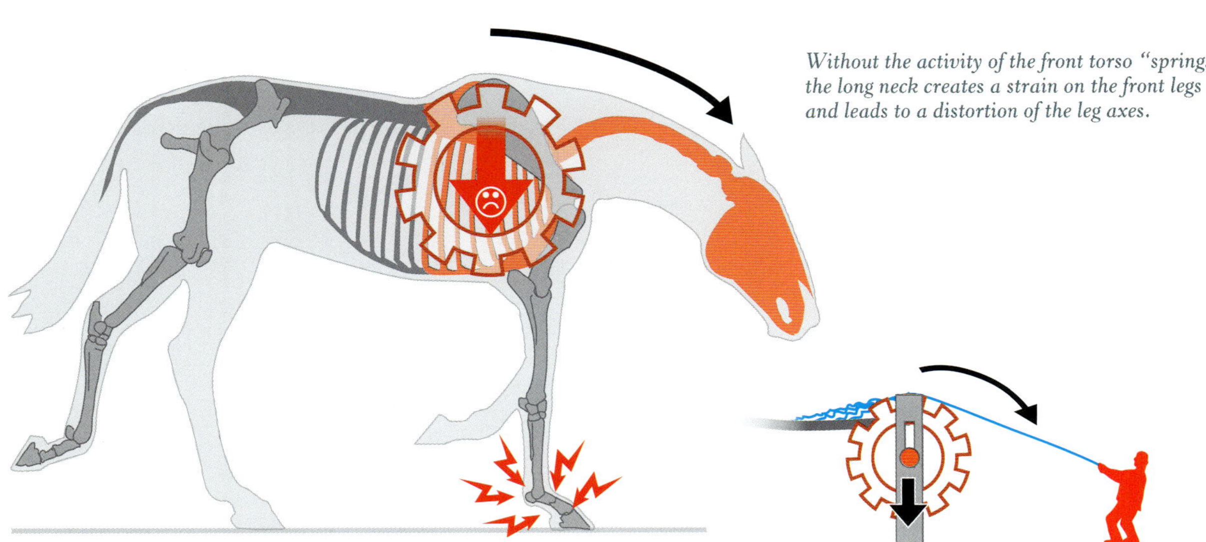

Without the activity of the front torso "springs," the long neck creates a strain on the front legs and leads to a distortion of the leg axes.

The FCPT—Passively Stabilized—Long, Low, and Relaxed

The misinterpreted and wrongly ridden variation of a forward-and-downward stretch is characterized by a horse without impulsion, with little to no willingness to go forward. He falls from one diagonal pair of legs onto the other. These horses very often move apathetically and indifferently. Others, mainly sport horses of the Thoroughbred type, react nervously and display a certain anxiety. The former are mostly overweight. The latter often remain too thin, even with the best of efforts to feed them.

Signs to Look For
- very little neck
- lack of back muscles
- pseudo "grass belly"
- pointy croup
- reduced general condition

Symptoms in Motion
- movement without impulsion
- setting the feet down hard and without elasticity
- the horse is looking for the "fifth leg" (leaning on the hand/bit)
- frequent tripping

The HCPD—Passively Stabilized, Limp

The distance from the hip joint to the abdomen functions as a long lever of weight mass, when it comes to the intestines. The total torque (rotational force) affecting the hip joint as a result amounts to more than a ton (1,000 kilograms), and is transferred to the tendon and joint system of the loin-pelvis passage.

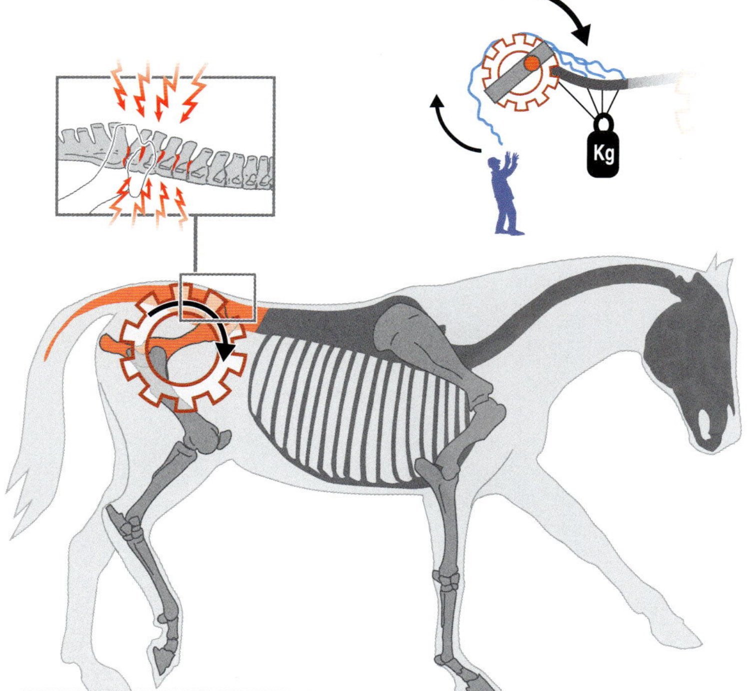

The mass of the intestines creates a downward force without any elasticity and pulls the entire loin-pelvis area down with it.

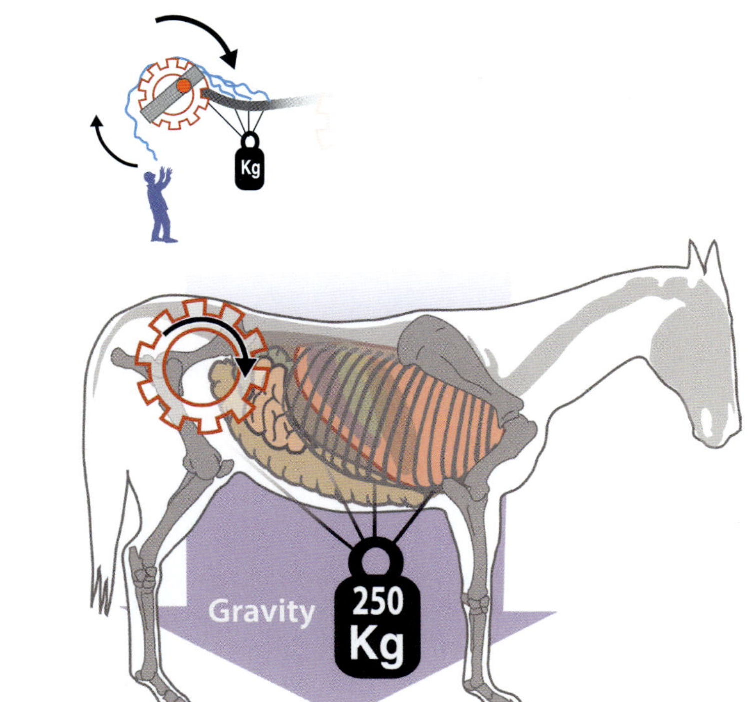

Standing Is a Strain

Due to the physics of leverage, a load of approximately a ton is dragging on the lumbar spine as the intestines pull against the hip joints, when a horse is doing nothing but simply standing in a stall. Therefore, those who think stall rest is equivalent to actual rest and will relieve all strain on a horse are wrong.

Once a horse is made to "relax" based on an incorrect understanding of that word, a system of strain on the passive structures develops simultaneously. The weight of the intestines literally falls down with every step or stride and pulls the spine along with it. The pelvis continues to rotate forward, and the leg axes become twisted. The horse loses his natural willingness to go forward, and becomes dull and sluggish. Due to an absence of swing in the back, forward-driving aids barely reach the horse.

This strain affects the spinous processes, the joints of the posterior thoracic and lumbar spine, and the passage to the pelvis.

The weight of the intestines bearing down on the spine can, in principle, only be reduced by movement.

However, incorrect movement leads to a significant increase in the strain caused by this weight.

Signs to Look For
- sunken in the loins
- belly appears bloated
- straight croup with "loose" tail, carried high

Symptoms in Motion
- horse travels excessively wide or narrow behind
- intermittent buckling in the hind legs
- lack of willingness to go forward
- dragging the hind legs

The Interaction Between the Passively Stabilized Movement Centers
There is no interaction between the FCPT and HCPD in a passively stabilized system. And the lack thereof is exactly the problem. Whether relaxed or tense, the rider feels a horse that is divided into forehand and hind end, without any connection between the two. Everything that riding is about cannot be felt. The horse doesn't give the rider a positive feeling of movement, which generally sets off a vicious cycle of incorrect reactions. If the rider uses more driving aids, the horse just goes faster; the forward-driving impulse doesn't lead to the horse actively arching his body, it only pushes him forward. If the rider tries to use half-halts, the horse simply slows down, as the rein aid gets stuck about halfway through the horse without ever reaching the hindquarters.

A glance at the statistics may prove interesting. Proportionally, recreational horses show slightly more damage to their locomotor systems than sport horses. Yet these numbers are misleading, as retired sport horses are counted in the group of recreational horses. Lameness and pain deriving from their athletic careers may initially be reduced by a longer break. As soon as a new owner starts working the horse without addressing old issues, however, the cycle of chronic overload, inflammation, and pain starts anew, even without the maximized stress an athletic career inflicts.

Summary
The natural movement pattern of a horse in trot and canter is characterized by "flight mode." The horse tenses his topline by lifting his head, pushing his chest and spine down into the strong tendon structures with his lower neck and back muscles. This directly transfers energy, with the legs acting as "catapults." This system is extremely powerful for a short time, and immediately accessible. It is ideal for flight on a slightly curved line that only lasts for a few minutes. Grazing with the nose on the ground and walking with a very low head position serves as passive relief and restoration of these systems. A horse can stabilize his movement in both of these systems with his passive structures, but that approach is not suitable for a riding horse in trot and canter.

Whether tense or loose, the horse's back and spinous processes are weighed down by gravity in both forms of passive stabilization. Inflammation, arthritis, and painful contraction and tenseness in the back muscles are the inevitable consequences.

It doesn't matter whether a horse is an overworked competition horse or an obedient trail horse. Both can develop the same pathologies if they are not trained according to the classical training principles for a riding horse.

3 The Third Dimension– Changing the Perspective

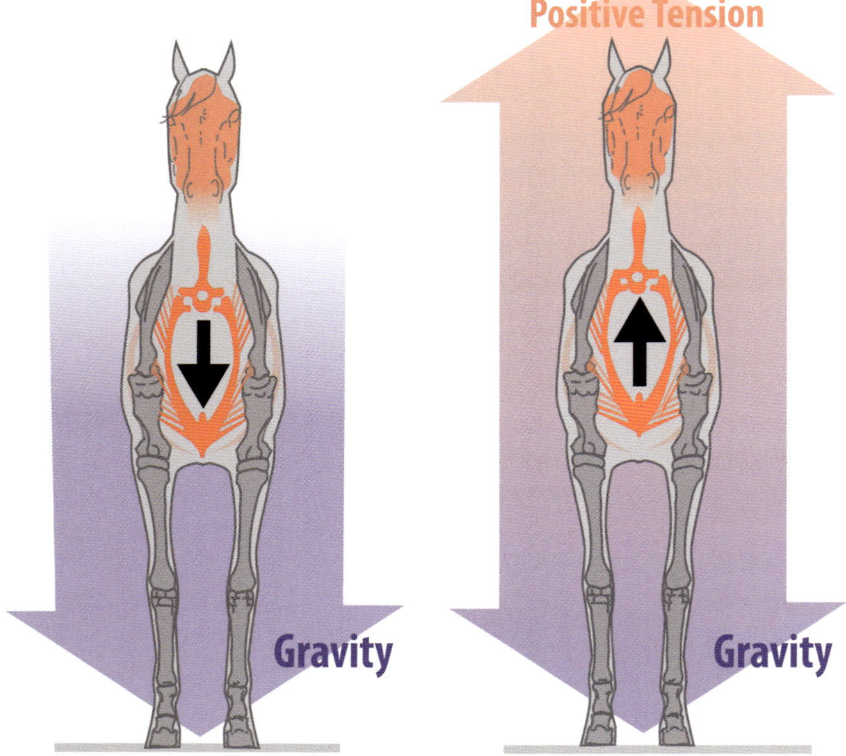

The effects of gravity seen from the front—stabilized passively (left) and actively (right).

The Biomechanics of the Horse in the Third Dimension

This chapter looks at the effects of gravity when observing the horse from the front or back. Most anatomical pictures that we see show a horse in profile, either standing or during the moment of suspension. A complete picture of the horse's movement can only be formed when the third dimension is included. If gravity works downward freely, the thorax falls down between the front legs. If the horse lifts his thorax, he develops a counter to gravity, and creates an active, dynamic balance. We will begin by looking at the horse from the front. From this perspective, which shows the horse standing on two legs, the weight of the torso is divided across two axes and supported on the ground.

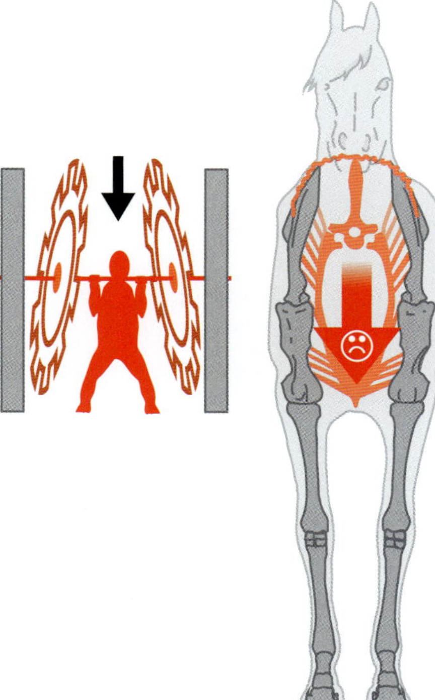 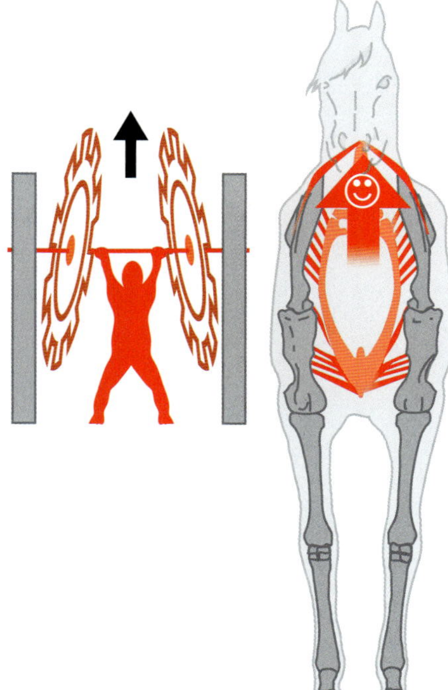

This image shows the shoulder girdle, which lifts the thorax equally on both sides. The upper structures of muscle and fascia around the withers are only arched when in a raised position. This movement can be felt when the horse is standing and a person on the ground prompts the horse to lift his thorax.

There is one muscle that matters most to the stabilization of the FCPT in the third dimension: the trapezius muscle. If the thorax is lifted by the shoulder girdle structures, it stabilizes the entire FCPT like a tent, where all the tent's sides become taut when the center post is set up.

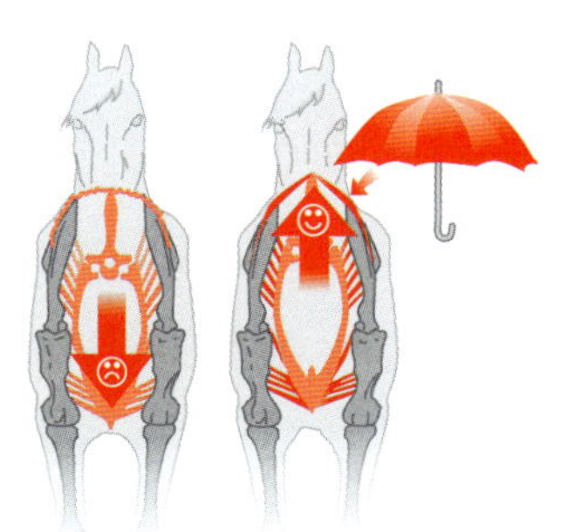

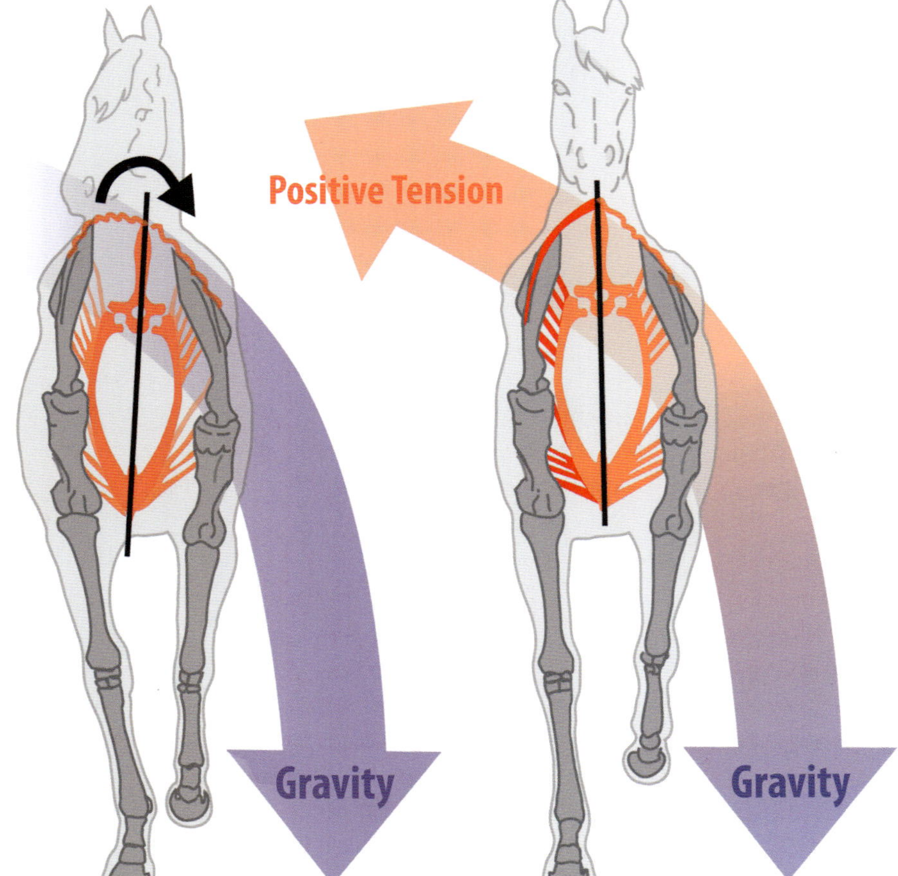

The effects of gravity seen from the front—stabilized passively (left) and actively (right).

The Third Dimension in Movement

The instant when the horse starts to move is interesting to observe, from a biomechanical perspective. To understand this important moment from this angle, we have to take a little tour of the world of leverage principles in physics. Once the horse starts moving, in terms of the FCPT and HCPD, there is almost always only one leg touching the ground. The thorax wants to lower, together with gravity, toward the side of the leg about to swing forward in the sequence of legs (the "swinging leg"), and it can only be held in place by the muscular activity of the other side of the horse—the side on which the leg is touching the ground and taking the horse's weight (the "supporting leg").

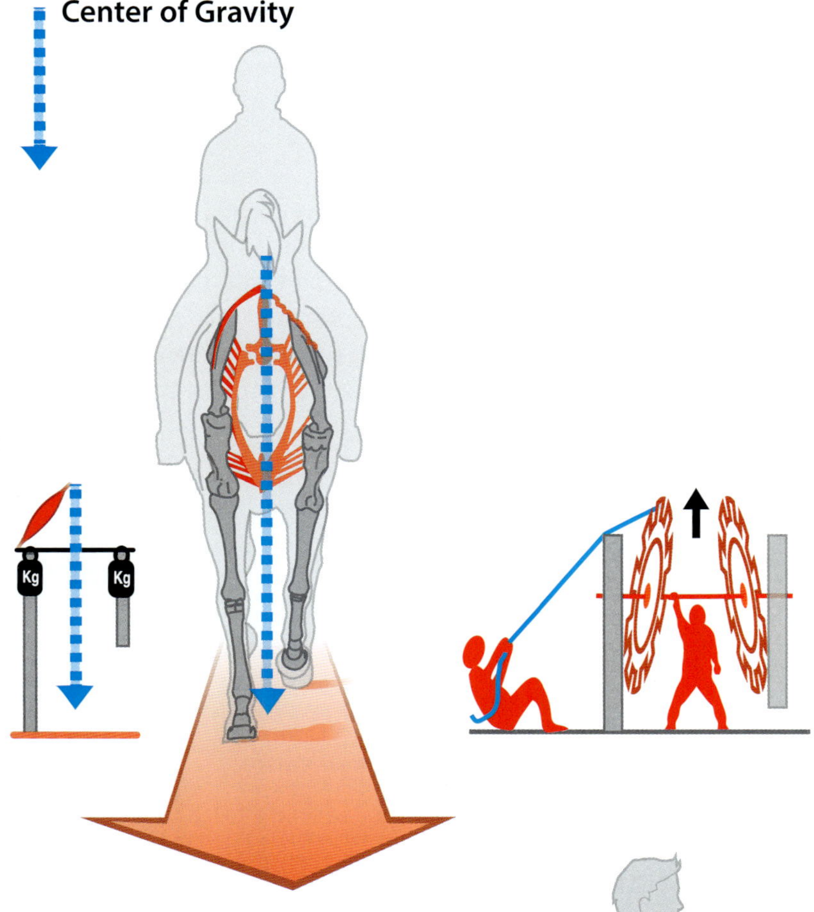

The processes occurring in the FCPT to stabilize against gravity, as a schematic illustration showing the body's center of gravity.

Levers Create Rotational Force (Torque)

The mass of the torso no longer has an effect on the axial position of the supporting leg. This creates a lever between the body's center of gravity and the axis of the supporting leg. Depending on the horse's reaction to this change, the rotational force created by the weight of the torso decreases or increases.

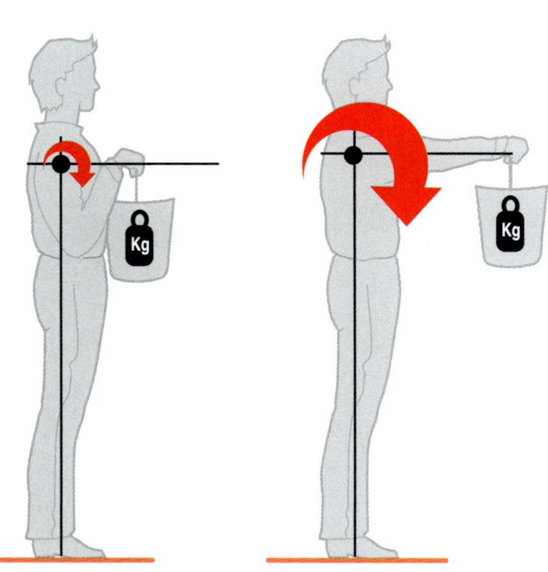

Even if the weight stays the same, the length of the lever can multiply the rotational force.

Rotational Force (Torque)

Balancing Rotational Force

There are different ways for the horse to balance against this rotational movement. He can use his neck as a balancing pole, he can lower his torso and twist it, or he can actively stabilize it through the development of muscles.

The Neck as a Balancing Pole as Seen from the Front

If the horse moves his neck past the supporting leg to the outside, the center of gravity shifts toward the axis of the supporting leg. The lever of the mass becomes shorter and relieves strain on the shoulder girdle. The rotational force is almost completely dissolved, and the resulting stress on the shoulder girdle is about the same as the weight of the forehand.

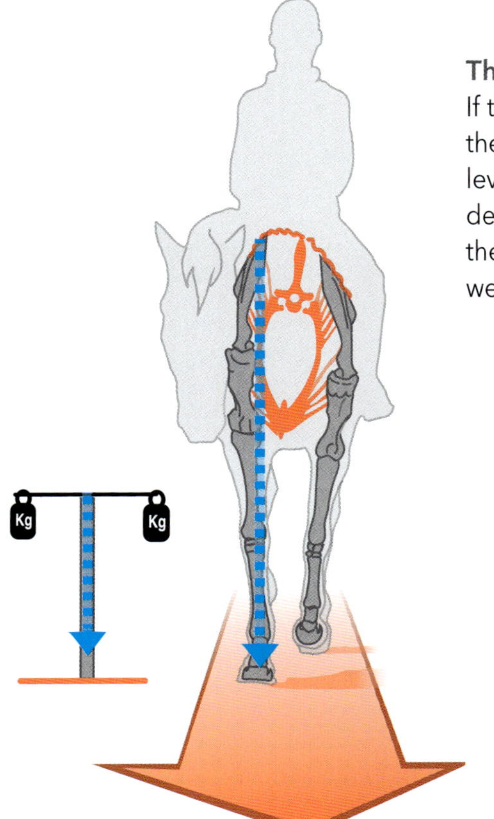

The neck, positioned over the supporting leg, acts as a counterweight to the mass of the thorax.

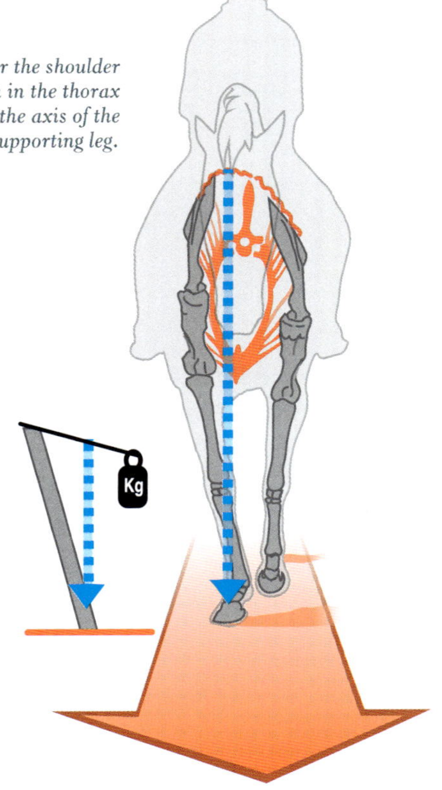

Falling out over the shoulder means a distortion in the thorax and a change in the axis of the supporting leg.

Falling Out over the Outside Shoulder

The second option for the horse to balance himself is falling out with the shoulder of the supporting leg. The horse steps toward the middle and under his center of gravity with his foot, and lowers his thorax toward the side of the swinging leg; this strategy also reduces the rotational force to about the same weight as the forehand.

Stabilization Through Active Muscle Slings

If the horse has to carry himself according to the classical principles of riding theory, this means a great deal of physical effort, especially in the third dimension. If the neck is to be carried firmly in the center (when seen from the front), the horse's center of gravity shifts away from the supporting leg and extends the length of the lever involved. Thanks to this added leverage, the rotational force that needs to be stabilized now amounts to about two-and-a-half times the front torso's weight, which means a load of over 1,500 pounds (about 700 kilograms) for a Warmblood horse. If the FCPT system is to remain in balance, its stabilizing muscle chains have to exert an equal amount of force to maintain balance and rhythm. Holding the neck in a central position in front of the body is by no means a given, but a goal of training! Therefore, a judge's note in a score sheet at a dressage show commenting that the horse is "swaying" or "wobbling" on the centerline cannot be corrected by strengthening the rider's aids, but only by strengthening the horse.

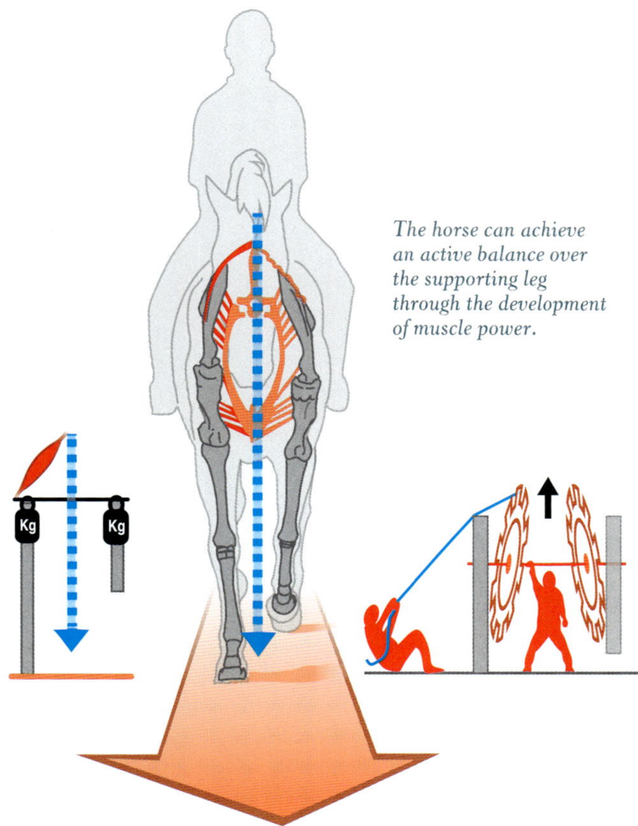

The horse can achieve an active balance over the supporting leg through the development of muscle power.

The Hollow and Stiff Side

A horse does not have two equally strong muscle slings in his shoulder girdle when he is first started under saddle. To relieve strain on the weaker side of his shoulder girdle, the horse will instinctively move his neck to that side—to use it as a balancing pole. This side is the "hollow" side. Being able to lead the neck away from the weak side of the shoulder girdle is dependent on developing the horse's muscle power. He has to build up a muscular counterweight in the shoulder girdle to control the weight of his neck. Straightening the horse cannot be achieved by improving mobility in the short term, but only through long-term gymnastic strengthening of the horse.

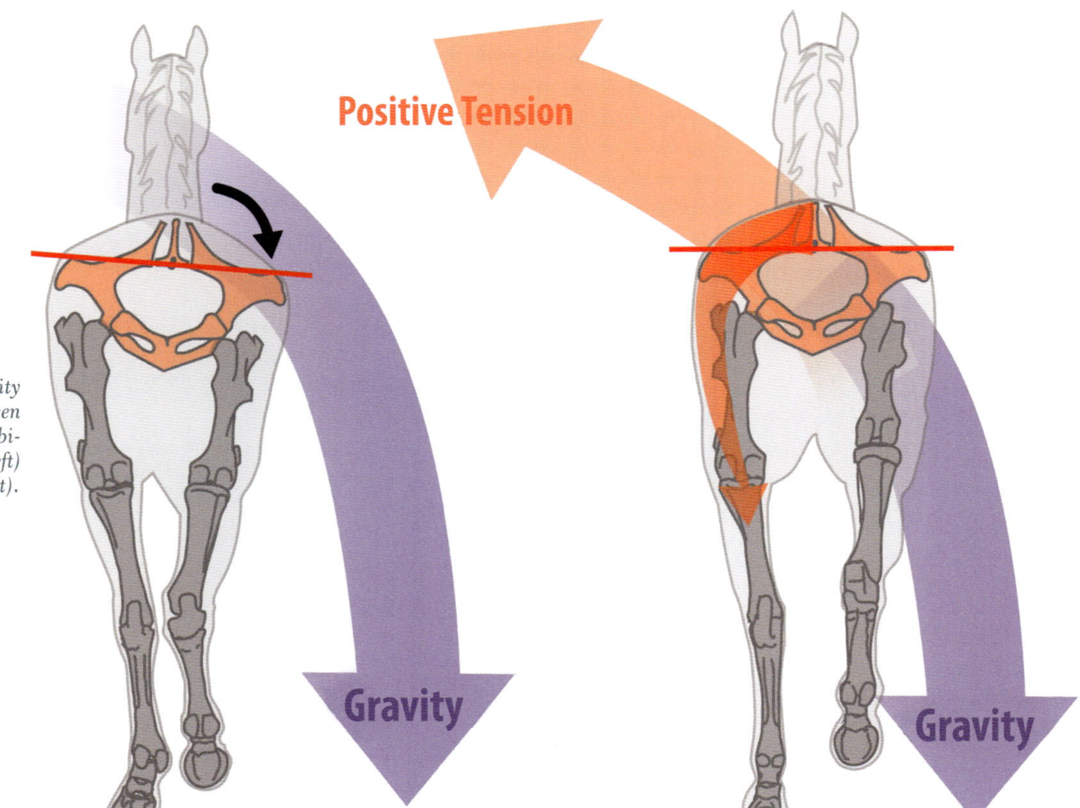

The effects of gravity on movement, seen from behind—stabilized passively (left) and actively (right).

The Biomechanics of the HCPD As Seen from Behind

The HCPD has a different approach to stabilization. The difference between the HCPD and the FCPT is that the HCPD is missing the balancing pole of the neck. Therefore, it can't be strained by a shift in mass—nor can strain on it be relieved by a shift in mass. The situation is different for those animals who walk on their hind legs. Bipeds step fully underneath their centers of gravity; in many bipedal or mostly bipedal species, like the kangaroo, or certain dinosaurs, a long, heavy tail takes on the role of supporting the organization of balance.

A crookedly held tail, in a horse, only indicates a potential problem in the balance of the hind end. A horse's tail cannot adequately counterbalance, compared to what the neck does for the horse's forehand or the tail does for kangaroo or dinosaur.

Animals whose hind end dominates and controls their movement have a distinct tail to help them balance.

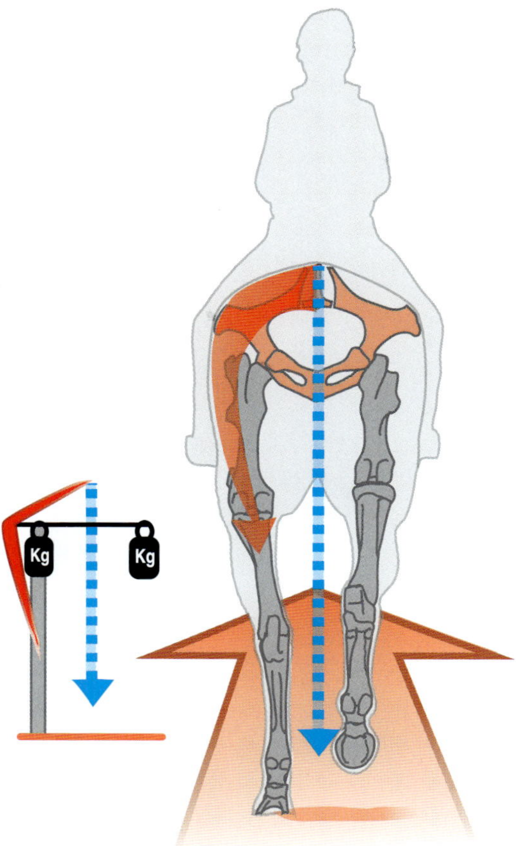

The internal processes taking place inside the HCPD to stabilize the horse against gravity, as a schematic illustration.

The Hip Joint As a Fixed-Rotation Axis

In contrast to the FCPT, the HCPD has a fixed-rotation axis in the form of the hip joint, around which stabilization or evasive movement is organized.

Stabilization Through the Outside Muscle Chains

The large lateral and rear muscle chains of the croup, together with their antagonists, the *oblique abdominal muscles,* take a particularly important role with respect to stabilization. Riding theory rightly pays attention to them.

Compensation Mechanisms of the Hindquarters

Due to the absence of a balance pole like the neck, and the presence of the hip joint as a fixed-rotation axis, the hindquarters have different compensation mechanisms from the forehand.

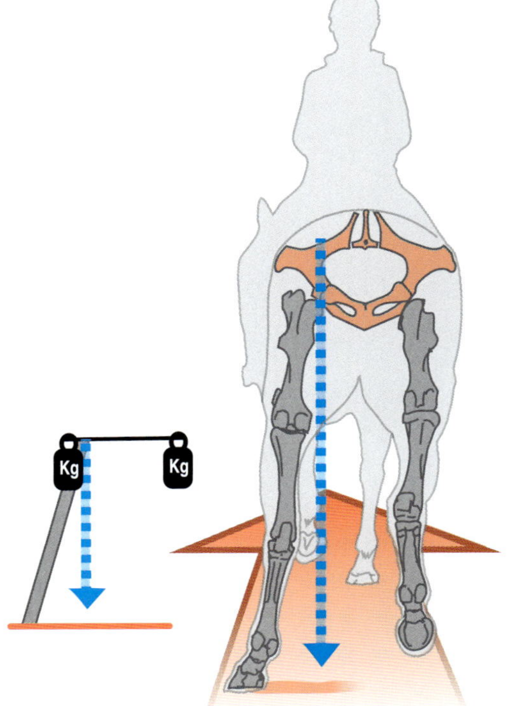

Drifting to the Outside with the Hind Leg

The hind leg of the weak side drifts to the outside to artificially increase the support surface under the horse's center of gravity. At the same time, the lever ratios for the lateral croup muscles are improved.

Drifting to the Inside with the Hind Leg

The horse travels toward the inside, under his center of gravity, to stabilize the FCPT. The combined rotational and tilting movements of the pelvis add up to a more obvious lowering toward the side of the swinging leg than is usually visible in the thorax, where parts of the evasive movement are swallowed up by the sliding motion of the shoulder girdle.

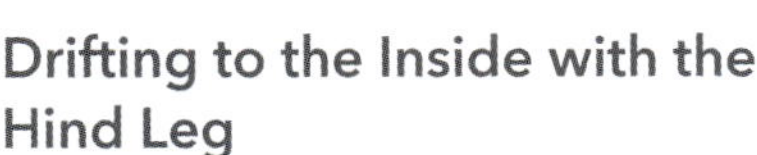

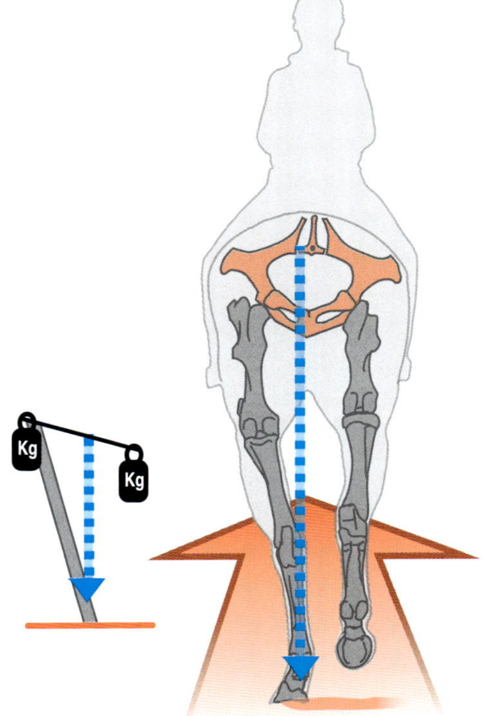

Stabilization Through Active Muscle Slings

The weight of the intestines, which creates a diagonal pressure on the hip joint, plays an important role in calculating the forces at work. Through the "lever effect," that 550 pounds (250 kilograms) will be multiplied three- or fourfold, depending on the horse's conformation. This means that we can safely assume a rotational force of approximately one ton must be stabilized by the horse. This emphasizes the importance of a powerful and well-coordinated musculature in the hind end, if the trainer wants to avoid these compensatory movements.

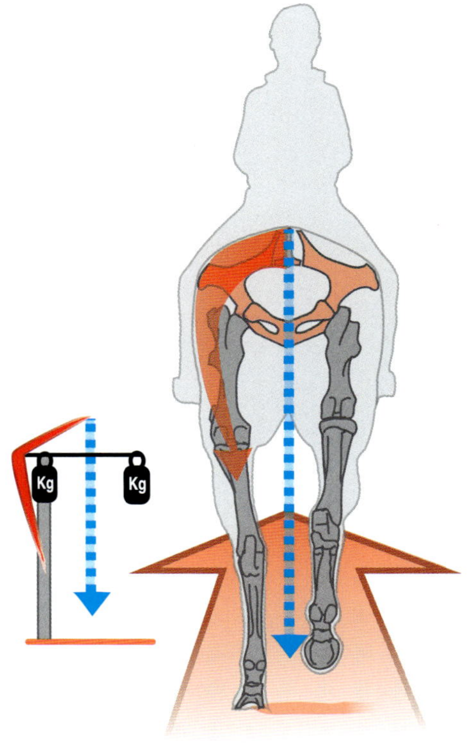

Summary

Knowledge of the mechanisms through which the horse stabilizes himself against gravity in the third dimension is a basic element in comprehension of classical riding theory. The evasive movement of the neck, contortions in the shoulder girdle, and different options of the hindquarters to evade correct work can be explained with physics. If a trainer knows the reasons for the horse's weaknesses, she can address them with appropriate training strategies. From this perspective, the development of a horse's athletic abilities is an important basic principle of training. Additionally, the principles of curved lines amplify the impact of such insights.

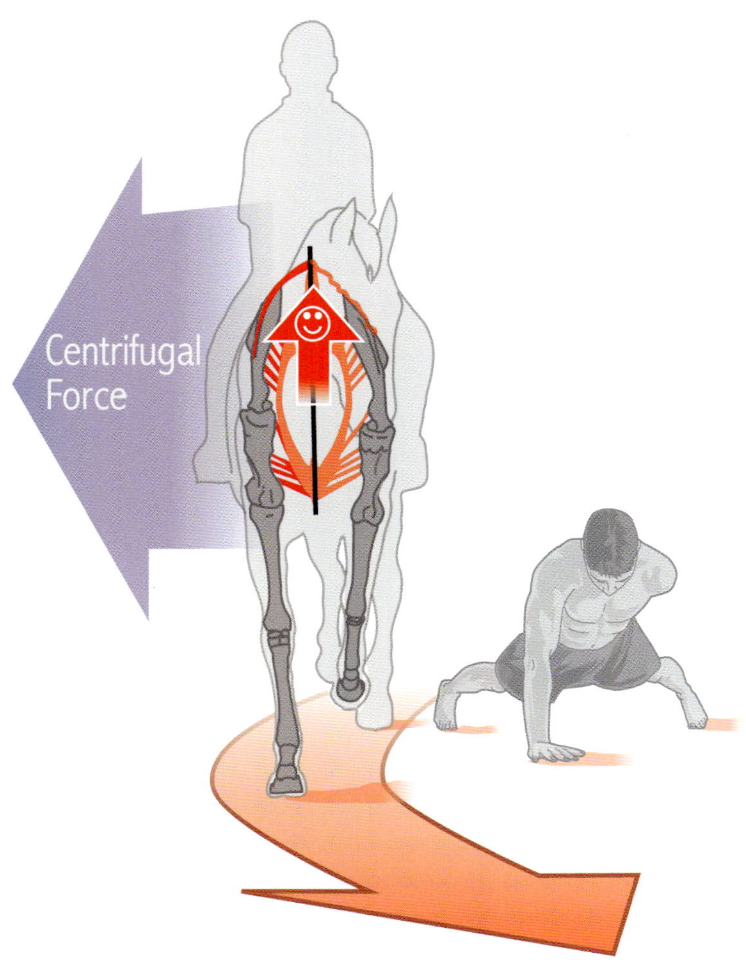

The Biomechanics of the Horse on a Curved Line

Thus far, we have only looked at the horse's movement on straight lines. To fully grasp the biomechanics behind the horse's stabilization, we need to examine movement for a horse on a curved line, too.

Centrifugal Force Illustrates the Principle

Generally, while in motion, the horse stabilizes his FCPT and HCPD with a rotational movement to counter gravity, determined in part by his sequence of footfalls. If a horse moves on a straight line, the stress of gravity is almost the same on both diagonals, in walk and trot.

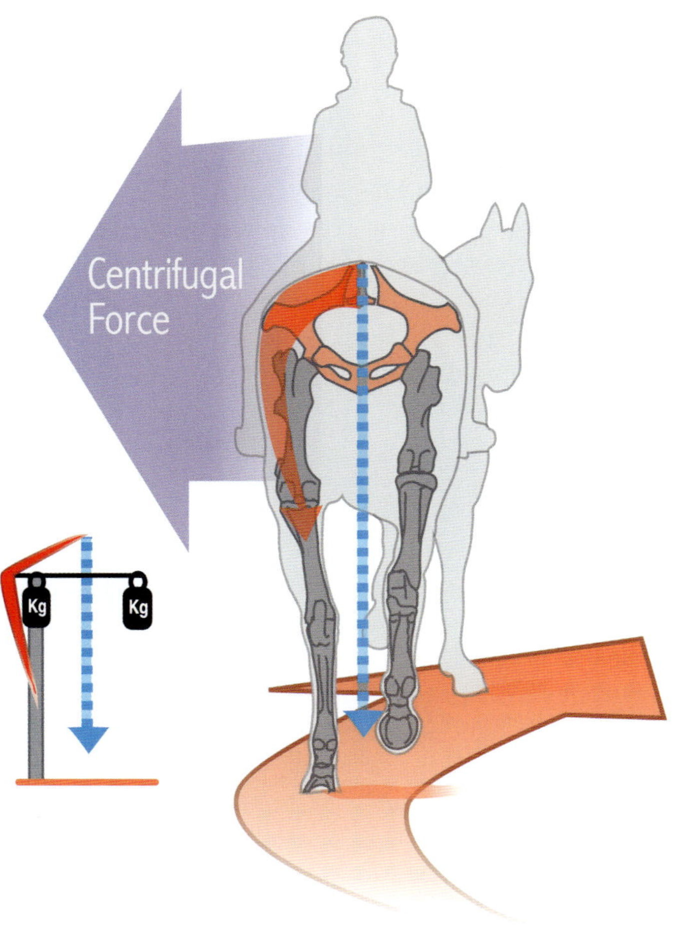

On curved lines, however, centrifugal force to the outside has an effect, together with gravity, and increases the strain on the outside muscle slings of the movement centers. On a curved line, the untrained horse will bring his head to the outside and shift his center of gravity to the inside in order to balance himself. When the horse is trained to align his body correctly to the curved line, he has to learn to deal with this new, completely foreign requirement. Much as when he is moving on a straight line, the horse has to learn to organize to counter the various forces acting on his body in a new way, in order to build active muscle slings. Only systematic training, together with the help of his rider, will enable the horse to actively balance on curved lines and maintain straight axes in his legs.

Without training, the horse organizes himself in a position that tilts him on his longitudinal axis when he travels on a curved line.

The Curved Line Will Expose Weaknesses

Weaknesses that may have been covered up on straight lines, through minor contortions and evasive movements, will intensify and become more apparent on curved lines. Problems with flexion and bend, or even with suppleness during seemingly routine movements, such as riding through a corner, can be explained, and hopefully solved. Stabilizing and controlling the thorax and pelvis against these contortions requires more than just relaxation, mobility, and individually powerful muscles. Complete functional muscle chains, sensibly working together, are needed to fulfill this task.

The FCPT's Balance in Correct Flexion and Bend

When the horse is correctly ridden, his neck should continue the torso's bend in the front. However, this directs the horse's mass even farther away from the axis of the outside supporting leg. The rotational force in the shoulder girdle is significantly increased, compared to movement on a straight line, and puts about 1,900 pounds (900 kilograms) of pressure on the outside shoulder girdle. If we add the effects of centrifugal force, we quickly reach force values in the range of one ton, approximately matching those forces that have an effect on the hindquarters. Physical calculations, and understanding the factors that contribute to them, can really help smooth the way to more balance and harmony with the horse.

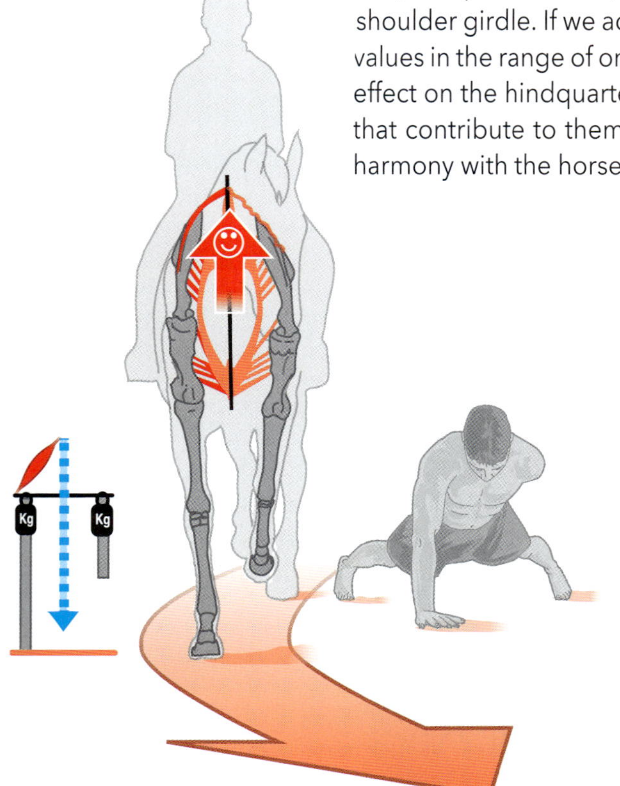

The neck position in front of the inside shoulder—the perfect alignment of the horse with the curved track—is seen as a significant element of the gymnasticizing work of a horse, and justly so. Positioning the neck past the inside shoulder is not intended—and also not possible, from a biomechanical perspective—without being harmful to the horse's health.

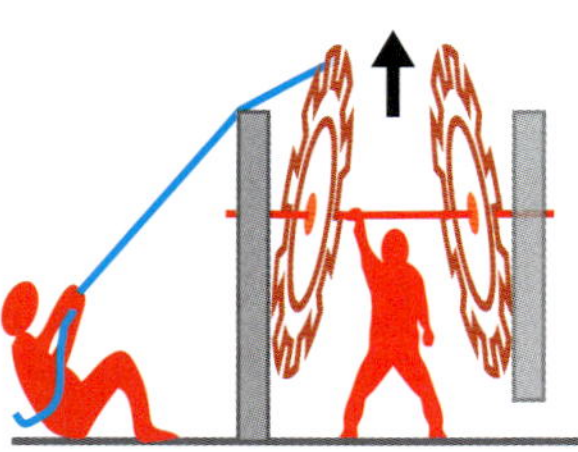

The more pronounced the horse's flexion and bend, the more muscle power is necessary to keep the horse balanced.

Lifting the Thorax
- large serratus anterior muscle
- straight as well as ascending and descending pectoral muscle
- long lower neck muscle *(M. longus colli)*

Rotation of the Thorax As Seen from the Front
- trapezius muscle

Rotation of the Thorax As Seen from the Side
- topline muscle
- straight abdominal muscles

If this group of muscle chains is functioning, muscular stabilization against the centrifugal force develops in the shoulder girdle. That means these muscle chains are the basis for the horse's ability to align with the curved track. When seen from the front, the horse remains almost vertical and his legs stay organized in their correct axial alignment under the shoulder joint. Therefore, straining rotational movements of the digital joints are slowed down or completely avoided—the best healthcare coverage for your horse.

Even a horse of average talent, especially in dressage, can be successfully taken to the highest levels by a top-class rider if this group of muscle chains functions properly.

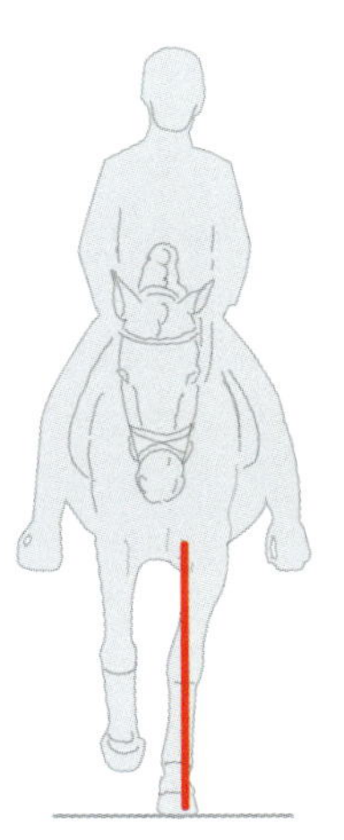

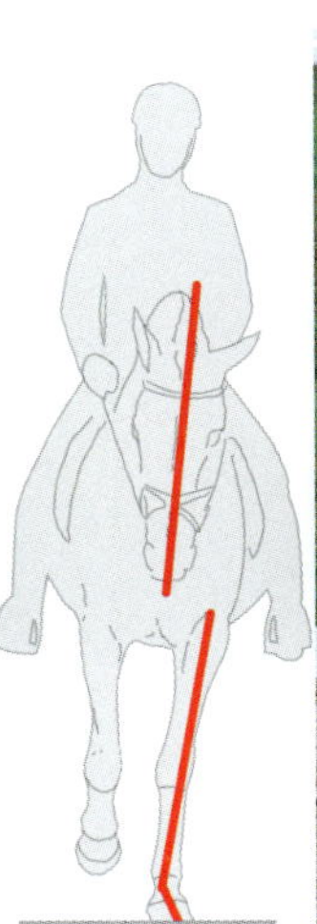

The difference between a stabilized (left) and a non-stabilized (right) thorax is clearly visible.

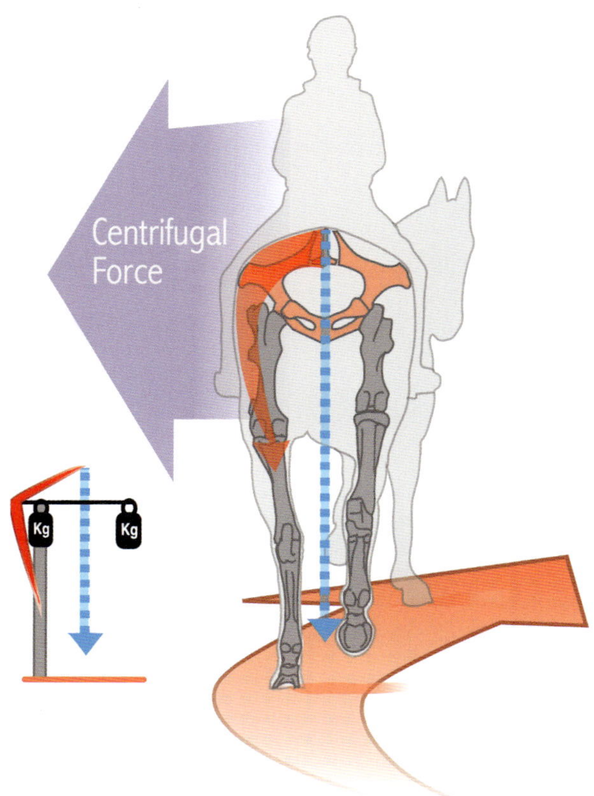

The HCPD's Balance in Correct Flexion and Bend

In general, when it comes to the FCPT, greater strain is placed on the outside of a horse when he is moving on a curved line, due to the centrifugal force. However, the situation is exacerbated for the HCPD. While the inside hind leg diagonally supports the outside shoulder girdle through its activity in trot, the outside hind leg takes on the actual work of lateral stabilization on a curved line. The hind end lacks the compensatory effect of the neck, with which the horse can vary the degree of stress on the FCPT himself. This is why the demands placed on the hind end are significantly higher on curved lines than on straight ones.

Lateral Stabilization

The centrifugal force generated by movement on curved lines has to be absorbed by the horse's muscles in the supporting leg phase of the outside hind leg. Here, the interdependency of the functions of the HCPD, when seen from behind and from the side, becomes clear. A curved line to the right will serve as an example.

Control over pelvis stability begins with stability through the left hip joint. The diagonally stabilizing muscles prevent a lowering of the right side of the pelvis during the swinging leg phase. The horse can clearly only step to the left of his center of gravity if the pelvis cannot lower in the swinging leg phase. The right hind leg becomes the supporting leg and prevents a lowering of the pelvis on the left side. Only the stable pelvis ring on can bring the outside supporting leg into the position needed to stabilize the entire hind end against centrifugal force. Thus, the task of the rider's outside leg is to control the rotational movement of the outside pelvis downward. In turn, this prevents the hindquarters from swerving to the side; the rider's outside leg acts in a "guarding" manner. The attempts of some riders to push the horse's outside leg toward the inside, inspired by a linear, two-dimensional concept of the horse's "bend," are doomed to fail.

This explains why the *timing of aids,* with respect to the supporting and swinging leg phases, is so much more relevant than their *intensity.* Through these movement patterns, mainly dominated by coordination, the hind end develops an additional elasticity in the loin-pelvis passage, which supports and controls the natural spring-like elasticity of the haunches.

Action and Reaction in the Hindquarters

On a functional level, the active approach of classical riding theory strives to stabilize the pelvis ring against centrifugal force in a three-dimensional manner, through the activation of various muscle chains. The fact that you cannot simply move or hold on to the hind end is the deciding factor here. Directly asking the horse's hind legs to move by using an isolated aid from your own leg may be a nice thought—but practically speaking, it's impossible. As described in chapter 2 (p. 21), the hind leg can only do its job if its movement energy is headed in a forward direction.

The hind legs do not act, they react. A rider has to learn to adjust her aids to the horse's balance, instead of trying to influence individual parts of the horse.

Summary
Compared to the forehand, the hindquarters lack the neck as a balancing pole. The hind legs are dynamic axes, which have to position themselves optimally under a shifting center of gravity. Control over the center of gravity can only be indirectly exerted by aligning the forehand with the hindquarters. The rider's action is to take control of the center of gravity; the horse's reaction is to position the hind leg accordingly—not vice versa.

The Muscle Chains for the Three-Dimensional Stabilization of the HCPD

Lateral Perspective
- croup muscle of the supporting leg
- long hip extensors/modular hip joint of the supporting leg
- oblique abdominal muscles

Diagonal Perspective
- abductor of the supporting leg
- adductor of the supporting leg
- oblique abdominal muscles

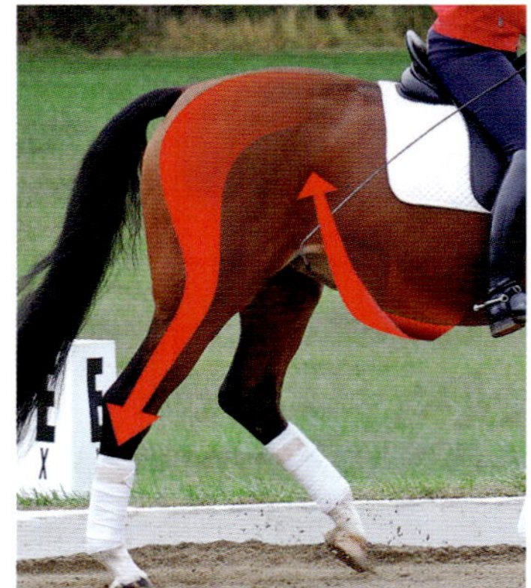

The muscle chains for the three-dimensional stabilization of the hindquarters.

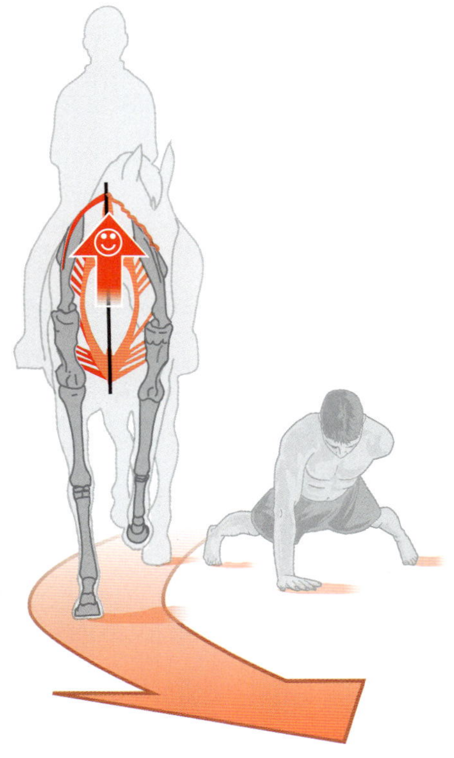

Riding a curved line: The art of convincing your audience that neither centrifugal force nor gravity exist.

Structure of the Muscle Chains of the FCPT from a Functional Perspective

1. Relieving strain on the horse's shoulder girdle on curved lines by bringing the neck toward the outside shoulder (inside leg–outside rein).

2. Activating the shoulder girdle through driving aids. Aim: The horse maintains his rhythm on a curved line and moves more elastically.

3. Activating the base of the neck through lengthening the neck. Leg and rein aids have to frequently stimulate and readjust the relevant muscle chains so the horse learns to balance himself through muscle strength.

4. Gentle guidance of the torso's center of gravity toward the outside shoulder girdle to improve straightness. The more centrifugal force the shoulder girdle can absorb, the more the neck can be brought inside and onto the curved line. This movement always originates in the weight shift of the torso. The rider's inside leg works lightly but dominantly toward the outside rein. The horse's topline becomes involved.

5. If all muscle groups stay active and are coordinated correctly, the head-neck axis can be guided upward more and more, without the thorax lowering backward. The inside hind leg can actively support this movement. The hindquarters virtually take over the job of counterbalancing from the neck, by holding the thorax in place through increased engagement under the horse's center of gravity. Any disturbance within the system will lead to mistakes in rhythm, especially on curved lines.

Correct Training Takes Time

After a while, the horse will be able to carry his neck slightly more to the inside, which will increase rotational force and thus the intensity of the training. The horse will be better able to carry his neck on curved lines and in the correct flexion, as an extension of his back, as his shoulder girdle strengthens.

Power acrobatics are the art of convincing your audience that gravity does not exist.

As soon as the FCPT can be controlled and stabilized, the hindquarters are able to diagonally support rotational movement through increased engagement of the inside hind leg.

Summary
Movement along a curved line notably furthers the athletic abilities of the FCPT. The demands on the strength of the outside shoulder and pelvis girdle triple when the neck is carried toward the outside during a correct bend of the entire body. Rhythm and suppleness, as the basic elements of the Training Scale as well as key factors in the athletic development of a horse, are inseparably linked. The biomechanical principles of movement on a curved line make this very obvious.

The Interplay of the Movement Centers on a Curved Line

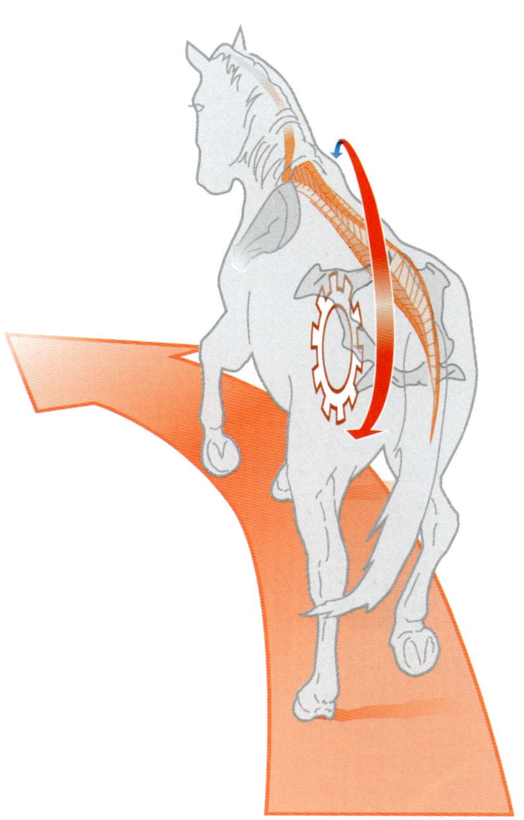

Curved lines and *lateral work* are very valuable when we talk about movement centers, because they offer the most effective options to strengthen the lateral muscle groups and simultaneously synchronize the two movement centers. If the relevant muscle chains are actively stabilized in front, meaning a diagonal rotational connection is in place, the inside hind leg has to automatically take on energy coming from the *outside* shoulder girdle.

Synchronization As the Key to Stability

What has been described in the previous paragraph can only be achieved through control over the thorax, and by *aligning the forehand with the hindquarters*. In response, the hind legs, stepping actively underneath the horse's body, travel more to the inside and toward the hip joint, when looking at the horse from behind. As a result, the track of the horse's hind legs becomes narrower on straight lines.

Synchronization of the movement centers.

Structure of the FCPT and HCPD Muscle Chains from a Functional Perspective

The curved line is the basic element for lateral stabilization. This is where the adductor and abductor muscle groups of the forehand and the hind legs are addressed and controlled through correct aids. The most important factor in controlling them successfully is always the rider's balanced seat. Any use of leg and rein aids can only be developed from a position of secure upper body balance for the rider.

The impulse from the rider's inside leg to the outside rein—the so-called diagonal aid—is responsible for the control of the FCPT. The control of the HCPD is mostly carried out by the rider's outside leg. Functionally speaking, these aids can only be effective together, when correctly synchronized, and never individually. Within this framework, lateral work is developed, which increasingly addresses and trains these pre-activated muscle groups in the movement of adduction and abduction, through the sideways shift of the horse's center of gravity.

- The better coordination and power have been schooled, the more correctly the entire body of the horse can fully align with the curved track he is following.
- The better and more correctly the curved line is ridden, the more intense the effect of training on the muscle slings, which contributes to any further athletic development of the horse.
- The better coordination and power are schooled, the more controlled, more correctly, and more tightly the curved line can be ridden.
- If a horse is ridden on a curved line without these athletic abilities, stress injuries will inevitably occur over the long term (chronic overload).

Interaction Between the Movement Centers

Muscle work cannot be forced; it has to slowly and continuously develop. This poses a challenge to the rider, in that she must constantly control the movement centers to maintain the horse's balance and catch evasive movement. Progress in training defines the correct amount of this control. The neck only serves as a balancing pole to add or relieve strain on the muscle chains. It is never the catalyst for movement on a curved line. The rider's diagonal aids need to be considered as stabilization for the thorax and pelvis—not as a two-dimensional tool to bend the horse out of shape.

Finding the Right Saddle

The saddle has a significant share in the development of correct musculature in a horse: It has to allow for the necessary movement in the horse's body. At the same time, it has to offer the rider the chance to optimize her own balance, and to influence the horse with her aids. To find and fit the right saddle requires complex knowhow. Knowledge from multiple different fields has to be collected to achieve an ideal result, especially for horses with problematic backs in the saddle area.

The Saddle-Fitter and the Horse's Topline

As shown, the organization of the horse's movement centers has a direct influence on his outer shape in all three dimensions. This leads to the following question when fitting a saddle: Which topline is used to fit the saddle, if the topline constantly changes during movement thanks to the influence of gravity and centrifugal force?

This question cannot be answered by the saddle-fitter alone; this takes an entire team, especially for problem horses.

Preferred Procedure for Saddle Problems

VETERINARIAN: Radiological imaging of the spine from withers to pelvis serves to illustrate problem areas and make unalterable movement restrictions visible. The vet also clarifies possible pre-existing inflamed or painful processes inside the horse. A diagnosis of lameness can be useful when assessing saddle fit, as oftentimes tension in the torso has its root in pain in the limbs. Therapeutic measures, before fitting the saddle, may be sensible.

PHYSICAL THERAPIST: Functional diagnostics help determine the relationship between the mobility and stability of the horse's entire locomotor system. Potentially mobilizing or stabilizing the buildup of the horse's spinal dynamics, before fitting the saddle, may be beneficial.

TRAINER: Evaluating the training level of horse and rider and their ability to achieve an active-dynamic stabilization against gravity and centrifugal force should be considered.

SADDLE-FITTER: The saddle-fitter has to draw the correct conclusions from all this information, and may potentially develop an individualized approach to support the horse in his build toward a functionally correct and stabilized topline. The saddle-fitter cannot forget to adjust the saddle to the rider with regard to the seat, as well as the length of his calf, thigh, and upper body.

Saddle Fitting Is Teamwork!

It Fits—It Doesn't Fit

A good fit is not easy to assess. Even a saddle that fits all the previously mentioned criteria can be problematic in the beginning, as horse and rider have to adjust to it. The saddle should facilitate correct movement and movement function. If a saddle feels perfect at first, but does not allow the horse to develop his topline in a desirable way, then the feeling of perfection is deceiving.

Moreover, assessing whether a saddle truly fits cannot be left to a measuring system. Studies conducted at the University of Zurich have proven that the way a saddle distributes pressure across the horse's back depends significantly on the technical abilities of the rider.

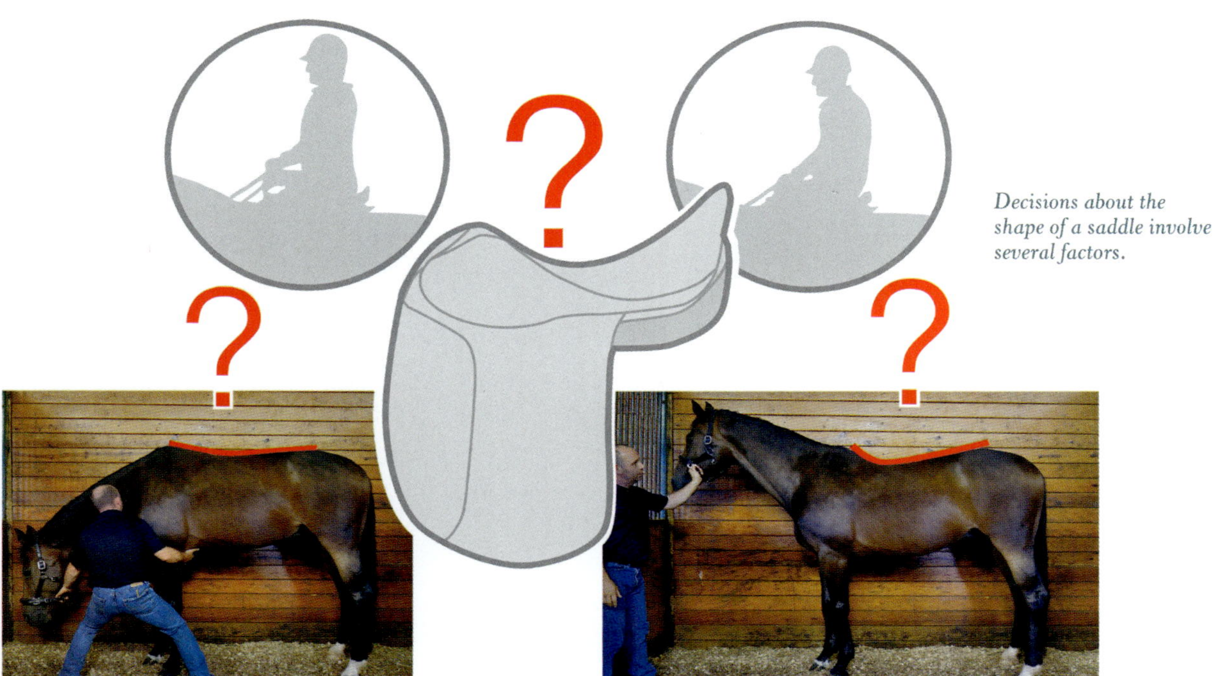

Decisions about the shape of a saddle involve several factors.

Custom-Made Saddles

Unfortunately, there are no characteristics that can universally define the term custom-made saddle. A saddle-fitter can easily measure a horse with a swayed and crooked back at the halt, and make a saddle tree—perfect for this exact topline, and a one-to-one image of the measurement. If the rider wanted to sit on her horse and read the newspaper, she would have the perfect custom-made saddle. But what happens once the horse starts moving? What happens to his topline?

Ultimately, making a good saddle is craftsmanship. It cannot be replaced by a fitting with solely technical devices, nor can its function be approximated by built-in cushions. This does not mean that there is no progress to be made in saddle fitting. However, not every new development is progress.

The Team

As said before, saddle fitting is teamwork. That is how it should be. Unfortunately, there are many therapists in today's environment who have gained their knowledge over the course of a few weekends. Due to this lack of experience and minimal training, they readily collaborate with a saddle-fitter who seems to have a solution to everything. Or vice versa: The saddle seller is looking for a therapist, who frequently "treats" deficits caused by their saddles but can fix these "problems" only for a short period of time. Teamwork in its true sense should involve good communication and collaboration between *professionals*. Surely, every therapist has her own trusted vets, saddlers, farriers, or trainers, with whom she has been working for many years—ideally, not just one of each, but several from each profession. And if a client leads to a new professional contact, everyone should engage in an exchange to understand each other's approach.

The Crooked Horse

Every horse is crooked, just like every human, dog, cat, and mouse. Nature does not produce absolute symmetry. Picture the horse's abdomen from the inside: cecum and liver to the right, spleen to the left. That is the opposite of balance. If you look at human portraits, you will not find a single head with an absolutely perfect horizontal eye line. If you have your picture taken and sit a little stiffly in front of the photographer, she will ask you to tilt your head to make the photo look more natural.

A few years ago, I was asked to contribute to an article where blockages in several horses' spines were to be assessed on the basis of only one photo. My comment was that this kind of photo assessment was dubious and gave readers a false impression of what an actual joint blockage looks like. I was cut from the "committee of experts" and my comments were not printed.

The Visually Symmetrical Horse
There is only one situation where I can imagine a horse standing almost symmetrically: It is a horse after a perfectly executed full halt, scored at 80 percent or better by the judges. This horse must be standing squarely on all four legs, with actively stabilized muscle chains.

When a horse moves, symmetry is equated with quality in the collected movements. Every movement that is asked at the Intermediate Levels and higher, should be symmetrical in its rough form and then developed to perfection in the Grand Prix.

Nature Does Not Do Perfect Symmetry
If you look at the right and left femurs of a horse, you will never see two perfect mirror images. You won't find two symmetrical bones—nor mirror-imaged tendons or ligaments, nor an evenly filled abdomen.

If a naturally asymmetrical system starts swinging, how is the living being supposed to *move evenly in a straight line?*

What happens if an untrained horse takes off at a full gallop? He will push off with one hind leg (usually the right one) and support with the other (usually the left). He certainly will not throw in a flying change about halfway to switch and ensure both legs get the same workout!

Blocked, unstable, or normal movement pattern? This cannot be determined from a single picture.

Example: Zebra

During the era of German natural scientist and zoologist Bernhard Grzimek, when no reliable tranquilizers were available, zebras were caught in Africa by driving right next to them at full speed, grabbing their tails, and then slowing down. This only worked because zebras flee like horses: on a slightly curved line, but never in tight turns. They move on a slightly curved line because one hind leg pushes, and the other one supports.

Crookedness Means One Dominant Diagonal

What is responsible for the difference between the two sides of a horse? There are several theories that attempt to answer this question, of which none has scientifically been deemed to be the only explanation. It may be due to automatic mechanical reasons, such as the differing structure of the left side of the abdominal cavity versus the right; or it may develop through imprinting of the mother's behavior; or it may be genetically determined to "align" the herd when fleeing.

It is not sensible to compare the horse's natural crookedness with human "handedness." In humans, this term relates to the hand as a prehensile organ. All training principles that aim to reprogram the horse on this basis are questionable. The comparison with a human's preferred "active" leg and "standing" leg is also off-base. Even in a soccer player with one very dominant active leg, this leg cannot be identified when he is running.

One movement precisely corresponds to deliberate *goal-oriented motor skills,* and the other to a *rhythmic movement pattern.* Horses do not use goal-oriented motor skills in their movements, only rhythmic movement patterns. A dominant supporting leg exists for goal-oriented motor skills, but a dominant swinging leg does not. A horse does not learn to deliberately cross his legs with the goal of performing a half-pass; he simply continues his *rhythmic movement pattern* with a shift in his gravity.

Hence, the trainer's thoughts and actions have to focus on the relevant supporting leg to transfer power.

"Bending" Does Not Mean "To Bend"

The term "bending" in equestrian language means the *sensible muscular stabilization of the movement center on a curved line*. The "bend" along the horse's longitudinal axis in terms of dressage training is a complex, three-dimensional movement pattern in the horse's body. It depends on the counteractive stabilization of the rotational movement of thorax and pelvis against gravity. Then—and only then—can the horse align with a curved track.

The phrase "the horse bends around the rider's inside leg" is a figurative term, but can easily be taken literally by inexperienced riders. The image it evokes generally tempts the rider to pull on the inside rein, hold the horse's midsection in place with the inside spur, and push the hindquarters in with the outside spur.

Uneven Steps in the Hind Legs—
Studying the Causes

Some horses take significantly shorter steps with one hind leg than the other, without any apparent or diagnosable reason as assessed by a vet. This also leads to many different approaches, especially from physical therapists. The most questionable one, when looking at the function of the hindquarters, is stretching of the muscles in the leg that takes shorter steps. Why? Try to mimic your horse's sequence of legs in walk on all fours. You will understand and feel quickly that it is easy to learn the sequences by heart to test your "horse knowledge," but to actively copy them is a lot more difficult.

If we analyze the sequence of leg phases, the lateral two-leg support phase catches the eye. It means that the horse has both left legs on the ground for a short moment, and both right legs suspended (and vice versa). This is a fairly complex position, which requires a high amount of coordination and power at the walk, if a horse has to maintain his rhythm. It's a position that is extremely unstable, as the horse could never maintain this position at a standstill, and it is not comparable to a human's cross-coordination when crawling. If, for example, the left side of the horse is not able to meet the requirements of stabilization, the right hind leg will want to touch the ground faster to compensate for the weakness of the left side.

To solve the problem, it might seem like a good idea to work on moving the right hind leg. But that approach is short-sighted. Instead, the rider has to walk down the long and arduous path of stabilizing the left hind leg.

Straightening through Stabilization

Generally speaking, it is completely out of place to cry out, "Help, my horse is crooked!" when a horse is first started in his training, and even over the course of his future training. Crookedness in the horse is absolutely normal and can only be improved through a long-term, correctly stabilizing gymnasticizing process, and should no longer be present when the higher levels of collection have been developed.

But why stabilize when I can simply make the horse's stiff side more flexible? This sounds reasonable at first, but on closer examination it does not make any sense. Why?

We have learned that the horse stabilizes himself by sinking passively down-ward, in his natural movement patterns. Since there is no symmetry at the level of bones and ligaments, the result can only be an uneven twist. Any correction when the horse is at this level may seem to work in the short term, but will ul-timately end in crookedness again. Active stabilization against gravity, carried out by the muscles and managed by the rider, is the only option to permanently straighten the horse's body. (This is called "riding" in expert circles.)

This means: A chiropractor can (re-)set, a physical therapist can stretch, an acu-puncturist can needle, and a vet can inject. But if the rider does not ride, the natural crookedness of a horse cannot be corrected.

Example: From the Horse's Perspective

I am being led on a circle by my rider and she wants me to trot and canter. I want to be good and do everything well. I balance myself by turning my head to the outside. My rider keeps trying to make me turn my head to the inside. But how on earth is this supposed to work? Whenever I turn my head to the inside, I fall on my inside leg. I simply can't maintain it. It is so exhausting for my outside shoulder. I make mistakes in rhythm, too, and that's not what she wants, either. It is doable to some extent on straight lines, but I become tense before every corner, in an effort not to lose my balance completely. Finally, she starts pulling on the inside rein. That doesn't feel good, but at least I have something to hold on to. My lower neck becomes pretty strong, and I get heavy in my rider's hands. Not really fun, but it works for the time being.

See? If a horse stiffens on one side, that's not the horse's mistake, but rather his
attempt to correct a problem somewhere in the training framework with the
short-term solution available to him. And that's the only method he has.

If you have arrived at the point where the horse has already become stiff and
strong, a bodyworker or physical therapist can certainly help bring the horse's
biomechanical system back to its original state of mobility. But if the second
therapeutic step, correct work under saddle, does not take place, a game of
ping-pong begins, where the bodyworker or therapist wins economically and
the horse loses with regard to his health. You are the one stuck with the short end
of the stick; it will cost you, and you still may not have a horse to ride in the end.

Example: Groundwork in Walk
*Groundwork in walk is a popular training and therapeutic approach. The horse
is often led over colored poles and around cones for months, or as long as he
needs, until he optimally turns his head and neck to all sides. Well, then you may
ride at the walk, and it is all good. But as soon as the horse starts trotting, he has
all sorts of problems again. Your horse is just as stiff as before.*

The reason for this is that the horse's
muscles can be *prepared* for gaits with
impulsion, namely trot and canter, in
the walk, but they cannot be *trained*
in walk. The coordination between
nerves and muscles differs massively
between walk, a gait without impulsion, and trot and canter with impulsion. Groundwork in walk has its uses
for certain objectives. It is, for example,
perfectly suitable for correcting a horse
that was incorrectly ridden. However,
groundwork cannot achieve muscular
rehabilitative training for gaits with impulsion, with respect to the *correction*
of *natural crookedness*.

Summary

Moving on a curved track places high demands on the athletic abilities of a horse. Used correctly, it is an ideal tool to develop these athletic abilities and protect the horse against chronic overload.

In most cases, problems on curved lines have their origins in poor stability, in terms of the horse's development of coordination and power, and they are not primarily a problem of mobility. Consequently, correction has to begin with the actively stabilized FCPT, with the support of the hindquarters, and not by overflexing the horse's neck. Reactions from the horse, such as becoming stiff in the neck or ribs, falling out over the shoulder, or tilting in the poll are normal signs of insufficient athleticism and cannot be considered mistakes on the horse's part.

The key to movement along a curved line is the active stabilization of the inverse rotation of the thorax and pelvis against gravity. The connection to the outside rein, as well as active engagement of the inside hind leg, support this task.

The basic property required for the horse to correctly align with a curved track, and to "bend" according to the meaning of the term in riding theory, is stability, not mobility.

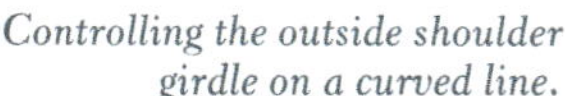

Controlling the outside shoulder girdle on a curved line.

The curved line is one of the most important training elements for a riding horse. Control over the outside shoulder girdle and pelvis girdle, in the supporting leg phase, is always crucial in this context. The work in the diagonal sequence of leg phases is the logical continuation of that control.

Diagonal supporting leg phase in the pirouette with correct flexion and bend.

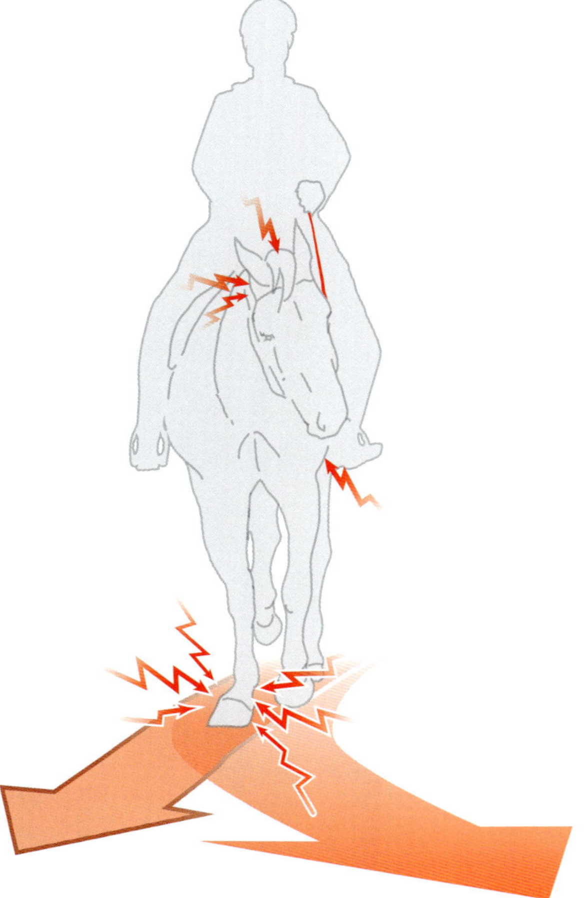

Strain on the horse when the horse is leaning or heavy on the inside rein.

Incorrect Movement Patterns and Their Consequences

FCPT—Evasion Mechanisms

Curved lines are not included in the horse's natural movement repertoire. If a rider asks a horse to move correctly along a curved line before he has been prepared with the necessary training and gymnasticization, he will inevitably take refuge in evasive movements familiar to every rider. Their biomechanical sources will be illustrated in the following pages.

Leaning on the Inside Rein

If the horse is heavy on the inside rein, he reacts to the weakness of his outside shoulder girdle by leaning on the rider's inside hand for support. He now has a type of anchor he can hold on to with his lower neck muscles.

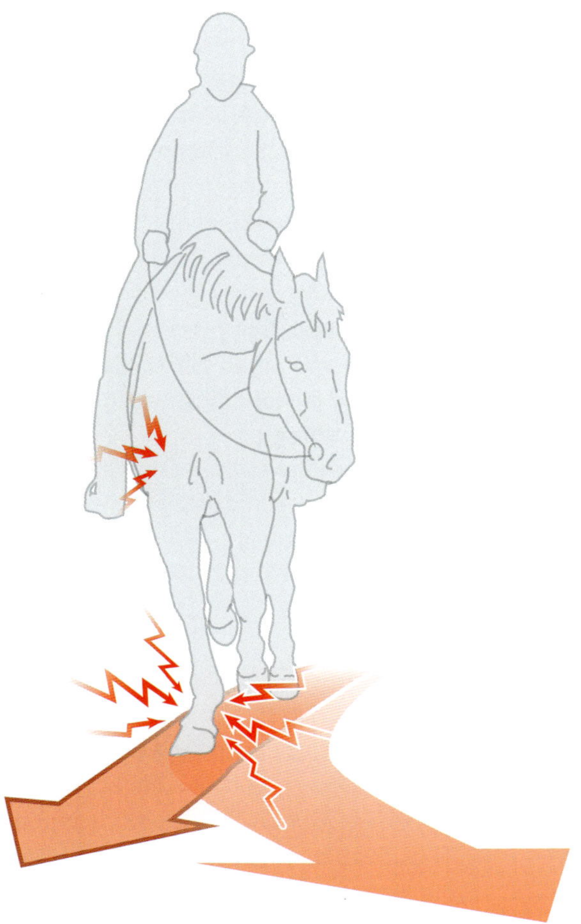

The tension in these lower neck muscles leads to a blockage in the entire shoulder girdle, and the correct muscle slings do not have a chance to develop.

Falling Out over the Outside Shoulder

In this case, the horse passively falls into and hangs from the ligament systems of the outside front extremities, since he isn't strong enough for the shoulder girdle's stabilizing work. By twisting the thorax until his movement limit has been reached, his muscle levers become so badly positioned that the muscles can no longer lift the thorax on their own. In the process, heavy strain is also placed on the ligament apparatus of the shoulder joint.

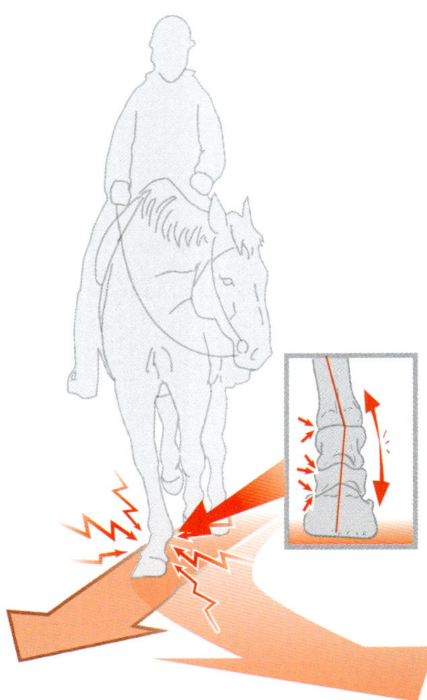

Distortion of the leg axes leads to compressive stress on the outer areas of the joints and tensile stress on the inner ligament and tendon structures.

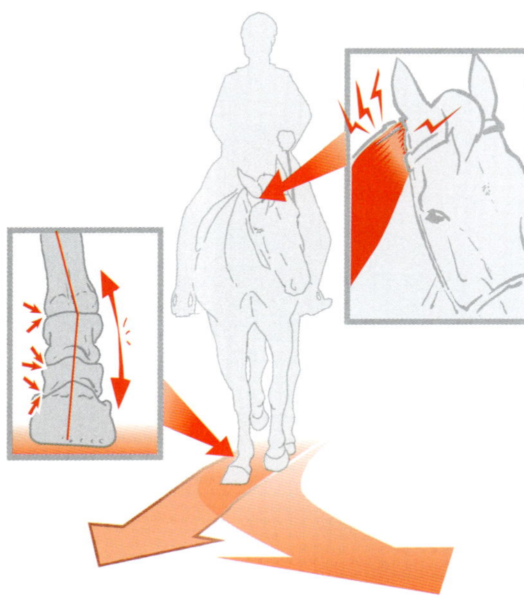

The horse's resistance on a curved line (he is "heavy" to the inside) is directly diverted onto the poll, the base of the neck, and the front legs through the tensed and hardened muscles.

FCPT—Chronic Overload Mechanisms— Without Tension

An unstable leg axis leads to an unnatural twisting of the lower joints of the leg. As a result, the joints, the inner parts of the suspensory ligament, and the inner and outer ligament systems, as well as the tendons, are subjected to high shear and rotational movements.

Associated Symptoms
- inflammation of the hoof joint, navicular bone, and surrounding structures
- tendonitis
- damage to the suspensory ligaments
- changes in the digital flexor tendon complex
- inflammation and degenerative changes in the cervical and thoracic vertebrae

FCPT—Chronic Overload Mechanisms— Negative Tension

This perspective clearly shows which structures are stressed if the rider tries to overbend her horse with the force of her rein and leg. Along with the visible spur marks, antagonistic lines of force meet mainly at the poll and also the joints of the lower leg, and cause chronic overload reactions.

Associated Symptoms
- problems in the jaw and poll
- degenerative changes and inflammation in the upper and lower cervical spine
- damage to the spinous processes ("kissing spines") and the small vertebral joints of the thoracic and thoracolumbar vertebrae
- hard, inflamed back muscles
- damage to the navicular system
- damage to the suspensory ligaments and tendons
- inflammation of the lower-leg joints
- recurring joint blockages, especially in the poll and the base of the neck

FCPT—Deviating Leg Axis

As previously described, the leg axes cannot be considered without taking into account their muscular connection to the torso. In general, deviation of the leg axis is a reaction to muscular weakness in this area.

The leg travels away from its axis to the inside. Depending on the shape of the hoof, the leg is going to be either set down levelly or tilted. In both cases, the fetlock cannot lower toward the center of the hoof, and inevitably has to perform a rotational movement. A share of movement energy is directed toward this rotational movement and places strain on *the outside parts of the joints, the navicular bone complex, and the inner ligament systems*. The remaining energy "catapults" the hoof to the outside in a whip-like movement during the swinging leg phase. The high speed also creates extreme stress in the ligament system of the lower-leg joints.

Signs to Look For
- dissimilar shape of the hooves
- faults in hoof conformation
- dissimilar deviations of the leg axes
- base-narrow or splay-footed position

Symptoms in Motion
- frequent tripping
- brushing of fetlocks
- long, sloping pastern with excessive stretch in the fetlock
- over-reaching (touching the underside of the front hoof with the tip of the hind hoof on one or both sides)

Other Associated Symptoms
- inflammation of the hoof joint and navicular bone
- unilateral inflammation of the suspensory ligament
- unilateral inflammation in the sesamoid bone
- inflammation in the lateral ligaments of the digital joints
- changes in the digital flexor tendon complex

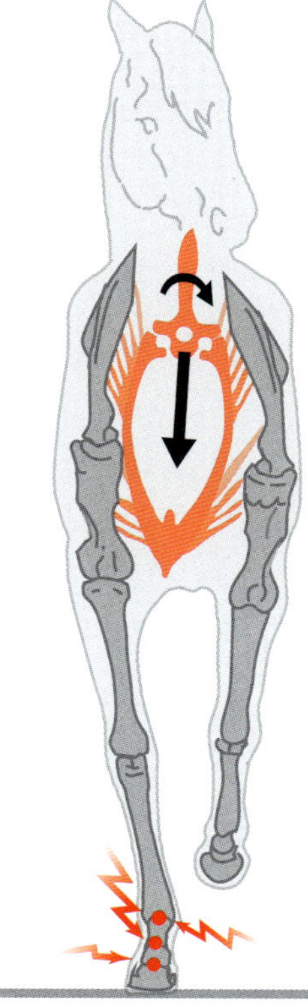

Whether unstable or tensed, the horse cannot set down his front legs with correct axial alignment—not without the muscles of the shoulder girdle working with suppleness.

An unstable leg axis during movement on a straight line.

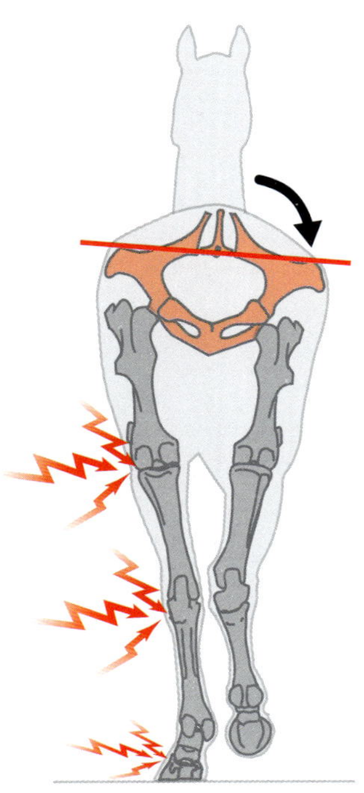

The biomechanics of an unstable pelvis.

HCPD Evasive Mechanisms—Without Tension

If the horse's movement is not stabilized securely by his muscles, then, in the "hanging" system described on page 30, the abdomen swings more strongly to the left and right. This leads to a lateral twist in the pelvis. The leg axes follow these rotational movements, and stress arises. The reason for this so-called "crooked pelvis" is very often a one-sided instability in the hindquarters.

Symptoms (X-ray, scintigraphy)
- inflammation and degenerative changes in the spinous processes
- inflammation and/or constantly recurring blockages in the small joints of the spine and the sacroiliac (SI) joint
- "loose" ligaments in the stifle
- osteoarthritis ("bone spavin"), often in the soft tissue
- strain reactions in the joints of the lower leg (most likely in the tendons and ligaments)

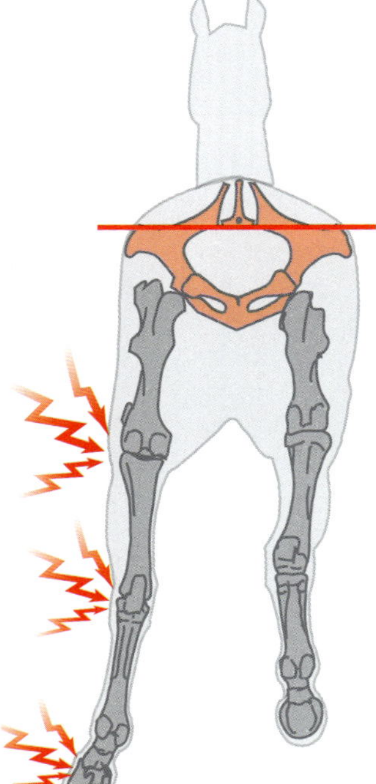

The results of a tense muscle chain in the pelvic girdle.

HCPD Evasive Mechanisms—Negative Tension

If the outside croup muscles become tense because too much has been asked of the horse, especially on a curved track or in lateral work, these horses usually start to travel wide behind. This wider track can be seen particularly in young dressage horses, and has to be severely penalized by judges.

Symptoms (X-ray, scintigraphy)
- inflammation and degenerative changes in the spinous processes
- inflammation or constantly recurring blockages in the small joints of the spine and the sacroiliac joint
- irritation of the stifle ligaments
- osteoarthritis
- changes in the digital flexor tendon complex

HCPD—Deviating Leg Axes

Deviation of the leg axis to the inside as well as the outside has massive effects on the joints and soft tissue of the hind legs. In both cases, the result is a quick left-right movement of the hock, which is then exposed to high rotational pressure. Osteoarthritis develops in the cartilage or soft tissue. The stifle is unnaturally twisted upward, leading to strain on the stifle ligaments. The rotational movement is diverted downward to the digital joints, resulting in tensile stress to the inner structures (suspensory, sesamoid bones, ligaments) and compressive stress to the outer structures. The navicular bone complex in the center of the hoof is equally overstrained in both cases.

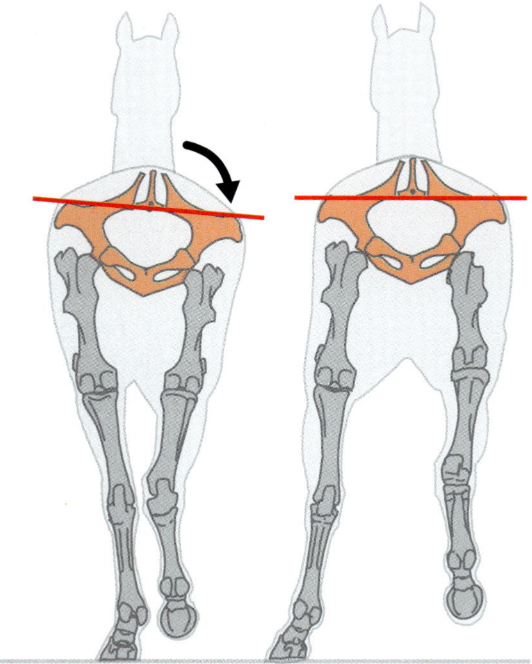

Deviation in the leg axes always has severe consequences for the horse's health, and definitely has to be considered in light of those potential consequences.

Signs to Look For
- hooves of dissimilar shape
- defects in hoof conformation
- dissimilar deviations in the leg axes
- cow-hocked

Symptoms in Motion
- frequent tripping
- brushing of fetlocks
- long, sloping pastern with excessive stretch in the fetlock

Other Associated Symptoms
- inflammation in the coffin joint and navicular bone
- unilateral suspensory inflammation
- unilateral inflammation in the sesamoid bone
- inflammation in the lateral ligaments of the digital joints
- changes in the digital flexor tendon complex
- problems in stifle ligaments

This shows how active wrong riding and passive wrong riding create almost identical pathologies.

The Farrier and the Leg Axes

As illustrated, deviating leg axes can lead to incorrect placement of the feet and, in the long run, deformations in the hoof capsule. Pathologies within the hoof capsule can also result from genetic predispositions or bad conditions during foalhood, and can cause muscular deficits and reactions. This means it's hard to be sure which deviation is a trigger or cause, and which one is a reaction to another problem. Everyone involved in treating a deformed hoof has to work together to achieve a long-term, solid result: vet, farrier, physical therapist, and trainer.

Functional Assessment of the Front Leg Axes in the One-Legged and Two-Legged Stand

This form of assessment yields important information about how the horse coordinates himself over the respective leg when standing. It can never replace assessing the horse in motion but provides a valuable additional perspective. It allows for differentiation between *structural* (attributable to the shape of the hoof) and *functional* (attributable to the stability of the leg axes) deviation during movement.

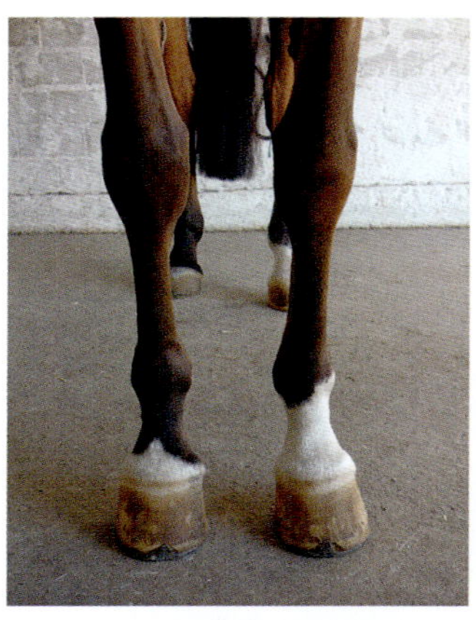
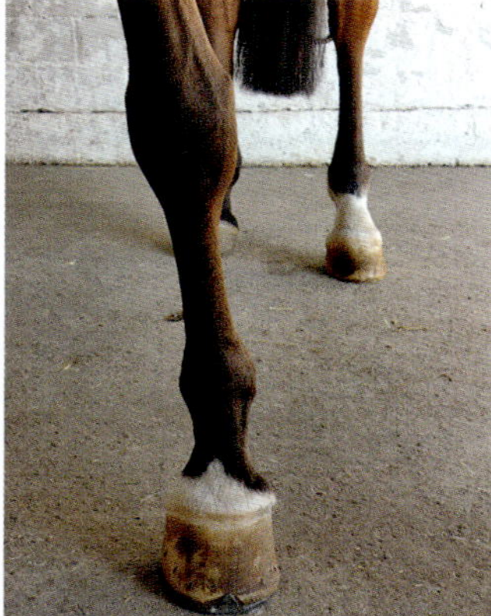

Correct shape of the hooves and the leg axis in a two-leg stand, with a clear deviation in a one-leg stand. This suggests a functional instability of the right leg axis, which can be improved through correct rehabilitative training.

Structurally changed hoof and leg axis in a two-leg stand. On the right: functionally stabilized. On the left: functionally unstable.

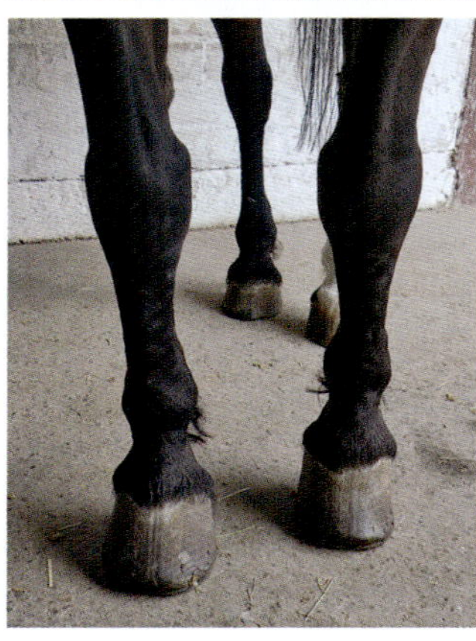
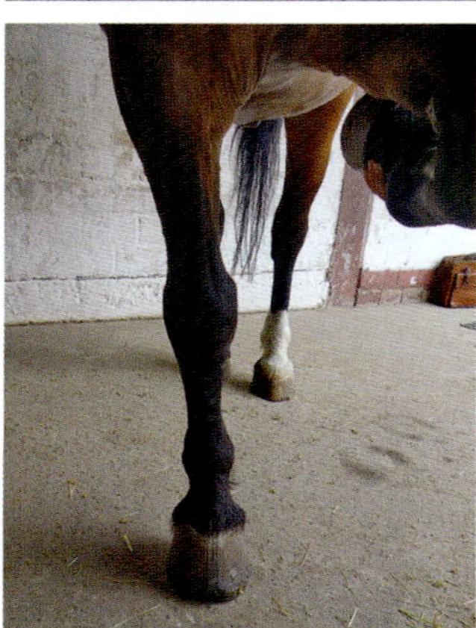
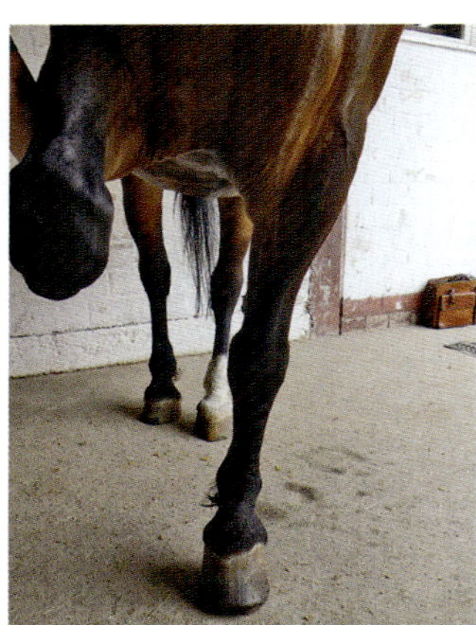

Preferred Procedure

VET: X-rays illustrate the actual situation between hoof capsule and joint surface. Simultaneously, the farrier receives information about the thickness of the sole. This determines the "wiggle room" the farrier has to correct the hoof capsule. In addition, the vet can straighten out inflammatory processes and chronic degenerations of the joint surfaces.

PHYSICAL THERAPIST: Functional analysis to illustrate the relationship between mobility and stability with regard to the leg axis.

TRAINER: Assessment of the training level of horse and rider, especially in terms of ability to stabilize the horse on curved tracks.

FARRIER: Assessment of the hoof capsule's shape and quality at a standstill and in movement.

After these basics have been clarified by each professional, an understanding of overall joint condition is developed, tailored to the individual horse. The entire effort is certainly significant in the beginning; however, in the long run, this is the only reasonable chance to permanently get ahead of any complex problems. In the end, this procedure is always faster and less expensive than everyone working in a "trial-and-error" fashion.

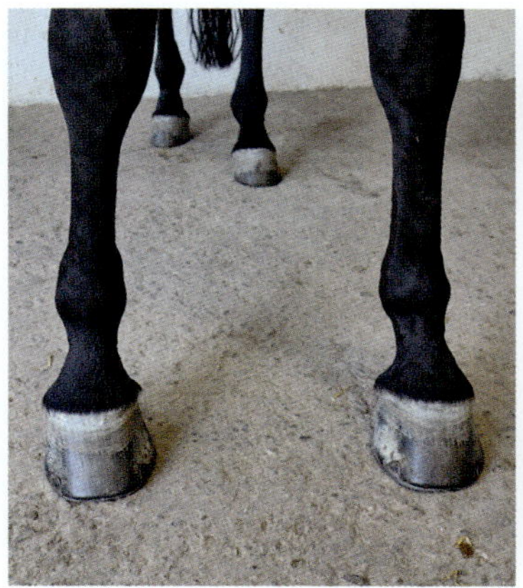
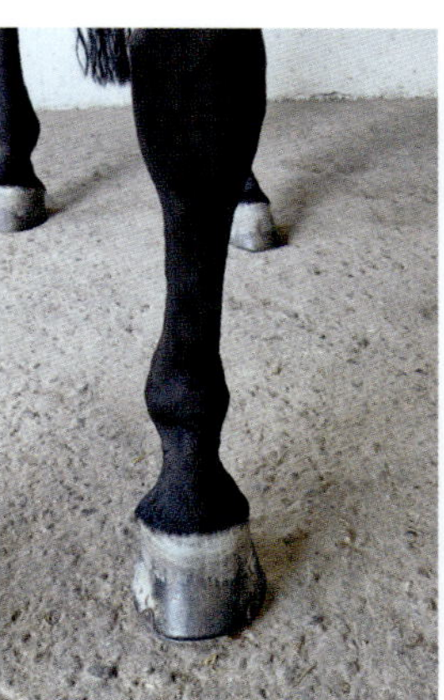
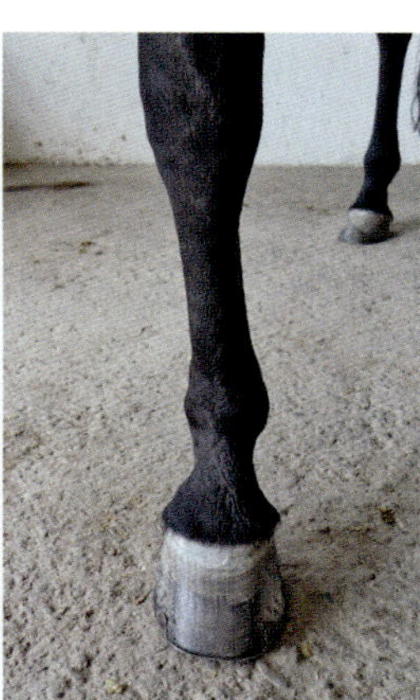

Structurally changed hoof capsule. Left and center: Alteration of the leg axis in two-legged and one-legged stand. Right: Functionally stabilized.

4 Positive Tension in Training

Gathering movement energy in the supporting leg phase.

At this point, the core statements of this book are:

- Correct movement with impulsion, on a straight or curved line, depends on strong, functional muscle chains and the development of positive body tension.
- "Positive tension" means the development of an additional muscular "spring" in the FCPT and HCPD.
- Alongside the schooling of certain movements, developing collection ability during the training of a sport horse mainly means adapting the level of tension in these elastic "springs" through the application of these movements.

Adaptation of the "Spring" Systems

The more movement energy is created in the legs, in their role as "catapults," the more powerful and effective the elastic "springs" in the horse's torso must be. The challenge this poses can be compared to the world of cars: The horse is equipped with a built-in engine, already capable of its maximum amount of horsepower, at birth. The transmission and clutch needed for a controlled transmission of this power, however, have to be built up over the years.

The connection between the classical principles of training a riding horse, and their influence on the development of these active torso springs, is explained in the next chapter (see p. 124).

Training Means Responsibility

Admittedly, it can be easy to lose sight of your goals when you're sitting on a young dressage horse that offers everything he can muster, everything he has in him in terms of elasticity and catapulting power. The rider can be tempted to frequently demand access to this talent and test its limits. Or even to develop movements within this unfinished system, movements which are only intended for a much later phase in a systematic training system. The temptation is just as great with a jumping horse, which, from a correct rhythm and basic tempo, almost explodes over the fence. Horses want to please their riders—they want to show, and to live up to their innate performance ability. They are the products of the fantastic breeding selection of the last decades.

However, as the performance ability of these horses increases, so does the responsibility of the rider and trainer to handle these systems within the horse correctly. The appreciation for a performance-oriented training structure must grow in step with the horse's performance ability.

To illustrate the connections, the model of the movement centers in a dynamic state of motion must be revisited. In the process, the concept of the "spring" system of the legs will be separated from that of the torso for a short time to demonstrate how the mechanisms of training apply.

The Training Scale in the Language of the Movement Centers

The Scales of Training are the guiding principles for any work with the horse, not just during the first stages of training. It applies to horses of all ages and training levels, even if the last three elements cannot always be achieved.

Rhythm

At first, the horse moves in his natural posture. The individual components of the movement centers are different in their muscle strength and have not yet become coordinated. In order for the horse to find an even rhythm, the development of trust and relaxation is the first priority. The flight reflex has to be replaced by the development of positive tension. The horse is expected to find an even rhythm on four "springs" wound to different degrees of tightness. This is only possible if two basic elements of correct movement have been achieved: the right basic tempo, and the right balance of the movement centers through the leg axes. In this case, "correct" or "right" is what leads to the individually correct rhythm of this horse.

This means that the horse is allowed to first adjust his balance to the various springs of the leg axes. His conformation determines the position of his movement centers and the use of the neck as a balancing pole. His individual speed depends on the basic tension of the tissue and muscles that were developed in his early years, genetic predisposition being a major factor. If all components have been ideally coordinated, correct rhythm is an automatic result.

Specifically, this means: If the horse's right shoulder girdle is weaker than the left one, he will use his neck as a balancing pole and position it toward the weak shoulder girdle. If the left pelvic girdle is weaker than the right one, the horse will lower his right pelvis, or travel more to the outside with his left foot. These changes allow the young horse to find his rhythm; he should not be interrupted in the process. In the early stages, rhythm is supported by promoting inner and outer suppleness, which, again, is reached by supporting the correct basic tempo.

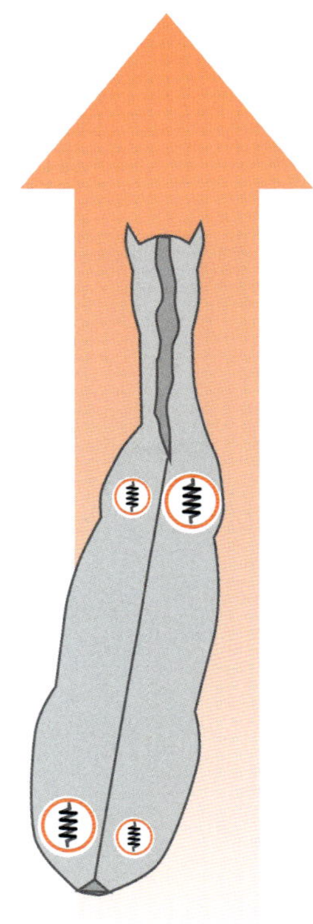

Leg "springs" wound to different degrees of tension are leveled out through the balance reactions of the neck and hind legs.

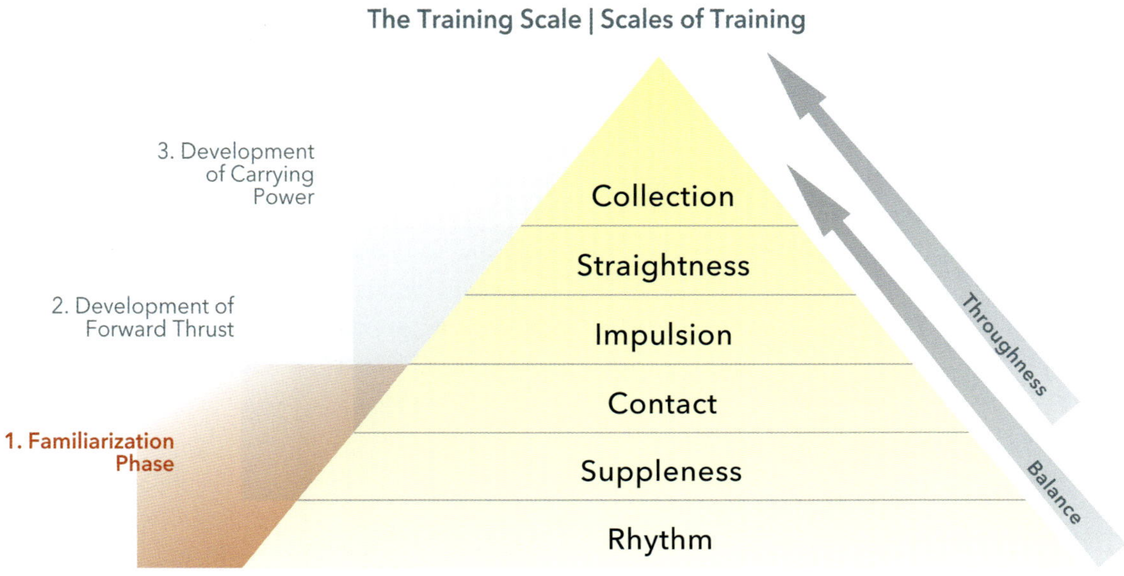

Through progressive improvement of rhythm, suppleness, contact, impulsion, straightness, and collection, balance and "throughness" are continuously refined.

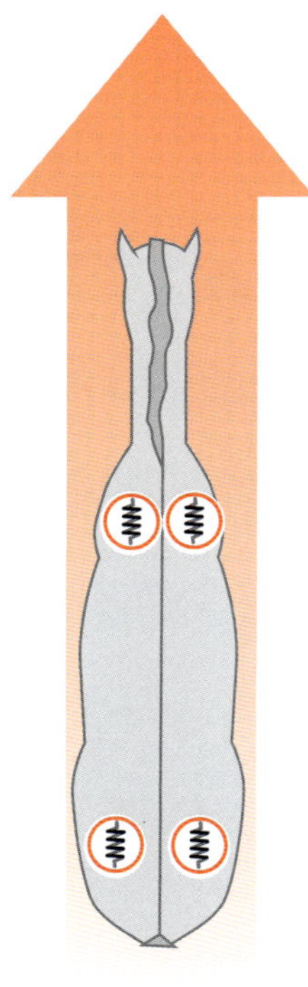

With well-balanced leg "springs," the horse can begin to straighten himself.

Suppleness

Once the horse has found his rhythm, his steps will be even and coordinated. He can then react to the rider's aids. Suppleness means the rhythmic contraction and relaxation of muscles within a movement cycle. The rider begins to form the horse's rhythm through development of positive tension. In doing so, she will encourage the relaxation phase for a horse that organizes his rhythm with a high basic tension, and curb the contraction phase through calmness and regularity. For a horse that organizes his rhythm with a lower muscle tone, the rider will encourage the contraction phase through activation and motivation, and simply accept the relaxation phase as it is. The trainer can push the intensity of the aids for as long as the horse's rhythm remains regular.

Contact

Once the trainer has all active muscle chains supple and rhythmically engaged, she can begin to change the position of the horse's movement centers. This means the FCPT starts to lift between the shoulder blades and is increasingly supported by the HCPD. The impulse of the forward-driving leg aid prompts the lifting of the thorax and increases the horse's willingness to stretch the neck toward the bit—which is to say, it's not that the neck stretches forward in a relaxed manner and brings the thorax with it, but rather that the lifting of the thorax allows the neck to stretch. In my opinion, believing that this body position begins with the stretching of the neck and ends in the thorax instead of the other way around is entirely incorrect, and one of the most fundamental misunderstandings of many riders of our time.

Contact begins with the rider's aids animating the horse to lift his withers actively forward and upward, between his shoulder blades. The pelvis supports this movement process by rotating backward, thus closing the "arc of tension." The neck starts to stretch toward the bit as a reaction to this process.

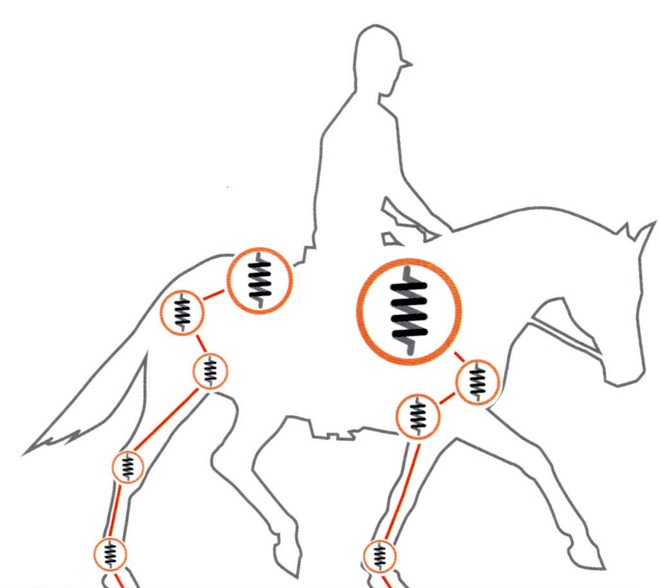

The development from untrained horse to riding horse begins with the activation of additional elasticity between the horse's torso and extremities.

Once this step in training has been reached, the horse has been "retrained" from his natural movement patterns to those of a riding horse, in terms of functional anatomy. He doesn't yet have the ability to bend equally to the left and the right, nor is he able to correctly process a half-halt. But he has a basic understanding of these movement processes, and even more importantly, is able to use all four limbs to absorb the force of gravity—even if he is not yet able to equally distribute that force. This is enough to maintain the well-being of a pleasure horse, if his workload is managed appropriately, and should allow a lower-level horse to perform a Training Level test with a score between 70 and 80 percent. However, if these requirements were asked of an advanced dressage horse, obviously this score would be devastating. For any horse that will be asked to participate in higher-level equestrian sports, this degree of basic training is not enough, and the deficit will be paid for with performance losses and injuries in the long run.

Impulsion

This is where the athletic training of the riding horse starts, on the Scales of Training. The movement centers take on more positive tension than is necessary to simply keep the horse healthy. The horse's musculature begins to visibly fill out. His lower neck becomes firmer and his topline becomes fuller. The FCPT continues to open up and unfold. The HCPD closes more and more. The movement centers increasingly take on movement energy through counter-rotation, which they then release in a controlled manner, according to the rider's aids, into more forward movement or into the first development of true carrying power to bear weight on the hindquarters. Maintaining rhythm and suppleness at the same time guarantees the balance inside the horse is not negatively affected.

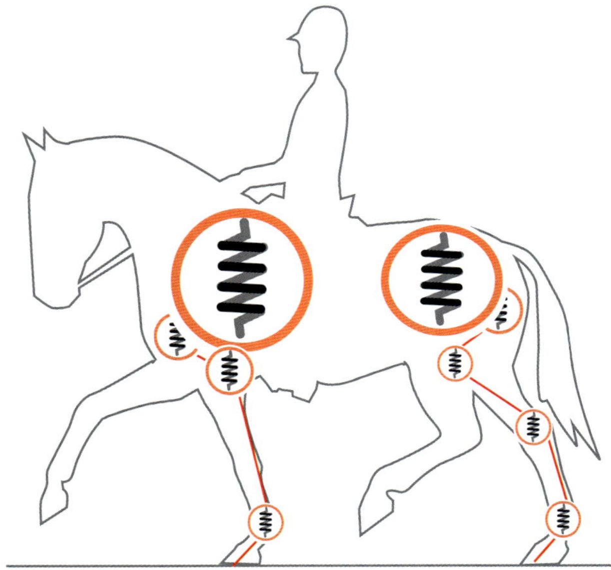

Any further development of the torso "springs" and their mutual interplay beyond this point is progress not from "untrained horse" to "riding horse," but from "riding horse" to "sport horse."

Straightening

Straightening is one of the most important and most interesting elements in the training of a horse. The muscle strength and positive tension of the individual muscle chains between the torso and the extremities are precisely addressed, from a functional perspective, through a lateral shift of the horse's center of gravity. An automotive engineer would refer to this as an "adaptive suspension" setup: the adjustment of the shock absorbers to allow them to handle the maximum speed involved in taking a curve, at its apex.

If a horse is stiff on the right, generally his left shoulder girdle is weaker than his right one. On a curved track to the right, the horse thus moves his neck toward the left shoulder girdle. This reduces the amount of force (torque) on the weaker side and allows the muscles to be worked in suppleness. To solve the problems of stiffness and leaning on the inside (right) rein, it is necessary to strengthen the left shoulder girdle, with the support of the right hind leg.

A logical approach would be to flex the horse's neck on the right rein in such a way that the horse can only just maintain the arc of tension between his inside leg and the outside rein. In doing so, the horse's head is positioned to the outside, between the outside shoulder joint and the sternum, with an open rein. The difference between flexion and bend is important here: Flexion in the poll has to be maintained, and the equal bend of neck and back is interrupted in the area at the base of the neck to develop the muscle slings in the thorax. Essentially, this is only possible with a certain basic strength, established by developing the previous elements of the Training Scale. If this is not the case, everything has to go back to square one (rhythm, suppleness, contact); nothing else will work.

When discussing dressage, it's important to understand that lateral differences up to the early advanced levels are quite normal, and not a mistake. Due to the horse's level of training, he is not yet ready to develop enough elastic force to absorb the impact to his body from both diagonals equally in the sequence of leg phases. However, if seemingly correct movement processes have been reached through the use of force, any effect of training is stopped in its tracks, and the horse drops in his scores in proportional relation to the increasing requirements of the movements and exercises (and in his physical development).

"Straightening" means the three-dimensional synchronization of torso and leg "springs."

Collection

Collection, as the pinnacle of the riding horse's training, is, on a functional level, about the movement energy of the hindquarters gaining more and more toward carrying capacity. The development of impulsion is strengthened further, but it is increasingly steered toward taking on and carrying more weight, due to the change in the horse's pelvis angle. In the process, the trainer's core task is the consistent, three-dimensional strengthening of the system, without negatively tipping the horse's balance in one direction or the other. The individual prerequisites of the horse play the most important role with regard to the result. Yet differentiation between a "leg mover" and a "back mover" doesn't only take place during the development of collection. The foundation is laid much earlier, in the correct positioning of the movement centers during the development of contact.

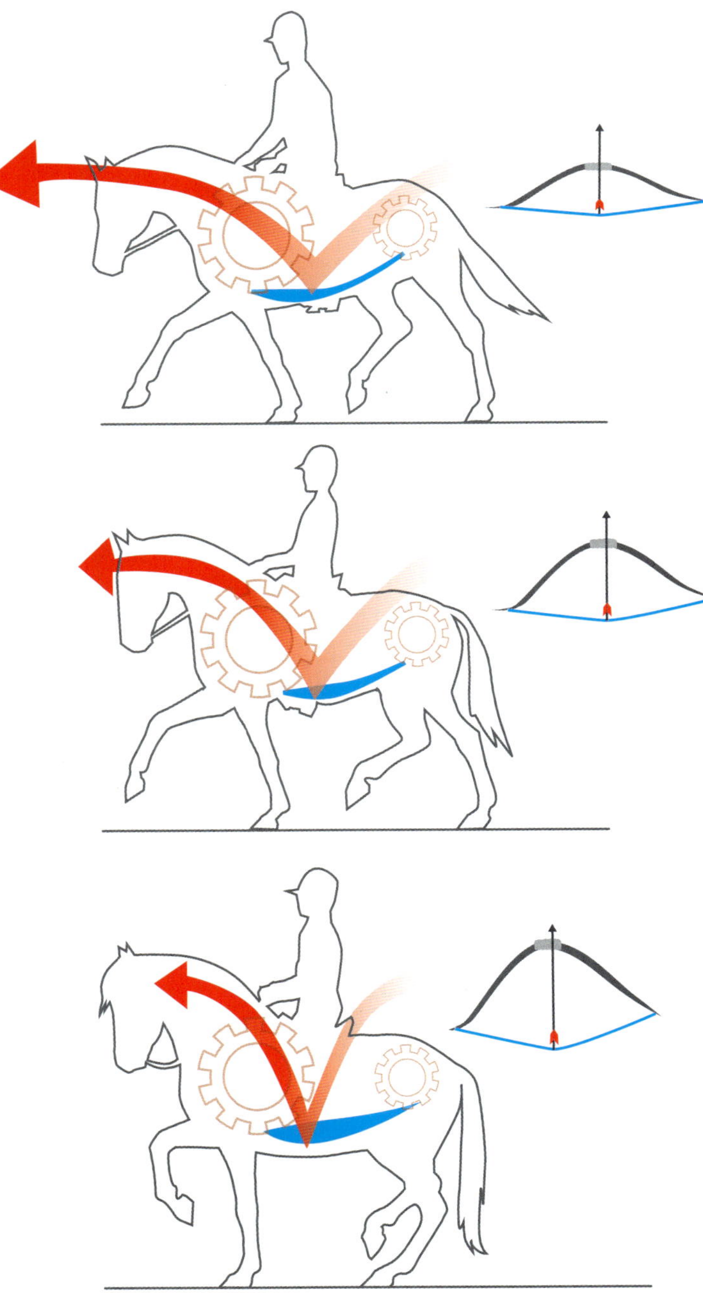

The development of collection means the consistent achievement of positive tension in the horse.

Flatwork—The Logic Behind the Movements

Every individual movement in dressage has a special gymnasticizing effect. All the possible individual movements, taken together, form a logical system. Every movement always shapes the horse in an athletic manner, and at the same time a foundation is laid for a new movement. It's worthwhile for riders to understand what the key motion and fundamental purpose of each movement is.

Quality Decides

A movement can only have gymnasticizing value to the horse when it can be ridden fairly well in its standard version. In the language of scores, this translates to 70 percent. For training purposes, this means: If a circle isn't awarded at least 70 percent for technical execution, it doesn't have a strengthening effect for the muscle slings of the movement centers–the rider is simply riding around in circles. Without this strengthening effect, the horse cannot be prepared for lateral work. The horse might cross his legs and trot sideways through the arena, but the laterally stabilizing muscle chains are not being reached. Without lateral stability, a horse cannot perform a straight flying change in one stride. He may throw his body from a right-lead canter to a left-lead canter during the moment of suspension, but this change of leg has nothing to do with a correctly ridden flying change. This chain can be continued on and on…

This fact can best be recognized when looking at a graph of a dressage horse's scores over the course of his career. Many start out as young horses with 80 percent and 90 percent. Over time, with continued training and increasing demands, scores go downhill until by Prix St. Georges, they're running at 58 percent. To face and handle this, it's absolutely necessary to ride seemingly easy movements with the same precision and care as more difficult ones during daily work. Or, in other words: It becomes easier for the horse to perform difficult movements when the basics have been thoroughly established, because the horse has been athletically prepared.

If problems arise in a collected movement of a high level, it is always sensible to thoroughly reassess the quality of the movements at lower levels.

"Riding on a Circle" or "Riding in Circles"?

In October 2013, the German Equestrian Federation (FN) published an article in their membership magazine by German riding master Hubertus Schmidt, where he dwells on the meaning and importance of riding on a circle in the horse's training process. He noted, among other things, that "there are Grand Prix horses out there that are not able to go correctly on a circle." In the following, I will explain the reasons for and the absolute importance of correcting these deficits.

The arena track or school figure *riding on a circle* takes the horse on a curved line. As previously explained, traveling on a curved line increases both the stabilizing force needed to maintain balance as well as the stress on the outside shoulder girdle significantly. That outside shoulder girdle has to manage approximately two or three times more stress than the inside one. Rhythm and suppleness can only be maintained if the horse can actively balance the outside shoulder girdle.

To do so, the rider has to activate the inside hind leg for support (so the HCPD remains stable) and maintain positive tension between the inside leg and the outside rein. This way, the horse's thorax remains in position and is prevented from tilting to the inside. If all these component goals have been reached, the training load on the active muscle chains is increased. They become stronger, and as a result are prepared for lateral work. If one of these component goals is not reached, the horse may move on a more-or-less round circular line, but that isn't the same thing as the arena track "riding on a circle." The circle does not have any gymnasticizing effects in and of itself *unless it's ridden correctly*.

The tighter the circle, the greater the forces acting on the horse's body that need to be stabilized. For an 8-meter circle, the athletic requirements increase by about half the weight of the forehand. Hence, the limit for quality—and the most common source for mistakes—on a curved line is lack of athleticism, not lack of mobility.

At left, the impulse from the rider's inside leg to outside rein stabilizes the horse on a curved line against the rotation in the torso. At right, the rider guides the horse's neck more toward the inside shoulder— the horse tilts and tenses in the poll.

"Half-Pass" or "Sideways Across the Arena"?

For a half-pass, both movement centers have to be inversely and actively arched. Once this has been achieved, the rider uses her aids to shift the horse's center of gravity from the center to the side. The legs react to this shift with diagonal steps. When first developing this movement, crossing the legs is not the priority. Rather, the horse must be flexed to follow the curved line, in terms of three-dimensional stabilization, and ridden straight in this position (travers); if these requirements have been met, the legs will react to the shift in the center of gravity with a movement sequence where the legs are crossing, and the exercise we call a "half-pass" can exert its gymnasticizing effect. The laterally stabilizing muscle chains are addressed and strengthened to facilitate straightness. Without correct positioning of the FCPT and HCPD, a horse may move through the arena, crossing his legs, but he will nevertheless be askew. The only purpose this movement can ever have, without correct positioning, is to reach the arena markers at the other end and cross the legs a lot on the way; it cannot develop athletic ability at all.

Only very close observation of the leg axes allows us to distinguish the stabilized horse on the left from the insufficiently stabilized horse on the right.

"Piaffe" or "Trotting on the Spot"?

Horses can always trot on the spot when they are sufficiently excited or want to impress. The correct development of the piaffe under saddle is something else completely. Functionally speaking, the thought of collection is simply extended. The front and hind movement centers continue to actively arch, and the pelvis angle continues to change, raising the pelvis. In the process, the movement energy in the supporting leg phase is continuously and vertically bounced into the "trampoline" of the horse's body—which means, in the end, there is hardly any forward movement but a forward tendency remains.

A piaffe with correctly and actively arched movement centers. A forward tendency is maintained.

"Canter Pirouette" or "Whirling Around in Canter"?

The same principle applies to the development of canter pirouettes. First, the horse must develop his maximum ability to collect. The two phases in canter, namely the development of uphill movement through the forehand and the preservation of that uphill movement through the hindquarters, are pushed to their maximum. The FCPT now has to elastically bounce itself upward without impulsion. Subsequently, the hindquarters can step under the horse's center of gravity, and movement energy can be absorbed and slowed down by the muscle groups of the HCPD. This is what athleticism is all about.

The canter pirouette is arguably the most important movement in upper level dressage tests.

"Cadence" or "Passage-Like Steps"?

The training of a dressage horse is the foundation for all other disciplines and is strictly guided by the aforementioned framework of the Training Scale. Within the Scale, the development of cadence is a central element. Defined by Colonel Waldemar Seunig as "rhythmic, elevated, and fluent steps and strides in the shortened and schooling gaits," cadence demonstrates the development of three-dimensional stability against gravity in trot especially well. When selecting a dressage horse, knowledge based on experience applies: He has to have a good walk and canter, but the trot, by contrast, can be "made." The trot is easiest to shape. Simply put, the development of cadence is about slowing down the supporting leg phase while extending the ground cover in the swinging leg phase.

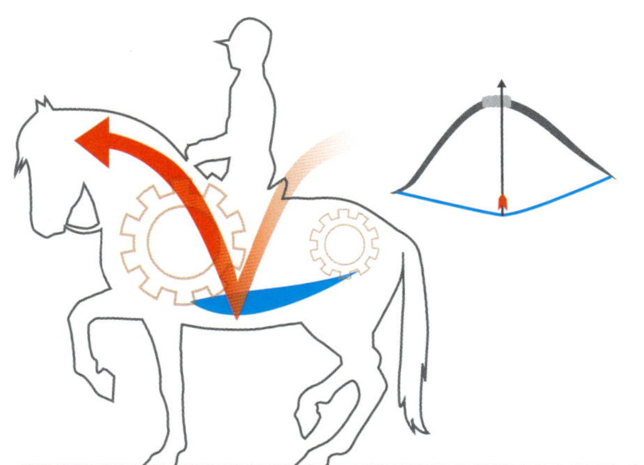
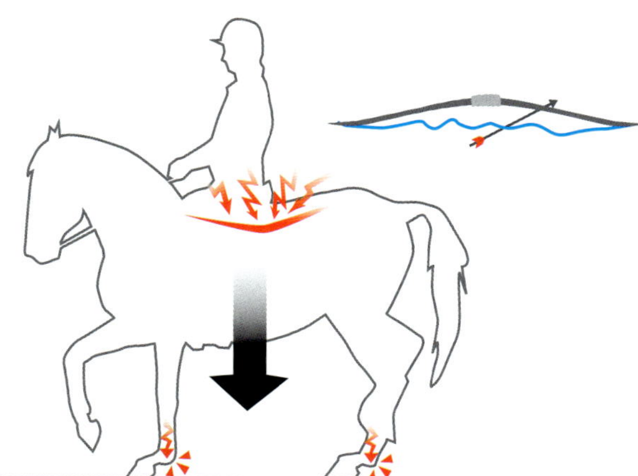

Development of the piaffe and "trotting on the spot" in comparison.

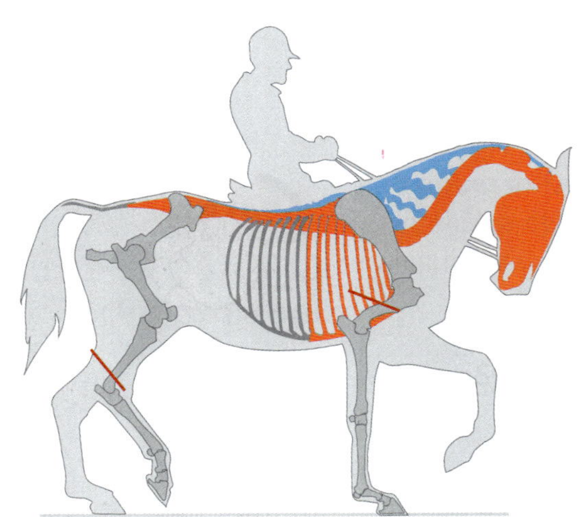

The broken parallelism between the hind leg cannon bone and forearm betrays a lack in quality of the horse's cadence.

This is only achieved if the horse's thorax and pelvis lower as little as possible during the slower supporting leg phase and are held in position by the muscle chains of the torso "springs." Only then do the swinging legs have the space and the time to be moved forward through a greater range of motion in a longer time span. Otherwise, the hind legs are yanked upward against the downward-tilting pelvis during "passage-like steps," and the front legs are hurled from the bottom-up, as a counter-movement to the backward tilting of the thorax. Both movement sequences together lead to a break in the parallelism between the horse's forearm and the cannon bone of the hind leg in trot. This creates an increased leg action, but in an incorrect space-time relationship.

Summary
The classical theory of dressage says the movement patterns of individual movements such as piaffe, passage, or half-pass are all already part of the movement repertoire of wild horses. This is true—but they can only ever be executed by the untrained horse in a passively stabilized system. Many young horses can trot on the spot when they are excited. But a piaffe in equestrian sports is more than trotting on the spot. Extensive lateral movements are part of horses' "threat" and "display" behavior. But travers, renvers, and shoulder-in are more than just trotting sideways. A movement can only exert its full gymnasticizing effect when it is performed with the horse's movement centers in an actively stabilized position. To control this position, the concepts of "on the leg" or "in front of the leg," willingness to stretch forward and downward, as well as rhythm and suppleness can be applied. If any one of these essential requirements is not met, the movement cannot have any relevant training effect. A difference can be seen in the dynamic and expression of individual cadence of a supple horse.

Principles and Methods of Flatwork

The "Half-Halt"

The example of a half-halt best illustrates the principle of developing uphill movement. From a functional perspective, the half-halt is the universal training method for the riding horse. In the interplay between the aids in canter, it effectively directs exactly those changes in the position of the horse's movement centers that have been described in previous chapters as necessary to balanced movement with positive tension.

Increasing the driving weight and leg aids encourages the shoulder girdle to lift the FCPT forward and upward. This allows the front legs to develop the ability to transmit power forward and upward. The angle of the horse's body changes and facilitates "uphill" movement. This automatically creates a willingness in the horse's neck to stretch toward the bit in order to maintain balance. Once movement energy is correctly directed this way, a retaining rein aid can direct the FCPT over the now actively arched HCPD. The HCPD is thus able–through the relief of weight on the forehand by active elasticity–to take up more body tension, due to its backward rotation. The horse closes his hind-end muscle chains, and his hind legs engage far underneath his center of gravity.

The difference here, compared to the usual understanding of how the canter stride is improved through half-halts, is due to our new awareness of biomechanical cause and effect: first, the forehand relieves itself of weight through the development of active elasticity and lifts the horse's longitudinal axis, and it is this that gives the hindquarters time and space to engage further under the horse's center of gravity and complete the movement sequence—not the other way around.

The Four Phases of a Half-Halt

1. *Increasing the rider's positive body tension–encouraging forward rotation of the FCPT through both forward-driving seat and leg aids.*
2. *Lifting the FCPT through retaining seat and rein aids.*
3. *Closing the HCPD through driving seat and leg aids–increasing the horse's positive body tension.*
4. *Verifying the horse's self-carriage through giving rein aids.*

This view of a horse's movement development also makes all other elements of riding theory, in terms of stabilization and development of positive tension, more comprehensible.

Cavalletti as a Training Resource

In theory, work over cavalletti is a wonderful tool to gymnasticize horses of all training levels. Cavalletti present an exercise with a strong visual stimulus, which animates the horse to lift his body and make room for his actively engaged hind legs. This encourages the horse to stretch more toward the bit and into the reins, and optimizes his body tension in terms of developing cadence. Muscular stress, especially on the shoulder girdle, is significantly increased.

That's the theory, anyway. Unfortunately, in practice, even trotting over cavalletti is not as categorically good for the horse's back as is often suggested. It may just as easily lead to the horse becoming so tense in the back that he increasingly throws his legs in the air. Only trotting with the correct rhythm and the right speed, with mental as well as physical suppleness—where the trainer has to constantly adjust the individual components of movement to the situation at hand—is actually relevant for training.

Work over cavalletti is a resource that can lead to improved cadence, if its use is correct and performed in accordance with the principles of the training method. The aim is not just to trot over poles, believing this alone will automatically lead to a supple back. The aim is to develop more cadence through the use of cavalletti, and maintain this cadence for as long as possible after having trotted over the poles. This may sound like an insignificant distinction, but it is vital to pay attention to these subtle differences when looking for the root causes of health issues in horses.

Even at the walk, it becomes clear how the positive tension in the muscle chains of the shoulder girdle (right photo) affects the lifting of the front legs.

Aids or Orders?

The foundation for a very finely tuned control over the horse is suppleness. Only a rhythmically contracting and relaxing muscle can react to nuanced impulses—the aids of the rider. Thus, the successful use of any aids depends on the actively stabilized basic position of the movement centers.

If the horse's system is in constant flight mode (tense), or is permanently loose and sagging, all communication channels for harmonious movement dialog between rider and horse are cut off. Correct aids from the rider become impossible. The horse cannot react to nuanced aids in a state of passive stabilization—he can only be controlled through coercion, or by calming him and teaching him tricks.

Without correctly, actively arched movement centers, all channels of communication for harmonious movement dialog between rider and horse are severed.

Horses are coerced using pure force on the part of the rider through sharp bits, spurs, or draw reins (auxiliary reins, which force the horse's head and neck into a fixed position with the use of leverage). Coercion can be necessary or even crucial for survival, in an emergency with a bolting horse, or during repeated, unfounded disobedience. However, there is no justification for it in regular training.

The Development of Positive Tension in the Jumping Horse

When looking at the jumping horse's movement pattern from the perspective of movement analysis, riding theory's call for significant education and training on the flat is validated. And not only that—analysis shows that this training is vital, without which a jumping horse rarely reaches the end of his career without any strain injuries. This fact helps to guide the incredible willingness that highly talented young jumping horses in particular show us in the right direction.

Generally, the jumper rider thinks from the ground level to fences of varying heights. The takeoff power needed to clear these heights mainly develops in the muscles of the hindquarters. Hence, the hindquarters have to be strengthened without compromise. But is this really the correct path for a young jumping horse? The development of power from the "catapult system" of the legs has been explained in chapter 2 (see p. 14). It is a known fact that young jumpers can already jump over 5'6" feet at just four years old. In the following pages, I would like to illustrate the development of a movement pattern for jumpers that will completely avoid chronic overload injuries in a horse, even over the heights of an Olympic course.

The Actual Jumping Height

If one measures from the ground to the horse's chest, this measurement amounts to around 3 feet in Warmbloods. To clear a jump of the same height, the horse only has to tuck up his legs, without even lifting his center of gravity. The development of an uphill canter stride through correct flatwork lifts the horse's body's center of gravity by about 8 inches. Together that makes 3½ feet or so.

Hence, the height required for a 3'6" jumping competition only requires the rider to canter a correctly gymnasticized horse over the fences. There is not yet any stress placed on the system in terms of jumping height, if the kinetic energy of the forehand and hind end has been actively built from the start. Subsequently, a correct bascule can be developed.

The Four Phases of the Jumping Effort

First Phase—"Catapulting" of the Front Legs

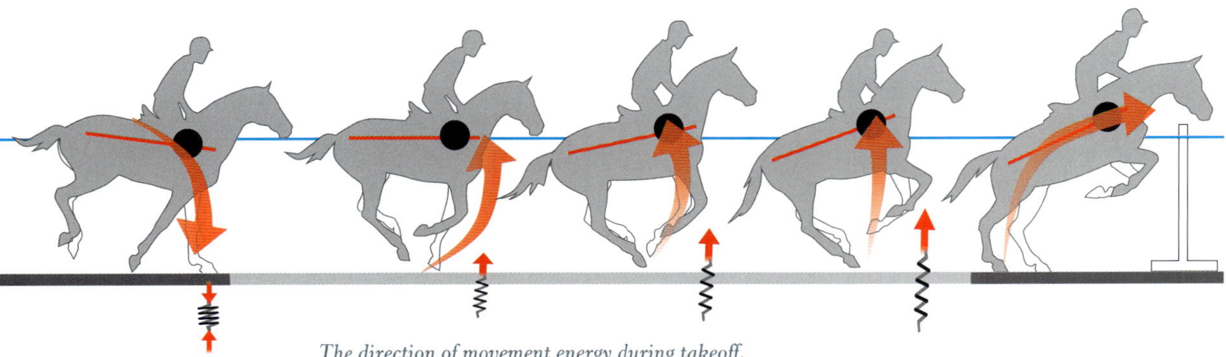

The direction of movement energy during takeoff.

During the first takeoff phase, the FCPT redirects the movement energy of forward movement, and the horse's forehand is catapulted upward. In doing so, the horse brings his longitudinal body axis toward a vertical position. The higher the fence that horse and rider are aiming for, the steeper the angle that must be created through the lifting of the FCPT. The front legs are completely suspended in the air during this phase and cannot support this movement pattern. The horse's bascule is developed in this phase—when the withers are catapulted upward by the muscular spring of the shoulder girdle between the front legs.

The "catapulting" of the front legs lifts the forehand, and defines the takeoff angle and thus the jumping height.

Second Phase—"Catapulting" of the Hind Legs

When the longitudinal axis of the body has been lifted, the hind legs and back muscles come into play. The long back muscles stiffen the entire longitudinal axis to protect it, and the hind legs "catapult" the horse forward and upward over the fence. In the process, the body's center of gravity only needs to be lifted slightly, between 8 inches and 1 foot—depending on the horse's size and the size of the gradient angle. It is this gradient angle, set up by the forehand, which determines the jumping height. The hindquarters can only change this set angle by a few degrees to achieve the total jumping height. And it is the forehand alone that determines the extent of the flight curve.

The hind legs "catapult" the horse farther forward and upward, at the angle defined by the forehand.

Third Phase—Suspension

Depending on the horse's bascule, a more-or-less harmonious flight curve is created. This flight curve isn't even; there is significantly more time between the jump's highest point and the moment the front legs first touch the ground again than there is between the hind legs leaving the ground and the jump's highest point. Physically speaking, the horse jumps down a drop. The reason, simply, is that the horse is about 15 inches shorter with his front legs outstretched than he is with his hind legs outstretched, due to his conformation. If we assume the angles of the body axis and speed of movement at takeoff and landing are approximately equal, the FCPT has to deliver twice the power to absorb the landing that the HCPD needs to deliver for the takeoff.

Due to the difference in length between the hindquarters and forehand in a stretched position, the horse essentially jumps down a drop, seen from a physical perspective.

Fourth Phase–Landing

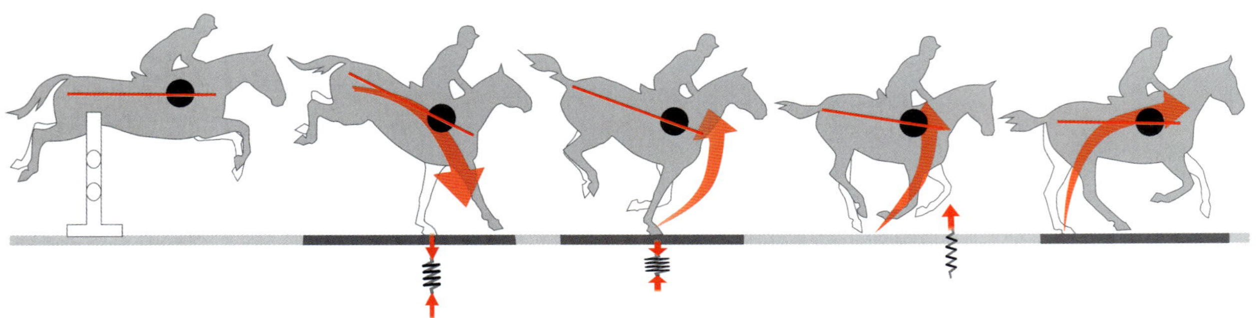

The direction of movement energy in the landing.

In the landing, that twofold movement energy has to be absorbed by the muscles of the shoulder girdle and transformed into forward movement. As shown before, this work can be done either by active muscle slings or by passive tendons and connective tissue.

During the initial landing phase, the forehand alone absorbs the strain of the movement energy of the flight phase and has to convert this energy into forward movement.

The biomechanical dynamics of the forehand during landing, seen from the front.

The Landing Is Key

As stated previously, the horse has to manage twice the power generated in the hind end with the forehand, in order to keep the system muscularly stable. However, since the forehand is less powerful due to its construction, excessive overload in incorrectly trained jumping horses is the rule rather than the exception. The result is horses who lose more and more of their performance capacity between the ages of four and nine years old. With time, the gradual chronic overload on the shoulder girdle no longer allows the horse to lift his forehand during the first takeoff phase. The elasticity in the shoulder girdle slowly disappears. The horse does not shorten himself well and pushes off the ground a lot less energetically. At the same time, his suspensory ligaments, flexor tendons, forehand hoof joints, and the joints in his spine become injury-prone—these structures being his main passive shock absorbers during landing. A talented horse can still win over a course of 4' or 4'6" with this kind of negative feedback system. Over even higher courses, with the help of drugs to make these strained structures temporarily pain-free, the pressure on the horse is increased through excessive body tension. But this kind of tampering would not be necessary if the horse had been correctly worked on the flat to begin with.

Summary

These facts lead to the following observations: A combination of different qualities is responsible for the high innate potential of a jumping horse. The elastic structures of the "catapults" of forehand and hindquarters have to transform their stored movement energy into actual movement, as efficiently as possible. The horse has to be willing to propel his forehand up as explosively as possible. He needs leg axes that are as solid as possible, to "catapult" his body's center of gravity forward and upward with the energy of his hind end. After his first attempts at this, the horse also needs the courage to tolerate the feeling of jumping down a drop.

All of these qualities are more or less a matter of genetic predisposition, and together they allow the horse to jump very high, very early.

Approach: Flatwork

But how should these willing, motivated, and talented horses be worked in order to keep them in the sport for a long time? After all, it is the horses who initially offer to jump these heights and clear them fearlessly. Isn't that enough? The answer lies in a statement by one of the old riding masters, who trusted the feel in the saddle 100 percent:

"Jumping is riding dressage over fences."
Those who follow this principle cannot go wrong. This will mean the horse is on the aids, and ridden toward the fence in a controlled and balanced manner, at an appropriate basic speed. The jumping effort and bascule develops from within the horse, without much help from the rider. She is mainly responsible for the technical and tactical finesse required to navigate the course. After landing, the horse finds his balance as early as the first canter stride. Those who follow this feeling in the saddle will find out the quality of the landing determines the possible height of the next jump. In turn, this depends on the horse's jumping technique, and therefore on how he develops his bascule from the first takeoff phase to the landing.

Bascule—Jumping "Over the Back"

The horse ought to jump "over his back." This phrase precisely describes the thorax's elastic "bounce" between the shoulder blades during the first takeoff phase (see p. 51). Many riders think the horse himself rounds his back, and specifically his spine, over the fence. This is not the case. The spine is slightly bent, with this bend originating at the pelvis, from the first takeoff phase to the second; afterward, the spine stays fixed in its stretched, unbent position until the landing. Ideally, the thorax stays in its raised position between the shoulder blades. The degree of movement in the thorax determines the distance available to the horse during landing for his muscular shock absorber to cushion the impact of the forehand. Hence, "bascule" means the upward movement of the thorax between the shoulder blades. This movement pattern sets the horse's takeoff angle through the muscles of the shoulder girdle. In a horse that does not develop a bascule, the takeoff angle is solely determined by the "catapult effect" of his tendons. During the landing, the tendon-ligament system in the shoulder girdle is placed under a lot of strain. Thus, a horse who jumps "over the back" is not any more powerful or capable over fences—but he retains that natural power and capability for a longer time, and can be ridden with finer aids.

Setting the quality of the landing as the standard for training the jumping horse pays off at the end of a course. Horses with additional muscular elasticity in their shoulder girdles don't just land better, they show more balance in their canter after the fence. This may save valuable seconds during competition.

Summary

Maximum elastic ability, and thus the limit for jumping height as well as impact absorption, lies in the system of the forehand. If the jumping horse is prepared for the respective flight curves through correct flatwork, the real tasks are of a technical nature. The rider has to be able to adjust the elastic "springs" of the forehand to different speeds, distances, and angles during takeoff. This can only be done when the horse is correctly on the aids and accepts these at all times, before and after the fence. This is the only way to coordinate the ideal rhythm between the first and second takeoff phases, as well as between the forehand and hindquarters during takeoff. If this is done correctly, there is no amount of strain when jumping that can automatically cause chronic overload damage for a horse that has been trained correctly and athletically on the flat. From an animal welfare perspective, we do not need statements against the sport, but rather statements in favor of correct training, no matter the discipline.

A horse that is correctly and athletically developed in his flatwork is subject to less strain on tendons, ligaments, and joints when jumping over a fence of over 5 feet than a badly trained horse being taken for a working canter in the woods.

An Example:

Goldfever, one of the most successful jumping horses of all time, competed for over 10 years at the highest international level, and today enjoys his retirement in a field in France. Next to his exceptional potential as a jumping horse, his strong basic rideability and his training on the flat—which was always a high priority to his rider, Ludger Beerbaum—were his greatest assets.

At two and a half years old, Goldfever was a well-proportioned young stallion, but he was visibly still growing.

Goldfever in 1999, at eight years old.

2008	2nd place, Grand Prix of Gothenburg (SWE)
2007	1st place, CHI Donaueschingen
2005	3rd place, Nations Cup at the CSIO***** in Rome
2005	2nd place, Grand Prix at the CSI-W in Vigo
2004	4th place, Grand Prix (Riders Tour classification) at the CSI**** in Munich
2004	1st place, Riders Tour team classification at the CSI**** in Hanover
2004	2nd place, Grand Prix (Riders Tour classification) at the CSN in Münster
2004	1st place, Grand Prix (Riders Tour classification) at CSI in Donaueschingen
2004	1st place, Nations Cup at the CSIO***** in La Baule
2004	1st place, Grand Prix in Vigo
2004	1st place, Grand Prix at the CSI***** in Zurich
2003	4th place, German Master in Stuttgart
2003	1st place, Grand Prix at the CHIO in Aachen
2003	8th place, World Cup final in Las Vegas
2002	1st place, Grand Prix at the CSIO in Calgary
2002	1st place, Grand Prix at the CHIO in Aachen
2002	1st place, Nations Cup at the CSIO in Lucerne
2001	1st place, Grand Prix at the CSI-A in Cannes

Goldfever turned out at the age of 23.

The movement dynamics of a dressage horse (top) and an eventing horse (bottom). Here, too, the front center of power transmission definitely makes a difference.

The Development of Positive Tension in the Eventing Horse

Combined, the qualities of a dressage horse and a jumping horse lead to the eventing horse. The analysis of eventing as an independent discipline takes place between two extremes: eventing as the crown discipline of equestrian sports, and eventers as the equine "jack of all trades, master of none."

Of all equestrian disciplines, eventing has undergone the largest changes in its requirements over the last few decades—not least because the risk of accidents and the number of fatal accidents are still too high. The limit of an event horse has always been, and still remains, the tough speed cross-country. For the horse's movement centers to be resilient enough for these speeds, a very firm elasticity is required. Mechanically speaking, this means a short range of the "springs," so the maximum movement energy can be processed. Only then can the required stability be achieved uphill, downhill, and over fences. However, that short "spring" range means both the cadence of a dressage horse and the bascule of a jumping horse are reduced. Both require a long and flexible "spring" range to process movement energy.

Changes in Requirements

Analyze the changes in the requirements for an eventing horse over the past years in this light, and the following immediately becomes apparent: Twenty years ago, the limiting factor in winning an eventing championship was definitely the cross-country phase. It was possible to win even from any position in the Top 20 after dressage, with one or two rails down in show jumping. Today, finishing the dressage phase outside the Top 5 will keep you out of the medals. Together with the removal of the stee-

The modern event horse can pose new challenges for a rider when it comes to his athletic training.

plechase phase, this has led to a trend to breed and select eventing horses with less Thoroughbred blood. A toughness meant to allow the horse to endure speed is exchanged for elasticity, in the selection of horses for the sport. Of course, this makes for much nicer pictures in dressage and jumping. But the responsibility to train correct technique and resilience against the demands of speed on a cross-country course becomes even higher.

Training Adjustment

The highest priority in eventing is the welfare of horse and rider. This has always been, still is, and will always be the case. No other equestrian discipline is so highly characterized by the companionship not only between horse and rider, but also camaraderie among riders. This makes it all the more important to adjust your training to the changing requirements of the sport. Where in the past, riders who were out of their depth filled the gap with fierce, Thoroughbred-type horses, today an ideal relation between elasticity and speed is crucial for the health and safety of horse and rider in modern eventing horses. A moment of inattentiveness on the part of the horse or rider can lead to an accident more quickly.

Following this line of argument, and despite all justified technical requirements as well as the high quality of the riders, the toughness and stability of the horse's "spring" systems has to remain the highest priority in the selection of event horses. This also applies to the management of an event horse. The focus has to be placed on *stability*, not *mobility*, particularly from a therapeutic standpoint.

The "Spring System" of an Event Horse

The "spring system" of an event horse is not a combination of the ideal "springs" of dressage and jumping horses. It has to be adapted for eventing as an individual discipline. This means a very short range of motion at maximum stability. Only this stability makes it possible for the horse to directly, reflexively, and independently react to uneven terrain or other unforeseen circumstances at high speed, without any direct aid from the rider.

Summary
The eventing horse requires toughness in handling speed and stability cross-country. This is a top priority to consider when devising a training plan—here, too, the basic training of a dressage horse, in terms of rhythm, suppleness, and contact, must form the foundation for stability. These are imperative in order to develop the ability to manage technical tasks in dressage and jumping.

The Development of Positive Tension in the Endurance Horse

Trotting or Cantering Over Longer Periods of Time

Water retention within protein structures allows for elasticity in muscles, tendons, and fascia. It also allows for a certain number of repetitions, during which a little bit of that water is squeezed out each time. That means this passive baseline performance capacity is finite, and is used up after only a few minutes (returning to our scenario of the wild horse in flight mode, it lasts slightly longer than the baseline movement energy of a lion). If the horse continues to be worked, (chronic) overload will inevitably occur in the body's micro-structures. As these micro-structures are damaged, the horse will lose more and more of his performance ability over time. This form of fatigue leads to similar injuries as overload through maximum stimulation, especially in the passive shock absorber systems such as tendons and suspensory ligaments. The phrase, "My horse needs 30 minutes before he is supple," should be reason enough for concern. *A horse is not supple after 30 minutes, he is tired.* And once he is tired, harm to tendons and joints begins.

Endurance sports also need a clear focus on flatwork, especially in the basic training of the horse. Paying attention to only blood levels and cardiovascular performance inevitably leads to strain injuries in the tendons and skeletal system.

The "Spring" System of an Endurance Horse

Endurance also has to be considered as an individual discipline. Over a distance of 75 miles (120 kilometers), it isn't possible to consistently canter "over the back," as a dressage horse does, nor is it sensible to solely put weight on the connective tissue structures. The combination of connective tissue elasticity and muscular coping has to be individually adjusted to the distance. In the process, flatwork can be done separately from strengthening work for the connective tissue structures, the better to, ultimately, combine both for an upcoming competition.

The Diaphragm in the Endurance Horse

To illustrate the importance of flatwork, I will reiterate the diaphragm's role in connection with the position of the horse's movement centers. If the thorax and shoulder girdles are lifted against gravity and positively, actively arched, then the diaphragm also has its optimal basic tension and can provide the body with the maximum amount of oxygen. This corresponds to contact in the Scales of Training. An endurance horse has to be perfectly trained up to this point; then, this system can be perfected to achieve lasting power and trained to maximum performance. Training toward impulsion, straightness, and collection would only serve to compensate for deficiencies in conformation, at best. Dressage training, with the aim of collection, would massively increase energy consumption over long distances and lead to a loss of performance in the long term.

Case Study
Vizrah, 18 years old, out of the premium Swiss mare Rishah (by Rihan Or.Ar. out of Jezabel) and the Russian stallion Versal (by Naftalin out of Pernataja), trained and ridden by Elisabeth Stöcklin, Switzerland.

Vizrah is used in versatile ways—mainly for endurance riding, but also for dressage, occasionally for jumping, and, more recently, for mounted archery and other games. He participated in his first endurance race over 12 miles (20 kilometers) at five years old, in the summer of 1999. Since then, he has completed over 1,500 miles (about 2,500 kilometers), with consistently good results. He was always in the Top 10 up to 75 miles (120 kilometers), and in the Top 5 in shorter and medium-distance races. He won the Arabian Trophy of the Swiss Arabian Association in 2003, was fourth in the Swiss Championships over the 75-mile distance in 2009, passed the performance test of the Swiss Arabian Association three times between 2005 and 2009, and was voted the Arabian of the Year by the WAHO Switzerland in 2009. In 2012, he won the Ämmitaler Endurance Race over 38 miles (62 kilometers) and was awarded the fitness prize (as the oldest horse participating in the event). He has shown against Warmbloods in dressage at Training Level.

An example of how endurance sports can be further developed through versatile training of endurance horses.

The Pleasure Horse

There is no other area in equestrianism where the interpretation of riding styles is as diverse as in the field of pleasure riding—from the ambitious recreational rider who wants to teach her horse the movements of the "High School" to those who want to take a break from life by hacking their horses at a walk on a long rein.

The Prerequisites Are Key

Of course, both are generally possible, but success in either is strongly dependent on the prerequisites of horse and rider. As noted in the section on the Scales of Training (p. 91), every riding horse should be trained at least to the point of the element of contact to promote their welfare. For the averagely talented horse with normal conformation, this can absolutely be achieved through hacking out, as well as a manageable effort in an outdoor arena. Rhythm, suppleness, and contact can often be better schooled when hacking than in the indoor arena; outside the arena can provide motivation and fun for horse and rider. (All of these also benefit the body and soul of any veteran show horse.)

Better Than You Thought ...

During my daily work, I do notice that recreational riders who do everything right in this respect often sell themselves short. I very often hear them say, with the air of a guilty conscience, "I only ride for fun, and I only ride my horse in the arena two or three times a month." When I assess their horses, I often find them to be in a very good condition; they are well-muscled for their purpose, and in good general health. The balance between what is demanded of the horse and his development is absolutely present.

... But Not All the Time

Unfortunately, there are also examples of the opposite, where horses who are not suitable for their purpose, due to their conformation or character, spend their entire day in a small paddock—"they are always outside and able to move around"—and then have to endure trail rides, three to four hours long, every other weekend, without any preparation. Or there are those riders who are told by third parties, magazines, or barn friends that a horse "will not survive without lateral work in the long run." Having been confused by this, they start to try out lateral movements without first working on the basics—often with the support of self-proclaimed trainers, who make their money by sowing feelings of insecurity. It is not uncommon that after many happy years of hacking out, horses have to see a vet for the first time in their lives after only a few months in such lesson "training" programs.

Summary
Even pleasure horses should receive a certain degree of basic training, not only for the sake of control and accident prevention, but also to maintain their health. If the horse is suited for his job, the effort asked of him by his work can be kept quite manageable. Once the horse has mastered the basic gaits and moves on trails with rhythm, suppleness, and contact, the necessary level of training has been reached. These three elements have to be frequently revisited, without long breaks in between. Those who like the work and have enough time and joy to do it can use these basics to continue schooling their horses, even those without fancy gaits, and even up to the movements of the High School. (But, please, not with force, nor with the underlying idea that "the horse cannot survive without lateral work in the long run.") No rider who adheres to these rules needs to feel guilty about her treatment of her horse–even if she does not spend four days a week in the dressage ring.

Training Different Types of Horses

Thus far, I have explained the basics of biomechanics with reference to an average horse type. In reality, we deal with many different types of horses, which can sometimes greatly differ in their attributes. I would like to introduce a few of these to give you a small glimpse into the impacts of training for different types of horses.

The Ideal Horse

The FCPT and HCPD are optimally balanced and actively arched. This state is rare but possible, even in young horses. Usually, these are compact horses of medium size, which look like finished riding horses at only four years old. If these horses are worked at a correct basic speed, it is easy for them to follow the individual steps of the Training Scale. Their movement centers swing steadily, with little downward movement, and bounce powerfully forward and upward in a secure rhythm. They can be worked with a focus on exercises and movements early on in their career.

But they still have to climb the individual steps of the Training Scale sequentially, even if it takes less time than it does for other horse types. What these horses have to offer can certainly be accepted, but their workload should only be intensified once they have been handled correctly at their initial level of training for several months. As jumping horses, they are characterized by their rhythm and safe landing. Solid, capable, and powerful, these horses are well-liked in all

disciplines. Even if they do not show the most spectacular movement to start with, they're perfectly suitable, because they display rhythm and suppleness in perfection from very early on.

The Long-Legged, Highly Elastic Thoroughbred-Type Horse

This type is the most difficult "system" to deal with during the first steps of training. An extreme lever length in the legs and elasticity from the joints creates tremendous movement energy, which, in the beginning, cannot be completely and correctly transferred to or through the movement centers. The horse often tries to manage his torso stability through a high level of tension in his back muscles. If the rider allows this, she will be able to obtain spectacular movement for a short time, but problems quickly become apparent when you observe the movement centers more closely.

The FCPT and HCPD are adjusted incorrectly. Long levers significantly increase these problems, and the transmission of power is increasingly blocked by stiff back muscles. A horse that was essentially willing to move at first loses his forward drive, and has to be urged along with the use of spurs.

The solution lies in the correction of the FCPT and in rejecting the movement pattern he is offering. For these horses, the only correct movement direction, in the beginning, is forward and straight. The neck, in its role as a balancing pole, encourages opening and lifting of the thorax in short reprises through a clear forward and downward position—yet there must be enough body tension to prevent the system from tilting over forward and placing strain on the forehand. Once the movement energy of the hind end is directed forward and is noticeable in the FCPT, it becomes necessary to collect it and transform it into additional positive body tension.

The half-halt, with all its contributions, is an effective means to achieve this end, always under the sole condition that the forward-driving aid also reaches the horse during the lifting and forward rotation of the thorax. These horses absolutely need a predefined frame given to them by the rider, but this frame should never restrict them too tightly.

Small indoor arenas, uneven or soft footing, and tight turns are poison for these horses. Those who are afraid of the movement energy of these horses have to seek the help of an experienced rider, who, by all means, must be willing to "let these horses go" in a controlled way—even though it may seem ironic to do so. These horses, who are bursting with energy, may initially not be containable. Their movement energy has to be guided forward in the right direction to open the FCPT. Only after the fact can it be controlled.

Jumping amplifies these horses' problems. They can jump very high, very quickly, with a lot of (negative) body tension over the "catapults" of their front and hind legs. However, during the landing, the FCPT is overstretched just as quickly, which can be felt as a deep drop into the shoulder girdle after the fence. With every jump, over several months, these horses will become worse in their bascules rather than better. They usually need three to four canter strides after the landing to balance again. This is the ultimate sign that their training must be shifted to stabilization, before a suspensory injury can occur.

In this case, jumping horse types need: flatwork, flatwork, flatwork. Not daily in the arena, but rather versatile work on hacks, in an outdoor ring, and over fences—a training concept, which, by the way, also works wonders for horses specializing in dressage.

Generally, this horse type needs at least two more years for his basic training than the average horse.

The Horse with a Long Back

From a mechanical perspective, a long back initially means longer levers for the movement centers, in the development of correctly and actively arched positions. Hence, the horse needs more en-ergy to achieve these positions, which, in the early stages of training, can be best realized through considerable forward movement. Once forwardness has been achieved, it should not be inhibited by any means, since this would inevitably move those long levers in the wrong direction. The obvious approach of shortening the frame at an early training stage automatically leads to a shortcut—in the wrong direction. Forward movement is the only option for a horse to slowly, but permanently, develop those muscles that configure the thorax and pelvis correctly to resist gravity. Doing this may extend the period of training by about one year.

A Difficult Topic

Unfortunately, the latter two horse types are destined to be overworked by ambitious riders too early in their career. They often fall through the cracks of excessively expedited basic training. Often, they then find their way to pleasure riders, who want to give these horses a second chance out of the kindness of their hearts—because, by that point, these horses are injured and very cheap. As admirable as this is, it does pose a great many challenges for these riders. Correcting such a horse is an art, even if the rider ultimately only expects an honest, well-behaved horse. The requirements that are placed on rider, trainer, tack, and the horse himself are very high, and can only be achieved through a high degree of experience and patience.

The Clunky Horse with a Large Frame and Minimal Body Tension

In the beginning, it is not easy to correctly position the movement centers of this type of horse. But at least this horse does not work against it. Next to a challenging conformation, it is mainly the horse's drive that is missing. These horses can best be started out on a hack with a motivated, forward-going equine friend. The basics of flatwork, up to contact, can also be established when hacking. You do not have to force yourself to ride in the sandbox. This horse type will later thank you with motivated cooperation, when he has built a basic level of athleticism.

The Short, Stocky Horse

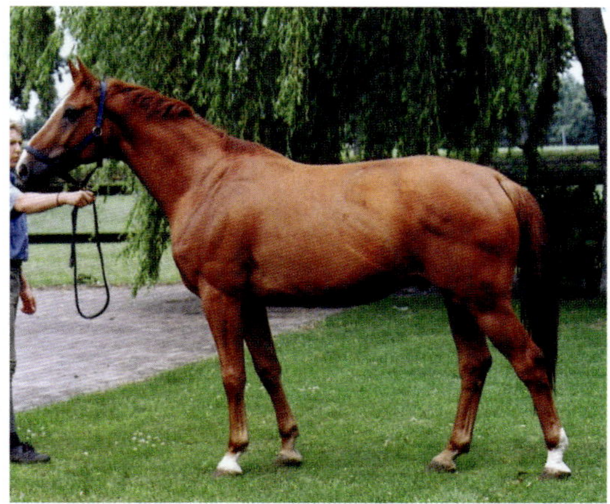

Due to their conformation, these horses have a high degree of basic stability, which makes them very suitable as pleasure horses for the less experienced rider. They need the least gymnasticizing work, in terms of the strengthening required for them to carry a rider. In their case, movements can be used as a mobilizing tool and are less prone to errors. Long walk breaks, where they can maintain elasticity in a maximally stretched position on a loose rein, are important for these horses.

Summary
Universal schooling and training principles are only as good as the rider's ability to adapt them to her horse's individual qualities. This adaptation does not mean dismissing the Training Scale, and it may not be used as an excuse for incorrect implementation. However, the trainer has to have the opportunity to veer off the proven path, for a short time, to give a horse the right guidance. Fairness and respect for the horse are of the utmost importance.

Implementation in Daily Work

How can all these theoretical lessons be implemented in daily work? All those who demand instant recipes for the training of a riding horse will continue to be disappointed.

What happens if 25 riders receive 10 identical exercises from one trainer to improve their horses' movement along curved lines, and they all meet again after a year? Most likely, you will see 250 different manifestations of mistakes along a curved line. But what happens if the trainer tries to teach the same 25 riders the strengths and weaknesses of their respective horses while moving on a curved line, and simultaneously motivates them to intensively engage with those strengths and weaknesses? After one year, you will see each individual rider having made some progress, depending on the talent, motivation, and ambition of horse and rider.

Rollkur: "Hyperflexion" or "Training"?

To wrap up the chapter, I would like to mention a topic that has shaken and divided the equestrian world: rollkur.

By now, even the smallest deviation of the noseline behind the vertical is condemned as rollkur and animal torture, by certain circles. If this head-neck position is achieved through a lot of pressure on the reins, a sharp bit, or the use of draw reins, this is absolutely true. But there are situations in which a horse escapes the aids and comes behind the vertical for a short time. For the topline muscles, this can indeed provide short-term relief of strain in their position.

This is against animal welfare!

If the young, immature horse is not yet able to actively carry his neck along its entire length, he will automatically position his head behind the vertical in certain situations. In doing so, he shortens the lever of the neck's weight, relieves strain on parts of the FCPT, and potentially facilitates lifting of his thorax through his shoulder girdle. This means evading a correct position of head and neck in the area of the topline—for only a short period of time—can promote the activity of the muscles in the shoulder girdle, if the horse is going forward enough. This is, of course, not a goal of training, and in a sense it also means the horse is evading the work of the topline muscles. But such a position can be tolerated temporarily, if the horse gains enough strength through the activation of his hind legs and the control of his thorax upward that, after a few weeks, he becomes able to carry his neck in the correct position when stretching. If a qualified, reasonable rider chooses a somewhat deeper head-neck position for certain training sequences, this may also be done with the aim of controlling and strengthening the thorax more thoroughly and more intensively. This is also not rollkur, but an individual training variation for horses with a weak shoulder girdle. It is part of the job of a fact-based analysis to separate the bad riders from the reputable trainers.

The following generally applies: A mild position behind the bit causes neither damage to the joints nor pain. However, if this position is achieved with pressure on the reins or sharp bits or if it is excessively used, strong rotational forces are created in the poll. These forces are harmful and cruel. This position is not suited to use over the long term, because in using it, the horse evades the carrying work that should be done by his topline.

Excessive curling of the neck restricts the horse's range of vision, and should also be rejected for this reason. In addition, toward the end of a movement sequence, any relief of strain from rotational force is reversed through the tension of the neck's lower muscle chains.

Conclusion:

If the terms *rollkur* or "hyperflexion" are used to mean the intentional interruption of the horse's positive tension with aids, clearly dominated by the rider's hands working toward negative tension, this has absolutely no place in the warm-up rings of the equestrian world—not for 10 minutes, not for 10 seconds. A visible sign of *rollkur*/hyperflexion is a break in the parallelism between the hind cannon bone and forearm in trot, even if there is spectacular front leg action (see p. 100). However, if the horse avoids the aids and comes behind the vertical by himself for a short time, this can be seen as evading work in the necessary muscle slings. This horse is still immature in his muscular and coordinative development; the rider should think twice about entering this horse in a show, and the judge should definitely take this into account in her evaluation and score accordingly. Yet this is not *rollkur* or hyperflexion, and in daily work with young, immature horses, this evasion should not be blown out of proportion; there is no reason to anxiously put training on hold entirely, if the horse is able to actively arch his movement centers. The basic characteristics of rhythm and suppleness have to be maintained. The horse can then develop and strengthen his willingness to stretch forward and downward from this position through structured gymnasticizing.

Positioned briefly behind and then in front of the vertical, without negative effects on the movement of the horse through his body.

5 The Rider

The rider's seat is the basis for every form of influence on the horse.

Upright Walk—Upright Seat?

The principles of positive tension within movement can also be extended to the rider. As previously mentioned, human bodies have a completely different kind of structural engineering than the horse's body. But the laws of physics apply to bipeds as well as quadrupeds; they just have to be adapted to each situation. It is, therefore, more than useful for riders to familiarize themselves with the *biophysical laws* of riding—and, thus, with themselves.

"Seat" vs. Lack of Movement

First, I would like to take a critical look at the current realities in equestrian education. It is a fact that a large number of riding students are no longer able to securely stabilize their own bodies against gravity—when on foot. Up to 30 percent of schoolchildren display postural defects, and 70 percent complain about occasional backache. Many scientific studies over the last years have described this phenomenon in detail and have given us all valid reasons for concern. These postural defects and pain are caused by a lack of movement and the accompanying muscular and coordinative deficits.

This is precisely where equestrian sports can take on an important role for the health of children and teenagers. Humans are subject to the same physiological and physical laws as the horse, only at a different level. Both have to stabilize themselves against gravity when they are moving. The high motivation for movement that the horse offers, in connection with the development of an independent basic upright seat, are ideal conditions to prevent deficits in body posture. The movement options involved in horse care, as well as the responsibility and ethical competence riders of all ages can gain, cannot be appreciated enough.

Simple tests give a first impression of the basic power of the muscles stabilizing the spine.

Opportunities and Obstacles

If we take studies on spinal stability seriously, we have to realize that riding students can quickly be overwhelmed by common traditional teaching methods. If a trainer tries to implement the correct position too quickly, the student will inevitably have to carry out evasive movements—visible or invisible—due to muscular weaknesses.

About the Rider's "Seat"

It is not necessary to reinvent the wheel. And yet there are common terms that produce incorrect mental images. The rider's "seat" is one of them. Humans connect the word "seat" with sitting down, relaxing, sitting in a chair. All attempts to teach people—especially those who work long hours at the office—an upright seat will fail sooner or later, not due to a lack of good will or effort by the student, but simply because the term "sitting" always evokes a static, immobile image in people's minds. But to sit immobile for a long period of time is physiologically impossible for humans, because their muscles cannot carry out such static work.

The positive tension needed for our upright posture can only be created through movement. And the rider's position on the horse should be dynamic at all times and under all circumstances.

Two different dynamic-coordinative stabilization tests.

Many in-depth discussions of the "rider's seat" can be found in equestrian literature. For example, Susanne von Dietze, Isabelle von Neumann-Cosel, and Eckart Meyners have written books on the subject and have found many reasonable solutions.

If you spend most of your workday sitting, do not waste time practicing how to sit "correctly." There are three sound alternatives:
1. Get up and move around.
2. Buy a chair that keeps you from sitting still.
3. Buy a chair that fits you like a good shoe, and passively supports you in the ideal way when you're actually forced to spend a long period of time in this position.

Your horse—and your back—will thank you!

Lack of Movement

Humans are made to walk upright, but in many cases, they've simply forgotten how, due to *lack of movement,* or they haven't learned to do it correctly in the first place. Studies of newborns show that their mothers' lack of movement has a negative impact on the motor development of embryos. To correct this problem, the respective requirements for the components of *power, coordination,* and *mobility* are needed. These can be learned and practiced. Riding, in particular, can work wonders here.

However, it is not enough to sit on the horse—you actually have to *actively ride.*

The Position of the Rider—A Definition

Since I am an advocate of the power of an accurate definition, I have tried to define the rider's position on the horse:

The upright, dynamic, balanced, and supple position of the rider on the moving horse.

This includes everything that defines the characteristics of a good seat. If you, as a trainer, find that using this phrase to correct your students when needed takes too long and is too complicated ("Would you mind positioning yourself dynamically and uprightly, in balance and suppleness, please?"), you may continue to use the word "seat," but you have to know what hides behind the term. However, it is even better to treat the cause than to treat the symptoms.

Riding downhill while bareback.

An Analysis of the Rider's Position

As early as Xenophon, a rider's position was described as "upright, standing with the legs apart."

This is true for as long as the horse is also standing still. Once he begins to move, the rider's pelvis follows. In the best case, the rider takes on the horse's movement rhythm, and the horse rhythmically swings the rider's pelvis in time with his own movement. To add to this, you could use the following wording: "Being taken along, upright, via the movement of the pelvis, with the legs apart."

The rider's seat always has to be able to react dynamically to the horse's movement, to allow the rider to react actively from this seat.

The Role of the Rider's "Feel"

The sensory (feeling) system of a more advanced rider starts working, in this movement pattern. The movement of her pelvis gives her information about the horse's spine and pelvis. The rider has to read and interpret this information. Only if she feels exactly when a leg lifts off the ground or is set down again can she actively influence the horse's stride with her aids. Only if she feels how her aids affect the inside of the horse can she assess their impact and change them, if needed.

But which prerequisites does the rider need to develop this feel? Does it come by "sitting on the horse, relaxing, and feeling"? No, it definitely does not come by *relaxing*.

Feeling requires an actively open tendon, ligament, and muscular system, working in correct suppleness. Only tendons and ligaments in an open, wide-spanning position can transfer information—much like a "phone" made of taut string and a pair of tin cans. Formal language calls this sensory mechanism *proprioception*. To be able to handle this open, positively tensed tendon and ligament system, the rider first has to learn to *feel herself* in positions that are as correct as possible.

Just like a "tin-can telephone," movement information inside the body can only be transmitted in a system under positive tension.

How the Horse's Impulsion Affects the Rider

Theoretically, I think it's clear how the rider is supposed to sit on the horse. But if it's so clear, why do we continue to see unharmonious pictures? Maybe because we also have to ride the trot! What is so different, then? Isn't it possible to be able to find balance again, after a while, like riding on a bike?

The answer is no—because there is no *up and down movement* when biking. There is no acceleration against gravity affecting the cyclist's body.

This is different when you're riding. The horse's impulsion is transferred to the rider. During the downward phase of movement, the rider's torso functions as inert mass. Physically speaking, the weight of the human torso (usually somewhere between 65 and 90 pounds) is accelerated, and that acceleration has to be absorbed around the tenth thoracic vertebra. Depending on whether the rider's position is correct, rotational force develops that corresponds to three times the mass of the torso, since the upper body wants to collapse in the same place (synonymous with the horse's torso in the loin region). The more a rider collapses, the longer the lever around which that weight is rotated becomes. Therefore, a *stooped back* can very well turn into about 175 to 220 pounds of weight on the tenth thoracic vertebra, in an average adult.

Evasive Movement in the Rider

Just like the horse, the rider may develop different strategies to evade coordinated, dynamic stability. Initially, we must consider the previously mentioned collapse. The rider develops a round back, often in combination with a rhythmically bobbing head. The alternative model is a fixation of the back—a hollow back. A third evasive movement is collapsing in the hip (usually visible in the waist), combined with a twist between thorax and pelvis.

A hollow back (left) and a round back (right), as evasive movements.

Movement as a Sensory Organ

The horse's movement with impulsion has yet another effect: As a suspension system for the muscles involved in maintaining an upright posture, the rider's pelvis develops a new, unfamiliar dynamic. All consciously and unconsciously received information, from and within the entire movement system, suddenly becomes diffuse and has to be newly organized. Information is no longer absorbed and interpreted by the legs, but goes directly to the pelvis, which initially causes confusion in the body. Despite this, or perhaps just because of it, the horse's movement is ideally tailored to the human body—admittedly, to one that moves correctly, in a physiological sense.

Any deviation from the ideal position becomes immediately visible in the horse; reflexes and compensation patterns, perfected over years, suddenly no longer work. This effect can be compared to sitting in front of a computer keyboard where someone has scrambled the keys. Everything you need is there, but you still have to search for each key you want to press.

Riding as a Strategy for Movement Therapy

By the way, this is one of the reasons why riding in walk is successfully used as a therapeutic measure for non-riders with poor posture and people with physical disabilities. Their existing, incorrect movement patterns are "garbled." The horse in walk transfers a correct movement pattern to the rider's pelvis. This is why, with the help of equine legs, an "upright walk" on the horse is possible for some patients who use wheelchairs and could never achieve the same on foot. The effect sometimes continues long enough that patients who had to be lifted onto the horse from their wheelchairs can walk a few steps back to their wheelchairs after they have dismounted!

The Risk of Making Mistakes a Habit

The risk, however, is that humans very quickly develop new incorrect movement patterns. The importance of good beginner riding lessons on solidly trained school horses cannot be emphasized strongly enough. Once the process of automated movement learning on the horse has been incorrectly completed, it can rarely be corrected through conventional riding lessons. "Sit up straight," "Take your outside shoulder back," and "Look straight ahead, not at your hands," are instructions that are doomed to fail before they've even been uttered. Such corrections only cover up incorrect patterns in the rider's seat, and do not address the real causes.

Again, I would like to point at strategies that follow kinesiological or movement therapy approaches. Eckart Meyners and Susanne von Dietze use these approaches by initially making it impossible for riders to fall back on habitual movement patterns, through the use of unfamiliar, "outside-the-box" exercises. However, these exercises, despite looking like games, only work if the trainer has a high level of expertise and experience and can apply both qualities to affect incorrect movement patterns safely and purposefully. For the rider, especially an advanced rider, this is a physical and mental challenge that is difficult to handle.

Deeply entrenched mistakes in an athletic movement pattern can only be corrected with patience and competent instruction. The rider has to engage with processes that make her familiar movement patterns in the saddle impossible to use, through new and unfamiliar exercises.

Another promising approach to correct flawed movement patterns on the horse is targeted correction on the ground. Any kind of gymnastics that promote a stable core and co-ordinated movement of the joints can be useful. More stability in the upper body has an effect on the horse, too—but ingrained seat mistakes that are already habitual will not vanish by themselves.

Training approaches that directly affect the pelvis and reprogram the body's movement patterns do work. Un-conventional, but very successful, training devices for this purpose are the moving stool "BALIMO," developed by Eckart Meyners, and the bicycle-like neuro-bike "SNAIX."

Learning a Rider's Movement
Let us imagine the rider's thoracic spine in trot. The de-mands on balance and the ability to stabilize are colossal.

Example: "Halt at X"
The trainer wants to practice a "halt at X." Horse and rider know the basics of a full halt. The rider turns onto the center-line and focuses on arriving at X. She begins with half-halts two to three steps before X, and only thinks, "I hope he will stop at X." The movement is reduced to its result, not its development and prog-ress. This means every step of the horse is different, especially so shortly before a new movement.

If the rider is not able to feel this change, she is also not able to respond to it. Ide-ally, during this exercise, the angle in the horse's pelvis, the tension in both move-ment centers, and the angle in the major joints of the hindquarters (haunches) will change. The rider has to absorb and go with these movements to be able to actively guide and control them.

Disrupting a stiff position on the horse by "pedaling" the legs.

The SNAIX coordination trainer (the bike shown here) has a joint in the middle of its frame, and can only be steered and controlled through the pelvis.

Learning to Feel

There is only one solution for the development of "throughness" (in both horse and rider): The rider must never focus too early on the outcome of an exercise. Developing a feel for movement, dynamic balance, and the ability to follow the movement of a horse come first, second, and third, respectively, in the training of rider and horse.

But what happens with most riders at the beginning of their equestrian careers? They are given the reins and told to do something with them, even if it's just to hold them still, long before they have a dynamically swinging position. Or the aim of learning is not the seat, but something that "works"—this is how fake feelings of achievement are created, to the effect of: If the horse stops at A, *fine;* if the rider's basic seat gets lost in the process, *not a big deal.*

Rhythm and movement sequences in jumping can also be practiced without a horse.

Movement learning that is only aimed at proficiency and is about the superficial "what" instead of the fundamental "how" of a movement directly leads to the automation of incorrect movement patterns.

I would like to transfer this principle to the young horse for the sake of better understanding:

The trainer who wants to teach movement(s) to riders and horses has to know the key sequences of a movement—these sequences must never be learned incorrectly.

This demand isn't easy to fulfill. The path to movement learning, on and with the horse, is automatically studded with mistakes, which always have to be corrected—that is the only possible approach in an equestrian education that can lead to success. But mistakes made in the basic structure of a movement stay with you for life, and can be corrected only partially, when they can be corrected at all.

Example: High Diving

You have probably seen a competition for high diving on TV before. In this sport, athletes perform the most amazing somersaults and turns on their way into the water, movements which are incomprehensible to the layperson. The judges award considerably lower scores if the athlete causes splashes when diving into the water. Now, you may say: "That was such a fantastic and difficult thing to do; does a little splashing really matter?" But the splashing shows the judges the form of the diving movement's key sequence—and that is the balance within the entire routine. If that balance is correct, the diver hits the water perpendicularly, and splashing is minimal. If the balance is incorrect, the water splashes. Hence, splashing has to lead to significant deductions in scoring.

Carrying over to an example from dressage training, this means that if a horse cannot be brought back into balance with subtle half-halts after a diagonal in extended trot, then the balance on the entire line was incorrect, no matter how spectacular the horse's movements may have looked during the extended trot.

Entering the water with minimal splashing is an outward sign of proper balance throughout the dive.

When it comes to rider or horse, this means: At the beginning of training, any little disturbance of balance has to be immediately corrected—or clearly penalized, when at a competition.

A young rider, however talented, does not have a chance to become a truly good rider if her balance is not well developed in line with her age. A young horse, however talented, does not have a chance to become a truly good horse if his balance is not well developed in line with his age.

6 Training, Therapy, Rehabilitation

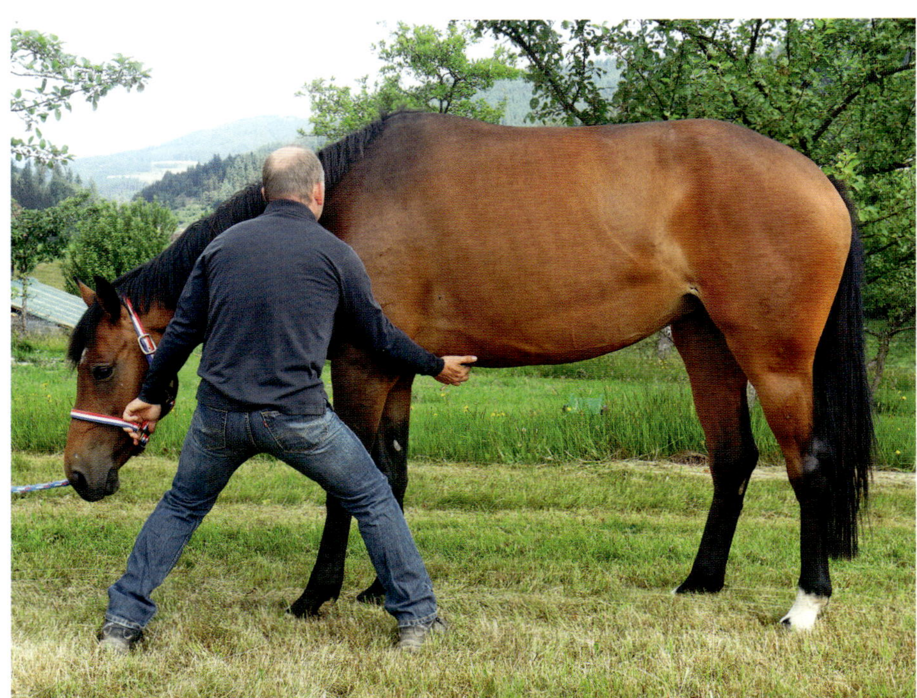

Training

With reference to chapter 5 and the functional connections involved in the horse's movement, the following can be established: There is no training without correct schooling. A horse can trot for miles without activating his shoulder girdle. He can canter and jump solely with the "catapult system" I've described, without using a single one of the muscle groups that are actually important in training. This background knowledge, which forms the basis of the horse's training, is needed to flesh out what follows. In the process, it is important not to cling to designated training schedules. The important step from schooling to training a horse can only be done correctly with maximum attention paid to the horse's individuality.

The different coordination requirements of trotting in a field versus on groomed arena footing significantly change the training stimuli for the horse.

The Four Pillars of Starting Young Horses
- in-hand work and work on the longe line
- free longing and free jumping
- gymnasticizing work on the flat, with a focus on developing and shaping the individual basic gaits
- cross-country training with and without obstacles

Decisions about the combination and intensity of these four elements lies solely with the rider, who works daily with the horse. She has to develop a feeling for which tasks can be fulfilled by the young horse to achieve optimal results. It should not be the aim of training to present a horse at a competition as quickly as possible, but rather to prepare the horse's body over the long term. Responsible training lays an ideal foundation to allow the horse, once he is of age and mature, to develop not only his maximum performance ability but also his maximum resilience.

Every rider of any young horse takes on a degree of responsibility. To do so, she needs knowledge, skills in the saddle, constant willingness to self-reflect, and—at least sometimes—the critical eye of an experienced trainer.

Ideally, the horse's muscular development should take place within this overall training framework. But what are the rules for building up muscles in ways appropriate to their function? Fattened pigs also develop lots of muscle, without ever having experienced one single training stimulus.

Even when the rider canters uphill on grass, the horse has to move in a correct working position if specific muscles for dressage are to be engaged.

The Basics of Muscle Training

Training a horse still leaves many riders with questions. "Strength training" is frequently connected with "riding uphill in walk." If an expensive supplement is fed to the horse, too, then it really can't be the result of a lack of muscles if a horse refuses a fence or does not perform flying changes. Right?

These or similar ideas are still around, and often they even come from experienced riders and trainers. If we want to talk about a well-executed and planned strength training, we first have to focus on a few physiological facts when it comes to training theory.

First, it is necessary to recognize the different characteristics of skeletal muscles, which can each be a limiting factor for loss of performance.

- contraction ability (power)
- contraction speed
- relaxation ability
- tightness
- stretchability (active–passive)
- coordination
  - o within an individual muscle
  - o between muscles, within muscle chains
- reactive ability (proprioception)

This is why a horse that can pull a beer cart cannot fly powerfully over a jumping course, even with a high level of strength and giant muscles, while an excellently trained dressage horse would be completely exhausted after a few minutes if he were used for logging. But even a dressage horse–if he is lacking both the ability to relax and looseness in his muscles, after having been overworked across a few weeks of training–will suffer from performance loss, even though he originally had a well-developed musculature. This problem cannot be solved with more training, more muscles, or by reaching into the feed bin for supplements.

If a horse does not learn to move as economically and light-footedly as possible–meaning he is able to divide work across as many different muscle groups as possible–he will always have to deal with problems from (chronic) overload.

Only knowledge of systematic training structure where the suppleness (looseness) of the muscles is constantly checked will save you from crucial errors of judgment in determining the workload demands to put on a horse.

A Diverse, Versatile, All-Around Training

Coordination, reaction, and speed are the factors that make muscles work. In the context of the horse, and especially the training framework mentioned in the first chapters, this clearly means: The horse has to stabilize his shoulder girdle and pelvic ring against gravity with every step and stride. The more he is gently thrown off balance every day and immediately regains it himself, the better this is for the development of the entire function of muscle control. If his control is correct, his system is dynamically stable and can react independently to any change.

In this process, the magic words from training theory are diversity and versatility of both movement and muscular stimuli.

Flatwork on a sloped grass field offers endless variations when planning training stimuli.

The most important tools from the classical, versatile basic training of a horse are changes of gait, speed, and direction of movement; combinations of straight and curved lines; riding on different terrain; and jumping natural and artificial fences. They all belong together and are a positive challenge for the horse's balance—but only in combination.

Controlling Training Load Through a Feel for Movement

Every athlete would like to have an instant recipe or infallible program for optimizing training stimuli. This is very easy to plan with strength training equipment, including defined angles and weights, like at the gym. For a horse and his many different movement components, however, these kinds of plans make very little sense. The difference that matters is whether the rider is or is not able to coordinate the muscle chains of the movement centers at any given moment. If the former, the horse's movement might feel light and elastic; if the latter, the horse's efforts will feel strenuous and heavy. In the first case, the horse still works optimally, and needs a break after a few minutes. In the second case, horse and rider might still need time to find their optimal movement rhythm. The horse may be trying really hard, but he doesn't yet work ideally. For these reasons, the rider's feeling is the most important factor in planning training stimuli. This rule of thumb applies: The more ideal the movement feels, the shorter the reprises become. The more laborious the feeling, the more correction–through thoughtful, methodical strategies–is needed.

Training should never continue if it feels laborious.

Therapy

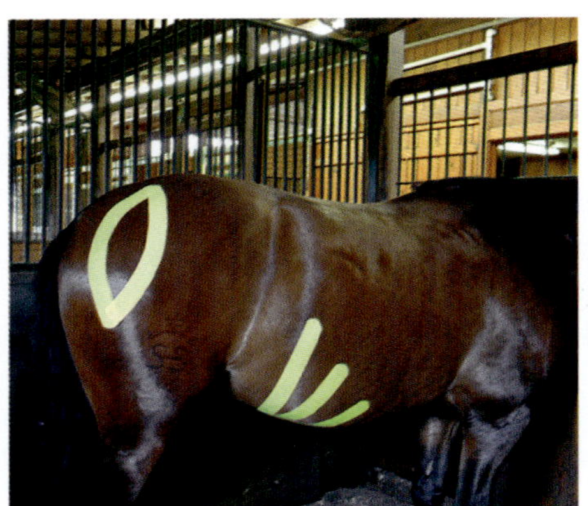

Application of kinesiology tape for the support of the horse's hind movement chain.

The field of physical therapy has changed significantly over the last 20 years. Where previously many therapeutic techniques were carried out to achieve individual effects, today, holistic conceptual frameworks are at the forefront. Where single muscle groups were stiff or painful, they used to be managed with stretching and massages. The use of physical therapies such as the application of cold, heat, or electrotherapy supported these treatment effects. Today, it is much more common to try to understand the mechanism behind the tension in any individual muscle group, and start there. Generally, everything is about entire functional chains, where weaknesses, instabilities, and movement restrictions take turns. Certain mechanisms within the body have to be examined to recognize problems within these functional chains. The aim of therapeutic work is to strengthen weaknesses, and at the same time maintain strengths.

Stabilization from the Inside Out

The organization of muscular stability from the inside out is an important mechanism within these functional chains. Studies on humans, examining the processes that take place within muscle chains, have shown that the movement of joints always has to be initiated by a stabilization of the musculature closest to the spine. If this is not the case, small shear and rotational movements are triggered, which will lead to inflammation or arthritis in the joints of the vertebrae and their ligament structures, in the long term. This mechanism can be observed especially clearly in patients with back aches. Over time, this will lead to a cycle of pain, fatigue, and instability.

With regard to a horse and the functional movement framework illustrated in earlier chapters, this means: Even from this perspective, guiding a horse to work "over his back" is not just a nice idea that will make it possible to ride the horse with very fine aids. It is a necessity in order to effectively maintain the horse's health in the long term. The muscles close to the spine can be used for direct stabilization, preventing those small shear and rotational movements, only if the lower muscle chains can functionally carry the horse.

Stammer Kinetics as an Independent Concept

The biomechanical model of the movement organization of the horse's body, as introduced in earlier chapters, is the foundation for a paradigm I developed for the analysis, therapy, and development of the functional movement patterns of the horse. Just like the training of a riding horse, this perspective follows the functional chains of the horse's body, which work against gravity and centrifugal force.

The muscles, the connective tissue structures, and all parts of the skeletal system have to be able to fulfill their *functions*. If this is not the case, any active attempt at correction of movement patterns during *training* is doomed to fail. It can happen that one dysfunction or another can be *corrected* in movement by the trainer. But if this is not the case after several days—or, in exceptional cases, weeks—these incorrect movement processes should be analyzed from a therapeutic perspective.

This book is not a therapeutic textbook, but I would like to give a glimpse into this kind of movement analysis of a horse.

The main parts of this approach are *active-dynamic myofascial mobilization* and *manual functional analysis*. In the process, the movement chains of a correctly ridden horse are triggered and assessed at a standstill, as realistically as possible. Depending on the diagnosis, these chains can then be mobilized or stabilized through different techniques. There are three different functional chains in this context, with corresponding therapeutic concepts.

- interdependence between mobility and position
- interdependence between position and function
- interdependence between function and training

Interdependence Between Mobility and Position
If a horse is to work "over his back," he has to be able to lift his thorax between his front legs, and maintain this position when moving his front leg forward. This skill can be tested with special therapeutic techniques.

Active-Dynamic Myofascial Mobilization
This somewhat awkward description disguises the basic understanding that a horse lifts and elastically bounces in his functional chains—which consist of muscles, tendons, and fascia—to counter the force of gravity, as has been explained in earlier chapters. During this process, the fascia systems are the key, and the link for the horse's catapult-like elasticity. The fascia are always the link between individual functional units, from the smallest bridging unit within a muscle to the large body sections of the torso and the legs.

The difference with this concept for the horse, as compared to classical, manual therapy for humans, is the work done by the active movement chains. During

Lifting the thorax leads to a lowering of the neck, creating the horse's willingness to stretch if the processes' coordination and dynamics are correctly observed.

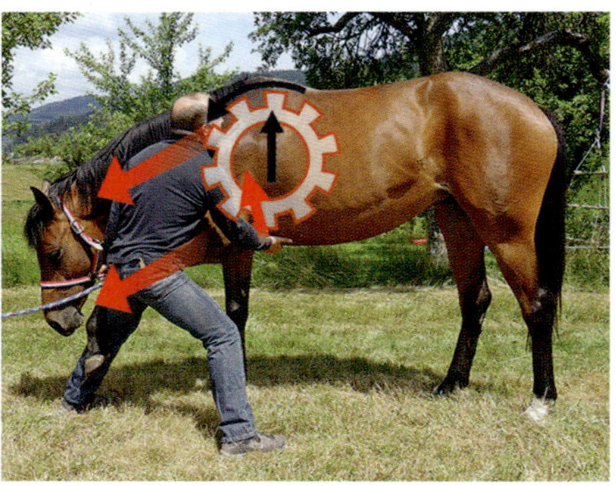

If the movement chains of the FCPT function optimally, the horse can maintain his topline correctly when stretching his front leg forward.

mobilization of the joints, a person is positioned in such a way that most or all of the muscles surrounding the joint are relaxed, and no longer work against gravity.

The therapist then moves the person's joints passively until their movement limit has been reached. She can give verbal movement instructions and directions, which can then be actively carried out by patients requiring special techniques. This is not possible with horses, obviously. If the horse's front leg is lifted, he has to rebalance over his supporting leg. It has been explained in chapter 3 (p. 52) how difficult this can be. If a horse is to avoid hanging in his passive compensation pattern and bringing his back into an unfavorable hyperextension, he has to find a way to actively balance. My approach is to integrate mobilizing techniques into dynamic activating techniques. In doing so, coordinative processes are encouraged in a way that's congruent with functional stability in the riding horse. The picture series above gives an impression of the procedure involved in this active-dynamic mobilization.

How It Works under Saddle

If you now think that riding only works with the outside help of therapists, we have definitely overdone the analysis of this entire system. Colonel von Stecken has it in a nutshell: "Riding right suffices." He is absolutely right when it comes to a healthy horse that hasn't learned any incorrect movement habits. The previously mentioned processes will work without additional help, if a young horse is professionally and correctly trained. Therapeutic options only start when a trainer reaches her limits and cannot find the reasons for these limits.

Dependence Between Position and Function

The capacity of the horse to carry himself, as postulated by riding theory, is not innate, but depends on his ability to actively change the position of his thorax and pelvis. Manual functional analysis uses this fact to get an idea of the actual condition of the horse's coordination. This gives important information to the rider, including how much she can ask of her horse and when the point of overload has been reached by demanding something of the horse that he can't physically do. Therapists can simultaneously use these techniques to break up or at least reduce existing movement restrictions in order to facilitate an improved elasticity against gravity for the horse.

Coordinative Processes

This example illustrates exactly how movement patterns can be observed and how deeper underlying structures can be reached through this treatment.

First, the therapist lifts up the front leg. This is where the active diagnosis of the supporting leg begins. How does the horse balance?

Where does the horse's neck move to? Does he stand securely on three legs, or not? How does he react if the therapist tries to unsettle his balance? In the process, the supporting leg's coordination and stability are checked. Once the horse stands safely on all four legs, the movement of the shoulder joint in extension begins.

The shoulder joints' flexors are those muscles that can slow down or inhibit movement. The horse has several of them. Some are fixed to the shoulder blade, and one attaches to the back fascia, close to the spine. Depending on which structures "brake" first and where the first resistance can be felt, the experienced therapist can find the affected structure. She can also feel whether these are stiff muscles or stiff tissues within the muscles by means of assessing the feeling of resistance.

The forearm is brought forward and downward.

- *Stiff muscles* can result from pain, chronic overload, or stress. Distinct tests can narrow down the options.
- *Stiff tissue* can also result from pain, chronic overload, or stress, but it generally takes longer for them to be affected, compared to muscles.
- In addition, *blockages* from different body areas (spine, inner organs, energy system) can lead to these symptoms.

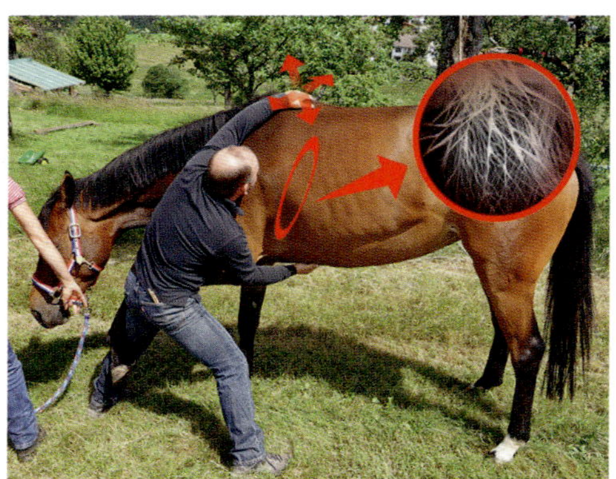

Including the deeper lying fascia structures of the torso in the analysis, through additional lifting of the thorax.

This list is not exhaustive but gives many potential reasons for a *movement restriction*.

If the movement is continued and guided toward stretching, more and deeper layers of fascial structures are incorporated into the movement pattern. I have already pointed out the importance of these structures within movement. Hence, a crucial focus must be placed on the elasticity and dynamic motion of the fascia from a therapeutic perspective. Soft, floating movement, which the therapist can carry out through either repetitive activation of the muscle chains or the dynamics of her own movements, is ideal to sustainably and effectively affect these structures. If all these structures are thoroughly mobile, we finally move on to the joint. Movement restriction—for example, in the shoulder joint—can be created through calcification; a joint can also be "jammed" by a free joint body (chip), irritated by a non-inflammatory arthrosis, or painfully restricted by inflammation. Blockage in the joint itself may stem from a neuronal reaction (a reaction triggered by the nervous system) inside the joint capsule, which limits movement. Depending on the root of the restriction, it may or may not be something that can be resolved by a therapist through manipulation. If it is resolved, the therapist continues to work more inside the deeper and functionally more demanding systems of liquids and the craniosacral system. However, if, for example, the horse's movement is structurally restricted by calcification, the possibility of mobilization is very limited, and may sometimes even be impossible without causing damage. In these cases, the therapist has to know and assess her limits honestly.

This little journey through the simple movement pattern of stretching the front leg clearly shows how many factors may be causing or contributing to a movement restriction. The training and experience of a therapist have to reflect this complex multitude of variables to work responsibly and with success.

How It Works under Saddle
In the end, the rider does not do anything differently when she works her horse correctly "over his back." His systems are brought into the correct position and are counter-mobilized. The image the rider has to internalize is the active lifting of the horse's thorax between the shoulder blades. The impulse of both seat and leg aids plays a decisive role in their connection with the rein aids in the development of this positive arc of tension.

The horse opens up forward and upward in his shoulder girdle and meets the rider on his way upward in between her seat bones. At the same time, the horse closes up behind, forward and downward from the pelvis, and thus actively engages under his center of gravity with his hind legs. The key to this element of movement is active forward motion. Ideally, the horse finds a way into this movement pattern during the warm-up phase, after an extensive walk phase. The described process is very demanding for the muscles of young horses who are not yet very athletically trained, and should always be combined with sufficient walk breaks.

Developing the willingness to stretch forward and downward during rehabilitation. Here, the system connecting the front leg, shoulder girdle, and neckline is shown. The nose line can only find its correct position in front of the vertical once the FCPT has reached its full movement potential.

Dependence Between Function and Training

Strengthening

The structural strengthening of the shoulder girdle begins once the horse's movement aligns with the first three principles of the Training Scale: rhythm, suppleness, and contact. The phrase "the horse carries himself" has to be taken quite literally in this context. If the basic gaits with impulsion are optimally coordinated, the riding horse elastically bounces his torso mass upward and "catches" it again in the supporting leg phase. His muscle chains can only be structurally and functionally strengthened within this movement pattern. Conversely, this means that any form of work in fatigued muscles has to be avoided, as the horse will initially lose the arc of tension between thorax and pelvis. The hind legs pushing forward can continue working for a long time, the neck can maintain its arched position, and the horse can still lift his legs off the ground with enough momentum for a while. Nevertheless, the very important athletic and coordinative training will be severely disrupted. The therapist or trainer has to use the principle of interval training to prevent this. Interval training means individual short, but intensive training units that engage the horse in correct movement patterns, which are regularly adjusted to the horse's performance ability. Compared to humans, this training method corresponds to gymnastics. Here, the athlete also trains solely with her own body weight, in different angles and at different levels, and not with equipment in the weight room.

How It Works under Saddle—Work over Trot Poles

Work over trot poles, as has been described in the chapter on training, is a good example. If the movement pattern has been correctly schooled, as described, and can be carried out by the horse in a manner governed by the first three steps of the Training Scale, it is not enough to work the horse over trot poles every now and then, once the horse has reached a certain athletic level. His training should be structured as follows to strengthen his shoulder and pelvic girdles:

Training programs only have a positive effect if all movement is carried out correctly.

Trot over five to seven poles five times back to back, then take a break of two to three minutes. Repeat this series three to five times, depending on the horse's current level of training. For the untrained horse, the two- or three-minute break should be in walk on a long rein. For athletically well-trained horses, this break can also be carried out more actively—for example, in canter.

Gymnastics (Grids)

In addition to preventing injuries, an athletically developed and shaped shoulder girdle is decisive for performance ability in the training of a jumping horse. A powerful shoulder girdle can save up to two-tenths of a second in the landing after a fence. On a course with 14 fences, this can mean saving up to 2.8 seconds. Gymnastics, or grids, have long been established in daily training routines. This effect can be significantly increased with ideal adjustment of gymnastic lines. The height of the fences should be chosen so the horse really takes off and shows a good bascule. In the language of the movement centers, this means the thorax is "catapulted" upward between the front legs. If this does not work, the trainer has to work with different methods for as long as it takes for the horse to automate the correct movement pattern. *Without this movement pattern, there is no training for the shoulder girdle muscles.* Once this has been achieved, the jump height should be set to between 3' and 3'6". A combination of three or four fences, set at a distance of one stride apart, is ideal for optimizing the stress on the muscles in a gymnastic. The horse should jump this line three to five times, back to back, per training set, followed by a three-minute walk break. The next set is then also repeated three to five times, depending on the level of training.

> **TIP**
> This training setup can be used every two to three days, for a duration of about 20 days, during the build-up phase of a horse between longer competition breaks—followed by a week of quiet gymnasticizing flatwork. The rider should feel a notable increase in the quality of the horse's jumping pattern after such a training sequence.

Rehabilitation

There is a clear distinction between regular training and therapeutically supported movement control, which should be used for rehabilitation after injuries or correction of incorrect movement patterns.

Medical Training Therapy (MTT)

The development of Medical Training Therapy over the last 20 years constitutes a milestone and a fundamental change in the development of rehabilitation concepts within physical therapy. In the 1980s, a cruciate ligament rupture was steadied and immobilized in a cast for six weeks after surgery; nowadays, the patient starts with easy squats and partial weight-bearing three days after surgery. Since then, the accompanying therapeutic measures also increasingly aim toward being able to move the body optimally as quickly as possible.

Arranging kinesiology tape on an insufficiently stable horse to help him find his balance.

For horses in particular, therapeutic work with the rider or trainer on site should be preferred to inpatient rehabilitation, wherever possible. The horse can remain in familiar surroundings, and the rider or trainer can perform many elements of movement therapy herself, with the respective therapeutic support provided. Only if the horse needs more therapeutic support, because the degree of discoordination or weakness is too great to manage otherwise, should the possibility of a professional inpatient rehabilitation be considered.

THE THERAPEUTIC TRAINING SITUATION

An aqua trainer alone does not make a rehab center. The following principle applies: Complex movement disturbances need complex treatment strategies, which have to be planned and performed by professional, experienced therapists.

Comprehensively trained therapists who have been theoretically and practically trained in their field for many years are needed to achieve this goal. Only they will be able to conceptually link individual techniques together. Unfortunately, the training situation for therapists in some countries is not optimal. It is sometimes possible for those who are interested to partake in a so-called "vocational training course," spanning 10 to 15 weekends, to become a horse physical therapist or bodyworker with a fancy name—without ever having to demonstrate any kind of previous basic training in the field.

This amount of training may suffice to learn single techniques, but these courses can never replace the structure of a physical therapy education spanning several years. Once these therapists go about their work according to the principle, "If your only tool is a hammer, every problem looks like a nail," the horse will pay dearly with his health in the end.

STAMMER KINETICS

The therapeutic framework of STAMMER KINETICS follows the principles of functional stabilization, as they have been described in previous chapters. The horse's stabilization against gravity is a central measure here—meaning the positioning of the thorax upward between the shoulder blades, together with the active stabilization of the pelvic girdle. If the horse does not find his way there with classical support through a trainer, the principles of movement therapy from the field of physical therapy take effect—for example, direct stimulation

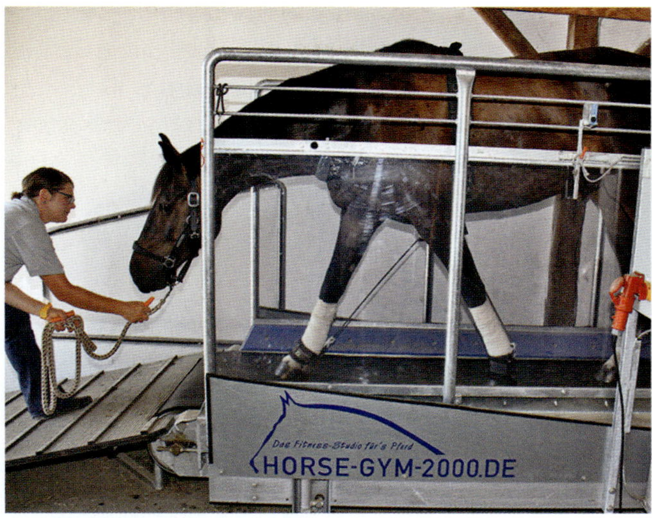

This page and facing: Precise pre-activation of the shoulder girdle muscles with movement therapy.

of the shoulder girdle through elastic resistance. It's important to remember the technical support is only as good as the therapeutic paradigm it's embedded in.

Summary
Modern therapeutic frameworks no longer aim to only treat individual structures such as back muscles, tendons, or joints. Instead, complex strategies are developed to affect and change the quality of overall movement patterns. Accompanying treatments such as massage and stretching techniques can also help. However, they can never be truly effective on their own. The main components of these frameworks are work within movement chains, schooling of movement feel, coordination, and responsiveness—always with the aim of developing or recovering functionally correct movement.

Movement Correction Example–Shoulder Girdle

Every rider likes an expressive front leg movement. *Freedom in the shoulder movement* is the correct technical term. The connection between stability and mobility has already been extensively explained. I would now like to describe the modus operandi that accounts for this connection.

Coordination

Once the shoulder girdle is flexible enough in all necessary directions to carry out the expected movement, the therapist can begin, together with the rider, to re-coordinate movement patterns. This may range from exercises at a standstill or simple leading exercises to movements such as *shoulder-fore* or *shoulder-in*. The degrees of discoordination, the horse's and rider's level of training, and the horse's muscular condition determine the approach. Hence, the therapist can, for example, initiate the correct movement pattern at a standstill through activation of the relevant musculature. After, the horse is led in walk, to transfer this pattern into movement. If this is successful, the next step is to transfer to trot. In principle, all additional measures for training and correction of a riding horse can be applied, as long as the fundamental elements of correctness, rhythm, and suppleness are observed. Elements from different concepts of groundwork can also be helpful.

Strengthening

Once the correct coordination of movement has been trained and the horse can maintain it for several minutes, you should automatically progress to strengthening the muscles. The rider has to be aware that the difference between an actively raised and passively stabilized thorax means a change in the degree of muscular strain. More specifically, the more intensive the correction of the movement pattern, the more quickly the horse will become tired. It is not uncommon in medical training therapy for seemingly well-trained sport horses with correctly raised thoraxes to show signs of fatigue in their shoulder girdles after 10 to 15 trot steps. These horses need a walk break on a long rein of about two to three minutes before they should be asked to repeat the same sequence three or four times. Every exercise load should be maintained for four to five days before it is increased. Progression is possible by increasing the number of trot steps, thus increasing body tension and the raising of the thorax, or by adding two or three more sets of repetition. However, it's important to only choose one of these options to increase the exercise load at a time, to avoid a situation of "overtraining."

Timing

The "rule of six" can be used as a rough guide. It takes approximately six days before the horse will take his first correct steps, in ideal coordination and with an ideal mobility. After six weeks, he should be able to securely hold this correct movement pattern over several movement sequences of about five minutes. With correct coordination, it takes about six months to strengthen the muscular system consistently. These time periods should be seen as estimates, and can be significantly more or less in some cases.

Summary
A modern therapeutic conceptual framework follows the principle of pro-
gressing from mobility to coordination to strengthening. In this framework,
these steps build on each other, and every step depends on having achieved
the previous one. The step from mobility to coordination is the most important
one. Compromises should be avoided at all costs. It may take several weeks
until the movement (pattern) has become soundly coordinated.

The Diaphragm as the Key Between Inside and Outside Systems

The *diaphragm* is a large muscle in the horse's torso, and separates the heart
and lungs from the abdomen. It is open and actively arched in the torso, spanning the area between the sternum, the costal arch, and the lumbar spine. The
diaphragm functionally connects the FCPT with the HCPD, and takes on a key
position for the horse's correct movement as well as for many other processes
of the inner organ system.

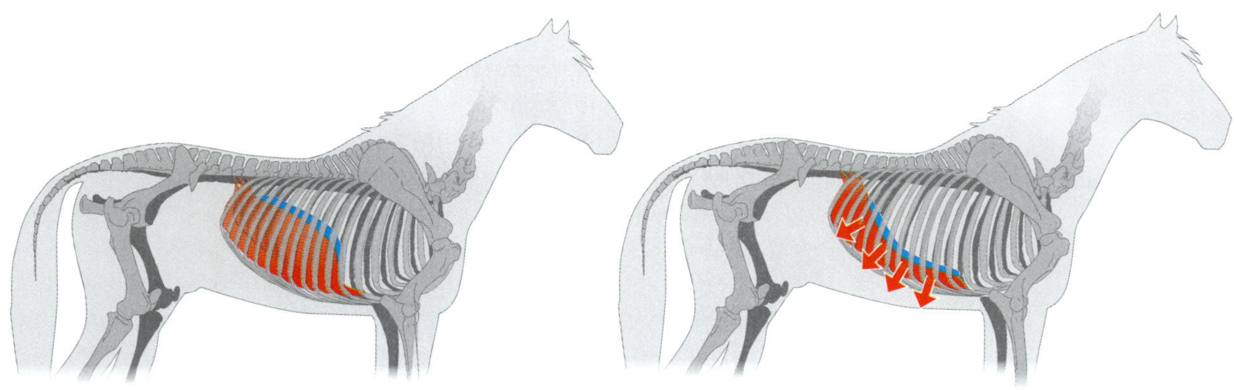

From a functional perspective, in addition to its role in respiration,
it is subjected to high strain during any movement. Canter strides
serve as an illustrative example.

The Diaphragm in Canter

The canter stride and a horse's breathing are inextricably linked. A
horse can take one breath per canter stride. He inhales during the moment of suspension, and exhales from back to front during the supporting leg phase. Deviations from this rhythm are impossible, due
to the high strain on the diaphragm in its function as a muscle that
actively supports both of these processes. This means that a horse who

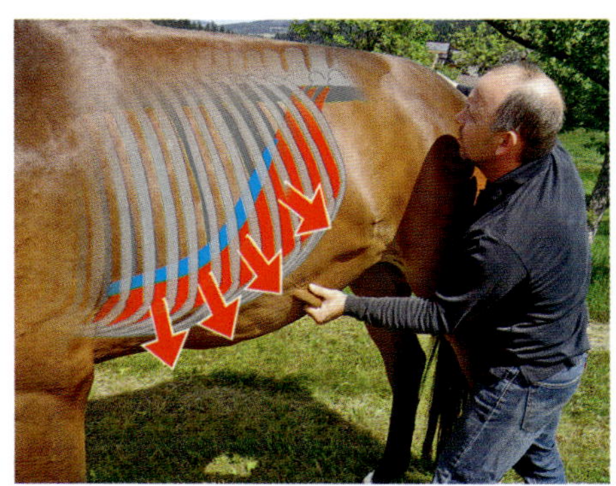

Therapeutic control of the diaphragm's function.

The end of the breathing-in phase in canter.

The end of the breathing-out phase in canter.

cannot breathe freely and without constraints also cannot canter freely and without impediment—and vice versa. The high strain the diaphragm is subject to thanks to its functions inside the horse can be demonstrated during the supporting leg phase of the front legs in canter. In this phase of "downhill" movement, the horse's intestines push their full weight—about 550 pounds—forward toward the lungs, and they have to be kept in position by the diaphragm.

The Diaphragm in the Jumping Horse

The strain becomes even more dramatic for a jumping horse during the landing phase. The higher the horse jumps, the steeper the angle with which the intestines push down on the diaphragm, and the greater the force that must be contained by the diaphragm during the landing. If this muscle tenses up after the seventh or eighth fence, the quality of the canter becomes worse and the horse's muscles are no longer provided with sufficient oxygen, due to the restriction in his breathing.

During the landing phase, the diaphragm is maximally stressed due to the massive weight of the intestines.

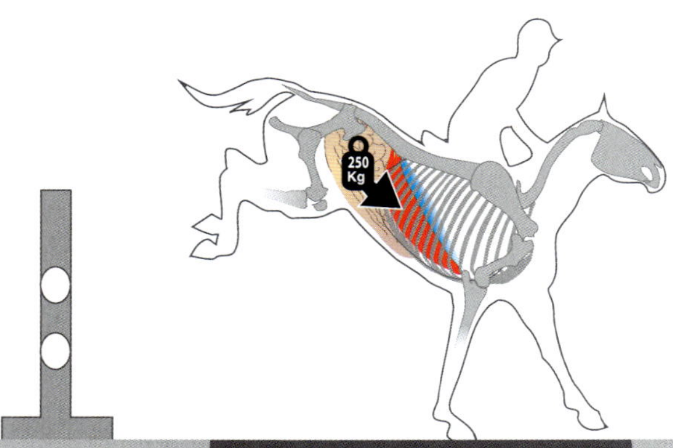

The Diaphragm in Dressage

The quality of the canter and its relation to the diaphragm has already been mentioned. But what happens during tempi changes? The moment of suspension is
usually shortened or made more difficult by a flying change. The horse has less
time to breathe in. If this happens once, it's not a problem. But the shorter the
series of flying changes, the more important the connection with the horse's
breathing becomes. This always has immense implications for the flying changes
at every stride. If the horse does not "jump" far enough under his body during a
single change, he hardly has the chance to inhale deeply enough. An error after
the sixth or seventh change will automatically occur because the horse cannot
maintain the rhythm of breathing and stride. This situation can only be corrected
by paying great attention to the horse's breathing during every canter stride and
taking every little disturbance seriously.

Diaphragm Problems—Causes and Consequences

Illnesses of the Respiratory Tract

Longer-lasting respiratory problems—for example, chronic bronchitis or permanent overload of the respiratory system during training and competition—lead to
negative tension in the diaphragm. Even if the underlying illness has long since
been cured, this tension may remain and permanently restrict the breathing
capacity as well as the overall movement of the horse.

WHAT CAN DIRECTLY EFFECT BREATHING DYNAMICS

- endurance capacity
- saddle fit
- rider's seat
- digestive tract
- cribbing
- inner suppleness
- stabling conditions (fresh air and movement)
- conformation (shape of thorax, croup-high)
- correctness of training (outer suppleness)

Since all of these aspects influence one another, it's obvious how important
functional, rhythmic breathing is as a control function within any movement pattern of the horse.

*Breathing is the most important element required to guarantee the suppleness
of horse and rider at rest and in movement.*

Disturbances in a Movement

Consequently, any limitation of the horse's movement patterns automatically involves restrictions in the horse's breathing, and vice versa. The horse can no longer freely move his thorax or pelvis, and develops movement disorders. He does not step evenly into both reins, does not react to the leg aid, or no longer engages as much as he used to. The horse can no longer functionally and correctly position his FCPT or HCPD.

The FCPT, for example, may keep "falling" backward and downward, which will make the sternum move forward. The result is a constant pull on the diaphragm, which triggers an additional contraction there. This negative tension can then be transferred to the HCPD. A downward spiral of incorrect movement and loss of performance is the result.

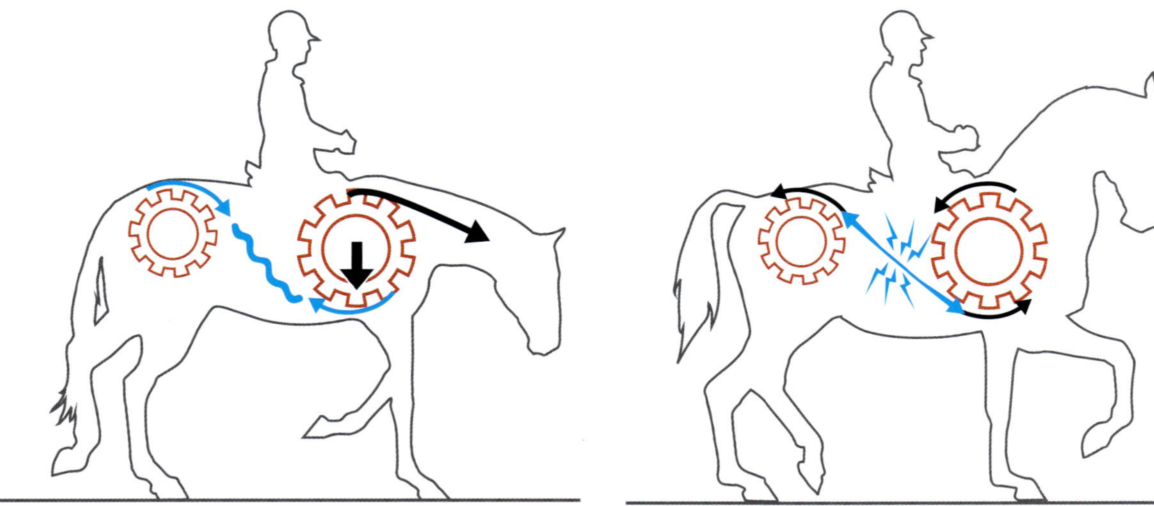

The diaphragm depicted without enough tension (left) and in a state of negative tension (right) from a functional perspective.

Influence on the Internal Organs

The diaphragm's movement has the same influence on the dynamics of the internal organs as on the external movement patterns. The diaphragm is capable of simultaneously moving the liver, the gastrointestinal tract, and all the other internal organs in the horse's trunk. Another important function influenced by the diaphragm is the dynamic of the lymphatic system and the circulatory system. The vacuum in the abdomen created by the act of respiration supports the flow of blood and lymph fluid through the body. This is why horses that tend to suffer from afflictions like stress-related colic or swollen legs should be checked for a malfunction of the diaphragm, next to more conservative veterinary diagnoses.

Manual Therapy of the Diaphragm

The exact positioning of all the systems the diaphragm is attached to leads to an increased breathing activity of the horse against resistance. Slight changes in this tension encourage the horse to reduce this resistance, which allows him to continue breathing more freely and deeply.

If this position can be maintained over several breaths, the therapist can positively influence the dynamics of the horse's fascia system inside and outside of the abdomen. Depending on the direction in which she guides the buildup of tension during breathing, the horse's internal organs shift along with it. This therapeutic technique is especially effective for releasing adhesions of the fascia in the abdomen and the encasements of the inner organs, and conforms to techniques of visceral therapy in osteopathy.

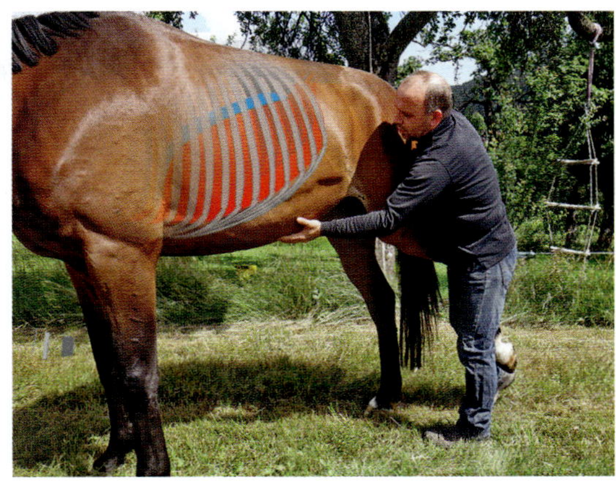
Manual diagnostics and therapy related to the diaphragm.

This example shows you how delicate and encompassing therapeutic techniques can work. 95 percent of the therapist's work is to "listen" to tissue. It is only after a full assessment that the therapist actively intervenes with a few very deliberate movements to alter the situation inside the body.

Dr. Andrew Taylor Still, founder of osteopathy for humans, said: "When a patient comes to me, I listen to her story, and while I listen, I see the different systems of the body structure in my mind's eye."

Summary
The diaphragm, as the most important respiratory muscle, is the mediator between inner and outer suppleness. An even and undisturbed breathing rhythm, which is required for suppleness, is the basis for any movement of the horse, any dressage movement, and any relaxation during the riding horse's training. If the breathing rhythm is disturbed, there are direct effects on the horse's movement, as well as his health.

7 Managing and Training Horses with Animal Welfare in Mind

Breeding and Raising Horses—The Four Most Important Years in a Horse's Life

No fence in sight—this space invites natural movement behavior.

Raising Young Horses in the Traditional Way

The horse's body, and especially his musculoskeletal system, develops in the first four to five years—not just the first three! These years determine how well bones, joints, tendons, and ligaments can mature, and how resilient the entire animal becomes. During this time, the foundation for the muscles' responsiveness in terms of the leg axes' stability is laid. This fact has been neglected for many years, and riders and scientists both used to pay little attention to this time in a horse's life.

Until modern times, it has been common practice to gather foals of the same age and turn them out to pasture in smaller or larger groups. These youngsters generally have ample space to move in the summer; however, in many places, space becomes scarce in the winter. During long spells of bad weather, foals are often put in a run-in barn, which many foals then do not leave at all during the winter months. In the best case, they have a small winter paddock. In the worst case, they stay inside a single stall or a small run-in barn, not only for several hours a day, but sometimes for days at a time.

At three years old, many youngsters move into single stalls at training barns. Time out on grass in groups is no longer taken for granted at this age, and a paddock for the winter months is often an exception rather than the rule. Talented sport horses, in particular, spend their riding horse lives moving between stall, grooming stall, indoor arena, and wash stall for their first months of training.

In a herd, horses of different ages live together in social groups.

Using a positive example for the raising of young horses, I would like to demonstrate through comparison what this means for the physical and mental development of animals that were once steppe inhabitants and highly specialized to be constantly on the move. The horse-keeping facility I will discuss, which has received multiple awards, offers an environment that meets horses' natural needs in a special way. Even if this "horse paradise" cannot be copied perfectly everywhere, the comparison shows precisely what is most relevant for the positive development of the bodies and minds of horses, when it comes to raising, managing, and training.

Example: "Les Dannes"

I have been serving as an advisor on a project called Les Dannes in the southeast of France for more than 10 years. Kurt Fuchs, a Swiss rider and horse lover, immigrated there more than 15 years ago for the sole purpose of returning horsekeeping to where it came from—back to nature. He has started to keep herds of horses of different ages on about 750 acres. The horses live outside 24/7 for 365 days a year, eat grass and hay, and have free access to minerals. Regular hoof trimming, deworming, and teeth checks are done, and the animals have regular contact with the Fuchs family. Apart from that, they get nothing else. No shoes, no blankets, no "extras" (supplements).

As teenagers, the three Fuchs children started to become interested in horses and in riding. There were a few former show horses among the group, which were to live out a handful of quiet years in the field as retirees. Many of them were still young and had already proven their potential at championships. Some of the owners no longer wanted to pay their bills after one or two years, although their horses were doing exceptionally well. Kurt Fuchs eventually took on these horses, and his children pursued an interest in show jumping. The horses had fun, and this is how a unique project was born.

The horses' maintenance continued as before. They remained in their herds, were jumped once a week, and went to competitions on the weekends. What was mocked in the beginning by those firmly established in the equine industry became a success story within a few years. Mind you, all horses at Les Dannes are barefoot, always live in their herd, only get grain at competitions, and do not have blankets, but grow their own winter coats. After six years, the Fuchs family won classes at national and international competitions over fences of up to 5 feet (1.5 meters), and the system is still working.

The sport-horse herd in movement.

Understanding the "Les Dannes" System

Projects such as this one are not intended to question the common equestrian schooling and training system. No one is being told to simply leave their horse alone during the week and then enter a competition on the weekend. The unique conditions at Le Dannes cannot be generalized, and it makes even less sense to copy individual elements from this system without recreating the rest of the conditions.

Yet I was interested in the system right from the start, even fascinated. I tried to understand why things that usually do not work would work there. How much training do we actually need to compensate for our horses' lack of movement? And, most of all, what can we learn from this system?

Lack of Movement

In the wild, a horse moves for 14 to 16 hours, mostly at the walk. Sometimes he trots or canters short distances during play. During flight, he gallops at a maximum speed for 40 to 60 seconds, across perhaps 500 to 1,000 feet (several hundred meters) at a time. This is the horse's baseline for movement; any less, to him, is a lack of movement. Even if a horse stands in an open field and grazes, this does not mean that he actually moves. Horses need movement stimuli to move! And a fence in his line of sight essentially poses a movement obstacle for a horse. He will not be motivated to move without a valid reason.

The GPS-monitored movement path of a horse at a different facility with year-round outdoor availability, in Haltingen, close to Lörrach.

The Development of a Healthy Skeleton

Bone Structure

The horse's basic physical structure consists of his tendon system and his bones. Together with the elastic force of the tendons and ligaments, the length ratio of the bones determines the horse's power development and power transmission. However, the outside forces which influence the bones have an effect on their development.

Osteoporosis Due to Movement Deficits

The quality, thickness, and shape of the various bones is determined by the nature of their workload. Research has shown that a bone can only be maintained or strengthened in its structure through dynamic bending during *medium to heavy strain*. A horse that stays in his stall or in a small field for most of the day, or just walks around, will not experience sufficient strain to strengthen his bone structure.

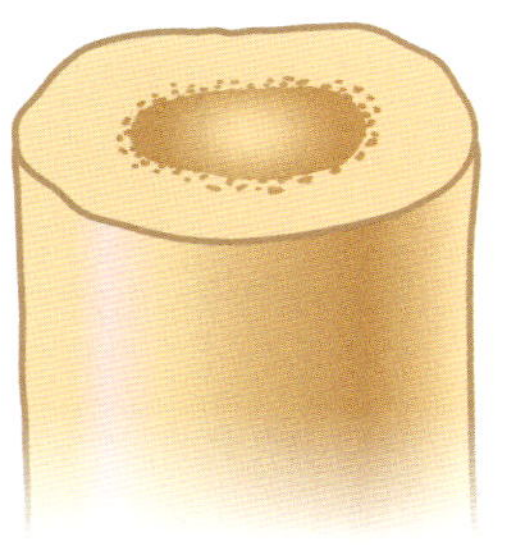

Various studies in human medicine have proven that bones and tendon structures can be weakened by too little strain, as a result of a lack of movement. Hence, they experience damage. These atrophied structures are then suddenly overstrained by the normal workloads intended by nature.

This graphic illustrates how the mechanism of bone development works. Bending strain leads to different loads on the convex and concave sides of the bone, respectively. The electric potential created by that difference is stimulation for the activity of bone-forming cells in the body, which they need to be able to work. However, these cells only respond once per stimuli, meaning a truly effective strain for a bone has to be dynamic. Static stimuli—bending once and then maintaining the position—will only ever get one response, no matter how long the position is kept. On the contrary, long-lasting, static bending strain can lead to damage of the bone's structures.

So bones need frequent and intensive dynamic stress stimuli to become strong. But this stress cannot be caused by unilateral or monotonous movements.

Thus, the development of ganglion cysts can more often be traced back to a too-rapid increase of stress in immature, young horses than an impact of excessive force.

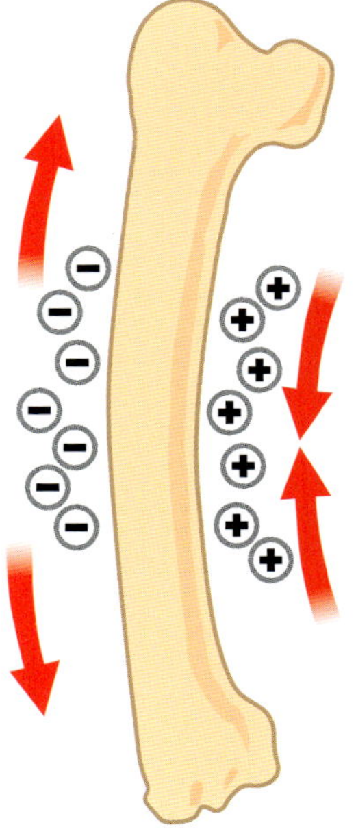

Dynamic movement releases electric potential in bone tissue, which positively affects bone density.

Fractures and *fissures* and osteochondrosis (often known as "chips"), which, nowadays, almost develop "out of nowhere" are very often the result of a lack of appropriate physical stress stimuli for foals and young horses.

The first four years (not just the first three) are the most important development phase of the equine skeletal system, during which daily movement in walk, trot, and canter on *different footing with short phases of stress* is absolutely necessary. This fact stands in stark contrast to young horses' typical environments today, including individual stabling of very young horses, which unfortunately has become the norm. If we assume that a two-year-old horse is kept in a small run-in barn with high bedding from October to April, this can definitely be assessed as *too little stress on the skeletal system*, which entails heavy *consequential damages*, not only to the bones but also in the connective tissue, especially in high-performance sport, later in the horse's life.

Bones, cartilage, and tendons need stress!

Numerous scientific studies have proven that the body needs regular exposure to stress for its development. When observing a foal in his natural habitat, you will notice that he leaves his mother countless times during the day in short sprints, only to return just as quickly. A horse is constructed for the hard footing of the grassland and has become specialized for exactly that terrain over millions of years. If we keep these animals on nothing but beautifully soft or deep and muddy footing, damage to the musculoskeletal system is guaranteed. Bones that grow without frequent stress do generally grow longer, but they are significantly less resilient. This is comparable to a tree that grows while protected under the best of conditions. It does look pretty and straight, but its wood is considerably less sturdy and durable than that of a tree exposed to the elements.

It's obvious that too much early skeletal growth without enough stress, in horses, leads more often to a negative prognosis for the stability and durability of this system, when using the horse as a riding horse. This contradicts a breeder's interest in three-year-olds that are "finished" as early as possible and have already reached the preferred height of 16.3 hands.

Breeding and riding competitions for three-year-old horses, where "premature" youngsters have chances to win a ribbon, reinforce the trend to breed and raise such horses—with a predisposition for degenerative illnesses.

The young horses at "Les Dannes" have stimuli 365 days a year to move around in large spaces, from feeding spaces to water holes to a natural shelter in the woods, or during playful races with their herd members. Their skeletal growth during their first three years is slower, and takes significantly longer. Four-year-old horses at "Les Dannes" often look like three-year-olds, compared to peers from different stables. From my observations, I can only confirm that their joints and cannon bones are strongly pronounced, above average. Once these horses are six or seven years old, they catch up to the genetically predefined longitudinal growth of their bone structure.

Quiet phases and phases in movement, during the horse's natural daily rhythm.

The Development of Healthy Connective Tissue

The "soft" connective tissue, meaning joint capsule, ligament, tendon, and fascial systems, takes on an outsized role in horses. Its importance in the movement and stabilization of the entire body has already been explained, in connection with the "catapult effect." In the following pages, the individual tasks of these structures are illustrated.

- support system within the muscles
- link between muscles and skeleton
- autonomous stabilization system within the leg axes
- autonomous stabilization system between leg axes and torso
- energy production through passive elasticity

Via the joints, this support tissue can build a *consistent system of tension* from hoof to spine. This is how, at rest, standing with almost *zero fatigue* can be done. In movement, this system absorbs energy in the supporting leg phase like a rubber band, and then converts that potential energy into movement energy for forward motion.

In addition to this contribution to forward motion, connective tissue also has a passively stabilizing function, as has been described earlier, in connection with the *passive stabilization of the spine*.

Adaptation Processes of Connective Tissue
Like bones, connective tissue needs dynamic stress stimuli to be healthy. For the most part, it is not the bloodstream that provides connective tissue with nutri-

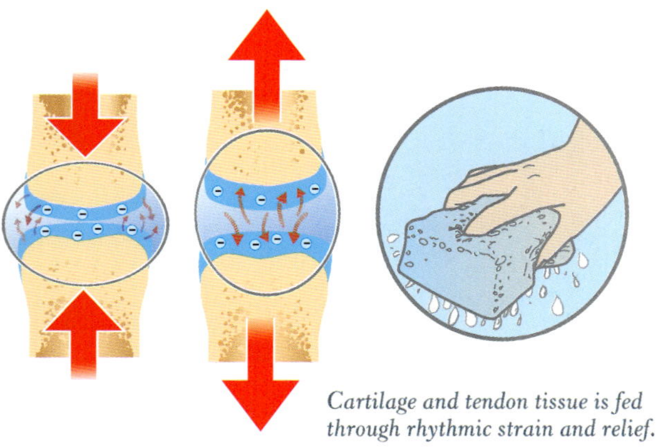

Cartilage and tendon tissue is fed through rhythmic strain and relief.

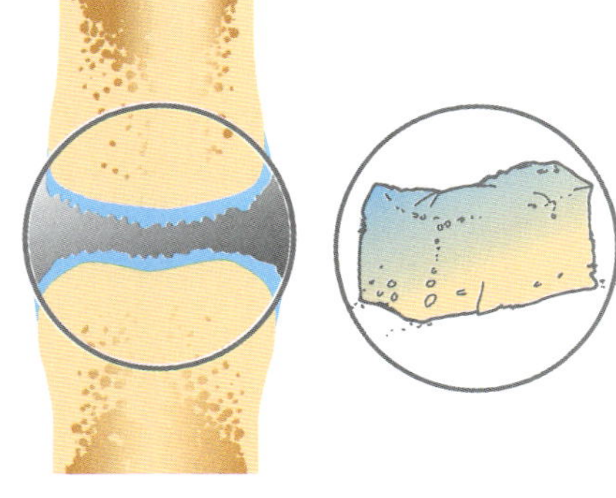

A movement deficit well and truly leads to "drying out," and thus to damage of cartilage.

ents, but the fluid systems in the interstitials, the lymph channels, as well as the synovial sheaths and joint capsules.

Just as the heart pushes blood into the capillaries, the body's movement serves as the pump for these systems; contraction and relaxation of muscles and joints moves these fluids and is responsible for supplying all connective tissue structures. Think of a sponge, which is squeezed and then, when released from pressure, soaks up new fluids. Joint cartilage reacts to compressive stress, and tendons and ligaments react to tension.

Lack of movement—or, better put, lack of stress—definitely leads to a deficient supply to these tissue structures, and therefore to degeneration and damage.

Horses need sufficient movement and reasonable physical stresses year-round, from the time they're foals until they retire.

Approaches that take these facts into account certainly do exist, but in my opinion they need to be much more radically implemented. Nobody is going to categorically deny that a paddock is "nice to have" for a horse. However, constructive criticism of horse-keeping conditions should be possible. Paddocks are a good option if the horses can decide for themselves when and how they use them, and when they have the option of a wind-proof shelter. If horses are just "parked" outside—wrapped in warm blankets which neither allow the sun to warm their coats nor help with the production of vitamins—good ideas are reduced to absurdities.

If large fields are divided into ever smaller sections, so every horse owner has her own private space, which she can carefully tend and where she does not have to walk far to bring her horse in for riding, we move toward conditions at equestrian facilities analogous to those at some modern campgrounds, where die-hard campers erect permanent wooden fences around their campsites. There may be valid reasons to categorically forbid letting horses run loose in the indoor arena—for example, to preserve new arena footing. But certainly nobody has asked the horses' opinion on this rule, horses which have to "let off steam" for their physical and mental well-being.

Horse-Appropriate Rules That Accommodate Their Need to Move

There are perfectly justifiable economic and management reasons for these examples. I also cannot offer a magic formula as an alternative; that would not be legitimate. But if the barn owner, trainer, and horse owner look over their facilities with the horse's movement needs in mind, individual solutions can always be found to at least improve the situation, with the horse's welfare as a top priority.

Even if boarders end up paying a few dollars more, even if the arena must be dragged one extra time every day, even if fences must be moved or removed (long and narrow for keeping a single horse, or over a large area for groups of horses at a stable), or the entire barn must be reorganized. After all, questionable supplements, tendon damage, or even the loss of a horse are always expensive, too.

The horses' claim to *horse-appropriate* keeping mainly entails *daily movement,* and better two or three times a day. *Variation* is the most important criterion: free movement and blowing off steam, longer distances in the walker, a little walk in the woods with or without a rider, sensible gymnasticizing work under saddle, or contact within their social groups. Ultimately, one form of movement cannot simply stand in for another. Of course, not every movement possibility has to be on offer every day, but ideally you should be able to check off two or three of them each week.

"Risk of Accident"–A Common Excuse

A horse that has not been allowed to run loose for months or years certainly cannot be locked in an indoor arena or turned out with a herd, and left there while we wait to see what happens. But with a little bit of creative thinking and preparation, a solution can and should be found.

And even if something happens: Responsibility can be taken and borne, where required.

Example: A Child

I like to compare the risk potential of free movement for horses with the development of a child. If one grows up on a farm and is outside every day, the risk of her breaking an arm or a leg is certainly higher in the short term than that of her friend, whose caring mother is there every minute of every day and sets out precise rules for the use of toys. Everything that is not branded "educationally valuable" is categorically removed and not allowed. Very often, this latter child loses all motivation for movement, and the computer becomes an easy alternative for activity.

The question is, who takes responsibility when children like the second girl become teenagers or adults with various movement deficiencies and illnesses, and become permanent visitors at orthopedists, surgeons, psychologists, and physical therapists–because every new stress stimuli in their lives leads to trouble spots that are tight or pinch, become infected or tear?

The Response of "Les Dannes" to the Question of Free Movement

The horse moves freely in the herd and sets his own daily routine, as well as his own regeneration and healing rhythms for affected structures, where needed. It is mind-blowing to see how sick horses band together with old horses in small groups. These small sub-herds follow a different rhythm, and they do not participate in every "kick-off" canter.

Nonetheless, these horses' connective tissue is exposed to thousands of different movement stimuli on a daily basis, to which it has to adapt continuously: uphill, downhill, different footing, forest, field, water, mud. The horse instinctively seeks out what he needs. It is not uncommon to see horses with a tendon injury with a mud pack on their injured legs, self-administered on the lake shore. There are always small setbacks during the first phase of recovery, and the horses do not become fit faster. But ultimately

a permanent relapse seldom—if ever—happens. Instead, horses who were considered incurable after exploring all conventional treatment and rehabilitation options have recovered. Sometimes, it took two to three years, but what difference does a few years make for an amazing five-year-old prospect that has his entire athletic career ahead of him?

The Development of Athletic Muscle

Example: "Les Dannes"

The horses are on the move from dawn till dusk, uphill and downhill, on an angle, to the left and right. They sprint in their passive mode, then present themselves and play in their active mode. They train coordination as well as active and passive stabilization the entire day, and if they need a break, they take it. The constant stimulation of the entire movement system is the big secret of "Les Dannes," in my view. The sport horses in the herds on site sometimes have five seconds on their competitors on a jumping course—barefoot, on wet grass footing. This is only possible because their legs have a better trained response capacity. They learn every day: If the hoof starts to slide, the frequency of their movement has to be increased. It is also this same response capacity that makes their muscles so quick and effective that they take action before the tendons are at the risk of being overstretched or the hoof actually begins to slide. Along the way, they learn to trust themselves and their bodies, even if they're in a tight spot.

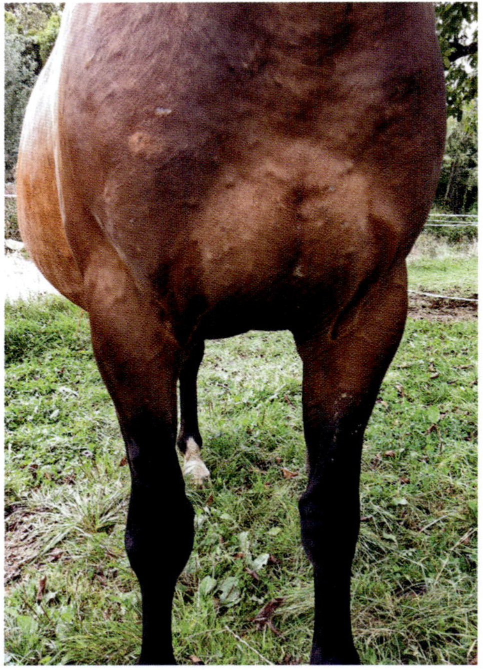

Pectoral muscles of a four-year-old at Les Dannes— "Selle Francaise," without grain but with 24/7 movement opportunities.

Transferred to conventional training, this means continuously varying the tasks asked of a horse. If a jumping horse is to hold his course in the jump-off, good flatwork is necessary. It is equally important to vary the movement speed, the angle of the horse's body axes, the footing conditions, and the rider's aids. Automatic habits in movement learning are the natural enemy of fine coordination skills. Control over the horse is an important part of the athletic performance of a horse on a jumping course or in the dressage arena, but it certainly isn't everything. In training, control can only be achieved with the opposite: constant variation and the horse's willingness to react to this change.

The most fascinating rides are those that demonstrate this to us. How else would Halla have been able to manage the second round at the 1956 Olympic Games in Stockholm, if not for her trust in herself, which her rider, Hans Günter Winkler, had encouraged through arduous training? The basis of his success was the *schooling and training of this wonder horse* that came to him as an unrideable problem horse. And this is exactly the trainer's job, in the end—on a professional scale in the saddle, as well as in the sense of horse psychology. Narcissism, over-confidence, and compulsive control of riders or trainers are the natural enemies of a sensible training structure, in this context.

With an acute hernia, under the influence of morphine to ease his pain, H.G. Winkler was only partially able to guide his horse.

The Psychological Development of a Horse

It is completely unnatural for the horse's development to be forcefully separated from his mother at eight months old or younger, and to then have to "deal" with peers or older horses, which supervise these youngsters, so to speak. The competitively oriented rearing and keeping of young horses of the same age in groups completely contradicts the natural herd structures of wild horses.

Pecking Order as the Foundation for Mental Stability

"Horses naturally accept hierarchies; they even need them to give them orientation." Christoph Hess used these words in the Personal Members' Magazine of the German Equestrian Federation (issue 11/12, 2013) to highlight the importance of the horse submitting to the leadership of the human "alpha animal" during daily routines.

Does this statement not apply even more so in horse rearing—and in that case, how is this supposed to work in groups with horses of the same age? Is the strongest two-year-old supposed to take responsibility for the entire group? Certainly not! Such a system is equivalent to a youth gang, and it produces mainly winners and losers, none of which are socialized correctly or brought up well. This has also been confirmed by the research done by Dr. Margit H. Zeitler-Feicht of the Technical University of Munich. In the new German Equestrian Federation (FN) "Guidelines for the Evaluation of Horse Keeping and Management from a Perspective of Animal Welfare" released on June 9th, 2009, it states: "It is of advantage to also keep older animals in young horse groups for educational reasons."

Horses of different ages maintain contact with each other and with humans.

Example: "Les Dannes"

The magic words are "mixed-age herd." Foals remain in their mothers' herds until they independently choose to spend more time with their friends. Eventually, the mothers are moved into a different herd, where they can care for other young horses or seniors as "aunts." All herds always display a mixed-age structure—from foals to a 35-year-old gelding. The different age groups take on social functions that are appropriate to their age. Foals and adolescents playfully fight and jostle; if it becomes serious, an aunt shows up and puts the brazen ones in their places. This guarantees life and movement in the herd; both young and old have manageable jobs within the social structure that are necessary for the smooth operation of the herd. Stallions of all ages and breeds stand together peacefully in a big herd.

A healthy mind and a healthy body always go hand in hand!

With sufficient space, foal and mare have time just to themselves.

One aunt babysits several juveniles.

Summary

The foundation for a healthy life as a horse is laid down in the first years after a horse is born. Failure to lay that foundation during this phase can't be corrected, and will be paid for dearly at a later point. Bones, tendons, ligaments, and muscles that haven't been exposed to regular, sensible work develop insufficiently in their structure as well as their function. The same applies to psychological development. It's hard to predict how much strain can be placed on these horses, and in part, they have to be worked like horses in need of rehabilitation before their actual training has even begun. Knowledge of how a horse was raised should play a more important role, to increase the pressure on those who are rearing young horses to make sure they do so with an eye toward the horse's mental and physical health and longevity.

True friendship rather than simply sticking together.

Transferring the Principles to Conventional Horsekeeping

The basic elements of horsekeeping as it's practiced at "Les Dannes" are a lot of space and a functioning herd structure. But what if you don't have 750 acres of grass fields and a consistent herd of 20 animals, which are always together, at your disposal? "Our Barn Needs to Become Better" is a public information campaign by the German Equestrian Federation (FN), aimed at promoting change at lesson barns, in terms of light, airflow, and movement. It gives encouragement and describes examples of equestrian facilities, and explains how sensible and horse-appropriate planning can lead to health-relevant changes, even with limited space. This is not about looks but about stimuli that can be provided for horses.

Small games of tag maintain the motivation to move.

Movement Stimuli—In the Group

With reasonable planning, movement-active "stabling" setups are much more doable than many people assume. Keeping horses in groups is also possible at show barns. But movement stimuli have to be set up to make the horses really move. Several different locations for food and water, artificially created round walks, and visual obstacles are some possibilities that can help keep a group of horses moving.

Movement Stimuli—Individual

Of course, keeping horses in groups is not feasible for every facility. Yet here, too, planning is key to many important improvements for the horse. If a horse spends several hours in a stall, there are certain minimum requirements: a sufficiently large, light, airy, clean stall, with the option for social contact with other horses. Treadmills and walkers offer additional possibilities for movement, along with work under saddle.

I would like to comment on this from a physical therapist's perspective. Even when using these tools, the rules of functional movement patterns still apply. Treadmills in particular are prone to incorrect use. Choice of location can also affect the quality of the horse's movement.

Distractions should be avoided, if possible, since the horse is limited in his reaction to external stimuli due to the configured speed of the treadmill. The individual setting of the treadmill's pace is especially important, along with a quiet and stress-free familiarization phase. This may sound trivial—but the expertise of an experienced trainer, who has an eye for the correct basic speed of a horse, should be sought. Even "a little too rushed" or "a little too slow," over 15 to 20 minutes of walking, repeated over several weeks, can lead to long-term movement disorders. From the beginning, the horse should move straight on the treadmill, with a low head-neck position. Rhythm and suppleness are indispensable basics of a horse's movement, even on a treadmill.

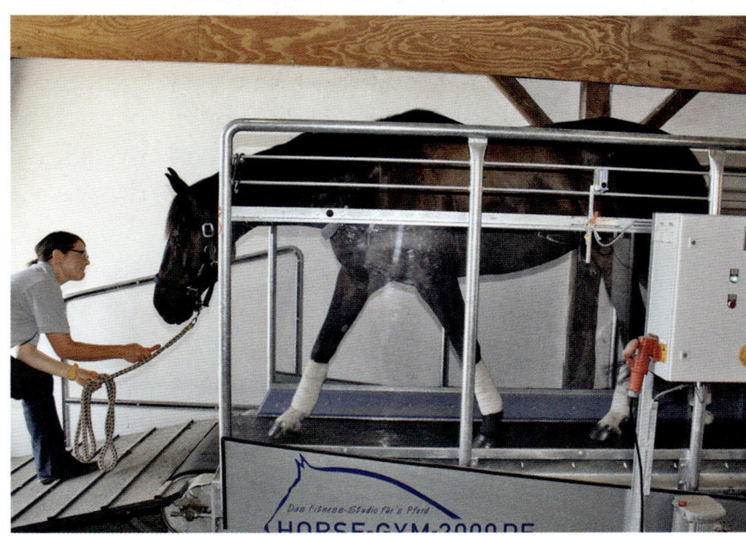

Correct movement on a treadmill, as well as managing parameters such as individual speed and inclines, should be trained with skilled personnel.

This applies to hotwalkers in much the same way, even though horses have slightly more opportunity to even out their speed due to the larger space of a walker. Important criteria here are a good, non-skid footing; solid, non-transparent side walls; and a radius of at least 50 feet (15 meters) to avoid too strong a rotational force in the horse's joints. If there are several horses in the walker, more time should be invested from the start to assign groups according to the horses' needs and preferences. The positive effect of movement will be increased by the positive effects of social contact. Conversely, movement under mental stress can negate any positive effect over the long term.

Summary
Treadmills and walkers can be useful instruments to offer stabled horses additional movement opportunities. However, they may not be used as a dull hamster wheel, where the horses just rattle off a few miles under stress. If you consider the first two elements of the Training Scale, rhythm and suppleness, as well as the correct basic speed, these tools offer a very good option to complement a horse's movement and exercise routines, as well as to create additional individual training stimuli.

Success in Equestrian Sports

Left to right:
Janine Fuchs, Marie Perron, Stefanie Fuchs, Andy Fuchs.

The impressive competitive successes of the Fuchs children and their horses show that this framework is not only suitable for retired horses and for raising young horses.

Stefanie and Janine started riding in 2005, and Andy Fuchs one year later, in 2006.

By 2008, they became French amateur champions with the team.

Ever since, they have been on the winner and result lists in the Franche-Comté region and beyond.

Nykos des Glays with Andy Fuchs.

Janine Fuchs with Amon ra van de Padenborre.

Year-end ranking, Championship Grand Régional Pro2 (up to 1.35 meters) for Stefanie Fuchs:
2011: 1st
2012: 3rd
2013: 1st
2014: 1st

Stefanie Fuchs with Storm d'Omael during a puissance class, jumping over 6 feet (1.90 meters).

Year-end ranking, Championship Grand Régional Pro2 (up to 1.35 meters) for Andy Fuchs:
2011: 3rd
2012: 2nd
2013: 3rd
2014: 2nd

Summary
Even though it might sound wondrous, all this has been achieved with horses who live outside year-round. They have winter coats, and no blankets in inclement weather. They do not have shoes, and they only eat high-quality hay and mineral feed; grain is only fed to them at competitions, if needed.

Acknowledgments

I would like to thank the entire team involved in writing this book.

The Team of Riders and Horses

- **Felicitas von Neumann-Cosel and Gene Freeze (First Choice Farm, Maryland)** Felicitas von Neumann-Cosel is a German Master Rider and Trainer, decorated with the Stensbeck Medal and, in her time, the earner of the highest ever marks given for the final "Reitlehrer" instructor's exam. Together, we have searched for new kinds of movement analysis. Over the years, we've spent many hours in the indoor arena on countless occasions to put the results of my therapeutic work into movement practice. I cannot honor enough the importance of Felicitas' skill in riding single sequences exactly to the point requested, and repeating them with planned but very minute modifications. Without the knowledge gained through her assistance, parts of this book could have never been written.

Gene Freeze, the owner of First Choice Farm as well as County Saddlery Ltd., England, and himself a very interested analyst in the field of hoof dynamics and saddle design, has been an important partner for discussion in reviewing my theories and findings. I would also like to thank the horses and clients of First Choice Farm, who have always supported us in our work.

- **Corinne Foxley** has always supported us, throughout the process of working on this book, and has become an important pillar of our team over the years.

- **Anica Fröhling** works as a trainer at the equestrian club in Mannheim, Germany, and she joined the cause of producing the pictures needed, and skillfully led her horses through the required movement sequences.

- **Beat Sax,** event rider from Switzerland, whose horses I have been taking care of for many years, represents the many riders whose exact feedback has always helped me to better understand my therapeutic techniques and to separate the effective from the less effective.

- **Elisabeth Stöcklin,** endurance rider from Switzerland, is also an example of the many riders in all kinds of equestrian sports and disciplines who have entrusted their horses to my care over many years. The focus was never on a short-term "fix" of things, but on a long-lasting development, during which I saw the horses two to three times a year and was part of their career for many years, on an international competition sport level, or simply as a preventive health maintenance measure for a pleasure horse. Photos of her were taken by www.lisart.de.

Illustrations

■ **Jeanne Klöpfer** made, without a doubt, a major contribution to the making of this book. When I check my email account, I can see the progress of the illustrations over the course of three years. What started as an ordinary project sometimes brought both of us to the verge of despair. When you see these illustrations today, one can hardly imagine how much effort went into them. I have always had certain images in my head that I wanted to see on paper. I simply didn't understand how complex it is to place a three-dimensional vision of an image onto a flat piece of paper. Jeanne, with her professional competence and imagination, has done an outstanding job in bringing these illustrations to life. A completely new aesthetic with regard to the movement functions of horses has come from this work.

"Jeanne, it might not have been fun all the time, but you can be really proud of your work."

Editing

■ **Isabelle von Neumann-Cosel.** As mentioned in the foreword, the production of this book was a long and at times onerous process. There were always points where that process came to a halt, since my job is working with horses directly, not writing. Isabelle literally took my hand and tried to keep me focused. When linking my topic to the theory of classical riding, she repeatedly advised and corrected me, if my wording became too flippant. Her experience as a trainer continuously allowed her to take the perspective of the reader and steer my ideas and conclusions in the right direction, so they helped clarify matters rather than add confusion. Most of all, she also motivated me whenever I reached a point where I wanted to drop the project because everything seemed to have become too much.

Layout

■ **Marianne Fietzeck** kept shifting all our illustrations, pictures, and text until every detail was just right. The pictures and the explanations of their connections with each other only work if they're visible on the same page. A nightmare for the layout...but it was worth it.

Clients and Their Horses

I also have to thank the riders and horses to whom I have had a close connection on a professional and personal level for many years and with whom I have always been able to discuss my ideas and thoughts. They represent all the other clients and their horses. Every single one of them has motivated me over the last 18 years to think a little more and never give up searching, even if I felt as if I had reached my limits.

- Elevage des Blés, Liliane Fromer, Hurbache, France
- Rhomberg family, Dornbirn, Austria
- Reitsport-Zentrum Hard, Austria
- Mareille Krause, Fulda, Germany
- Werner Scheidegger, Reitstall Mollishuus, Sankt Pelagiberg, Switzerland
- Sabine Ellinger Rehabilitation Center for Horses, Murrhardt, Germany, according to the STAMMER KINETICS concept
- Rehabilitation center Bertleinsbrücke, Daniela Frühauf, Weinheim, Germany, according to the STAMMER KINETICS concept
- Rhett Bird, England
- Good News Farm, Maryland, United States
- Cindy Rawson, England
- Peter Meneth, saddle-maker, Switzerland
- Equine hospital Dalchenhof, Brittnau, Switzerland
- Animal Hospital on the Racetrack, Iffezheim, Germany
- Dr. Patrick Luder, Veterinarian, Oberwil, Switzerland

To My Family

My kids: You are the roots that keep me grounded and give me strength and energy every day. I am so grateful to you for that. **My siblings:** Dear Andreas, dear Heike, dear Thomas—you are the best and most important support system in the world.

Index